the Computer

an everyday machine

second edition

enid squire

Addison-Wesley (Canada) Limited
Don Mills, Ontario.

MENLO PARK, CALIF : LONDON :
AMSTERDAM : SYDNEY : TOKYO

ENID SQUIRE took her B.Sc. at London University in London, England, and has taught in high schools in England, British Columbia and Ontario. Miss Squire is presently working for IBM Canada Ltd. as a systems engineer.

We wish to thank the following for permission to use the designated photographs in the book: City Hall, Toronto, Ontario (16.8); Control Data Canada Ltd. (3.7, 6.6, 8.5); CP Air (6.11); Hewlett-Packard (Canada) Ltd. (12.6); Honeywell Controls Ltd. (2.7, 6.2, 13.12); Howarth & Smith Ltd. (16.15); IBM Canada Ltd. (1.1, 1.2, 1.3, 1.4, 1.5, 1.6.1, 1.6.2, 1.9.1, 1.9.2, 1.9.3, 1.9.4, 2.1, 2.5, 2.6, 2.9, 2.10, 2.11, 3.1, 3.2, 3.3, 3.8, 8.1, 8.2, 8.3, 8.7, 8.9, 10.1, 11.1, 11.2, 12.1, 12.3, 13.1, 13.2, 13.3, 13.4, 13.5, 13.8, 13.9, 13.11, 14.2, 16.1, 16.2, 16.3, 16.4, 16.9, 19.1, 19.2, 19.3, 19.4, 19.5); Ontario Science Centre (1.4); The Royal Bank of Canada (16.12, 16.13); Sperry Rand Canada Ltd. (1.7, 16.5, 17.1). Illustrations on pages 168 and 170 by Will Eisner. We also wish to thank Dr. Thomas Hull and Mr. David Day for the use of the hypothetical machine and assembly languages used in Chapters 3, 5 and 6.

Cover design by Dennis Mason based on a mass storage system. (See page 107.)

PRINTED IN CANADA.

B C D E F 82 81 80 79 78 77

ISBN 0-201-07158-4

Preface

The objective of this text is to put the computer in perspective and introduce it as a tool that can be used and understood by the average person. The approach is to take a simple problem and to solve it using a hypothetical language and a computer consisting of the simplest units possible. One problem having been solved, other questions automatically arise, and these are tackled in a logical manner. Items of interest are included, and throughout the reader is reminded of the social problems posed by our "computerized" society.

Since the first publication of this book in 1972, many changes have taken place in the field of computing, and this edition of the text reflects many of these. Electromechanical equipment has become part of history and is treated as such. New techniques such as structured programming, database and virtual storage are introduced. New hardware such as mass storage and specialized terminals is covered. Increased attention has been paid to the need for regulations to protect privacy and security. The widening range of applications has been dealt with.

The emphasis and objectives, however, remain the same: to provide a basic understanding of how the computer works and to stimulate an interest in its vast potential in our world.

Contents

1 How We Arrived at the Computer Era

The purpose of this chapter is to put the computer in perspective and to show how it evolved.

What is a Computer?

Although the computer has been described as a giant electronic brain, it does not have many of the significant qualities of a brain, the human brain in particular. A computer might be referred to as a high-speed idiot, but high-speed data processor or general-purpose problem solver better describe its function. A computer is incapable of performing any action unaided by man with his remarkable brain. The value of the computer lies in its incredible speed and unfailing accuracy. Where humans tend to become careless doing repetitive tasks, a computer performs its assigned tasks twenty-four hours a day, seven days a week, with no loss of speed or accuracy—and no coffee breaks!

What is Data Processing?

In a literal sense, data processing is any processing of data or information. When exam marks are averaged, data is being processed; the exam marks being the data and the brain the data processor. Increasingly, the processing of data is being linked with the computer because of the masses of data that have to be processed in our technical and fast-moving society. Information must be checked, sorted, tabulated, listed, graphed, selected and dispatched to the right people.

The history of the computer is part of the history of the development of methods of data processing. Help in the solving of problems was originally sought by mathematicians. The machines and processes they developed were later adapted for other uses, including business.

History of Data Processing

Early man was processing data when he kept count of the number of animals he owned by using a heap of pebbles. If he needed something he could not himself provide, he traded with a neighbour. As coins were introduced as a medium of trade and transactions became more complicated, business methods and tools developed accordingly. More arithmetic became involved and a faster method of calculation became desirable.

History of Data Processing

One of the earliest aids to calculation, the abacus, appeared in a primitive form thousands of years ago in the Near East. The technique soon became well known throughout the civilized world and different versions of the instrument appeared in many countries. The Chinese abacus and the Japanese soroban were very similar and are still widely used. People using the abacus for calculations can become extremely skilled in rapid computation—in fact, in some tests, an expert using an abacus has proved faster than a person using a mechanical calculator.

On each string of the abacus, the five beads below the bar are each of value 1; the two beads above the bar are each of value 5. The parallel wires represent place values for units, tens, hundreds, and so on, starting with the units string at the right.

The beads do not take on their assigned values until they are positioned next to the bar. On the tens wire below, for example, the digit seven has been represented by moving a five unit bead, and two lower beads, to the bar.

During calculation, when the total value of the beads at the bar reaches ten (as on the hundreds wire), regrouping is achieved by carrying a bead to the wire immediately to the left.

Diagram 1.1 Abacus

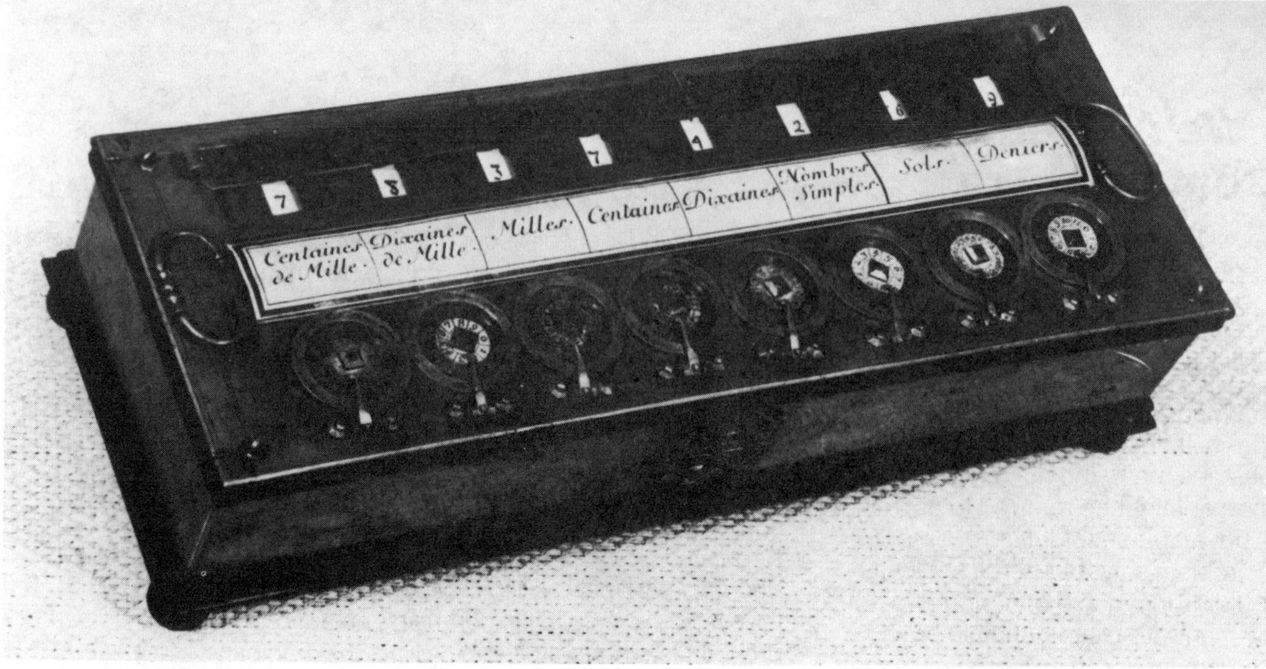

Diagram 1.2 Pascal's calculator

During the following two to three thousand years methods of data processing continued to develop and the next milestone came in the year 1642. Blaise Pascal, a nineteen-year-old Frenchman working on tax accounting in his father's office, decided there must be some way of relieving the drudgery of adding long columns of figures. He devised a mechanized calculating machine operated by a series of dials attached to wheels that had the numbers zero to nine on their circumferences. Pascal also invented a rachet mechanism that, when a particular wheel made a complete turn, advanced the wheel to the left one digit. Indicators above the dials showed the correct answers.

Pascal's calculator performed only addition. In 1671 Gottfried Wilhelm Leibniz started work on a machine that could multiply and divide directly, a working version of which was finished by l694. The stepped-wheel device Leibniz used in his machine is still found in some present-day calculators. "It is unworthy of excellent men to lose hours like slaves in the labour of calculation," observed Leibniz.

Diagram 1.3 Leibniz's calculator

Diagram 1.4 Jacquard's loom

Unfortunately Pascal and Leibniz were both ahead of the technology of their times and neither machine was dependable in its accuracy. This unequal advancement of technology and inventive ideas continued to be a problem for some years, and it has only been in the past twenty-five years that an answer to the problem has been found. It took three hundred years to solve the problem that existed and was identified in 1670!

Another milestone in the history of data processing was reached with the first successful use of punched cards to control a machine. In 1801 Joseph Marie Jacquard developed a loom for textile weaving that revolutionized the industry. Each line of the weave was represented on a separate punched card. The complexity of the pattern was unimportant; once the cards were punched and arranged in the correct order, they were put through the machine and the pattern was woven automatically.

When Jacquard first introduced his loom, he encountered a great deal of opposition and some scepticism. However, after the loom was exhibited at the Paris World's Fair, he sold a considerable number, and his basic technique is still employed in the textile industry today. In recent years his name has been used to describe certain fabric patterns or weaves, especially in towelling.

Diagram 1.5 Babbage's difference engine

About the year 1822 Charles Babbage, an Englishman, started work on a project he called a difference engine, which would be able to produce logarithm tables to six decimal places. Knowing the scientific need for a computational aid, he prepared an outline of his idea and made a small working model. On this basis he received a subsidy to build a full size-model. This project was never finished, however; the apparent reason being Babbage's growing interest in his "analytical engine". This machine incorporated many ideas that are used in today's computers. It used the punched card idea for introducing and storing operating instructions and produced printed output from the machine's own printing unit. Unfortunately, like those who preceded him, Babbage was far ahead of the technical development of the time and was unable to get the required parts built successfully. The analytical engine was never completed.

Shortly before the United States census was due

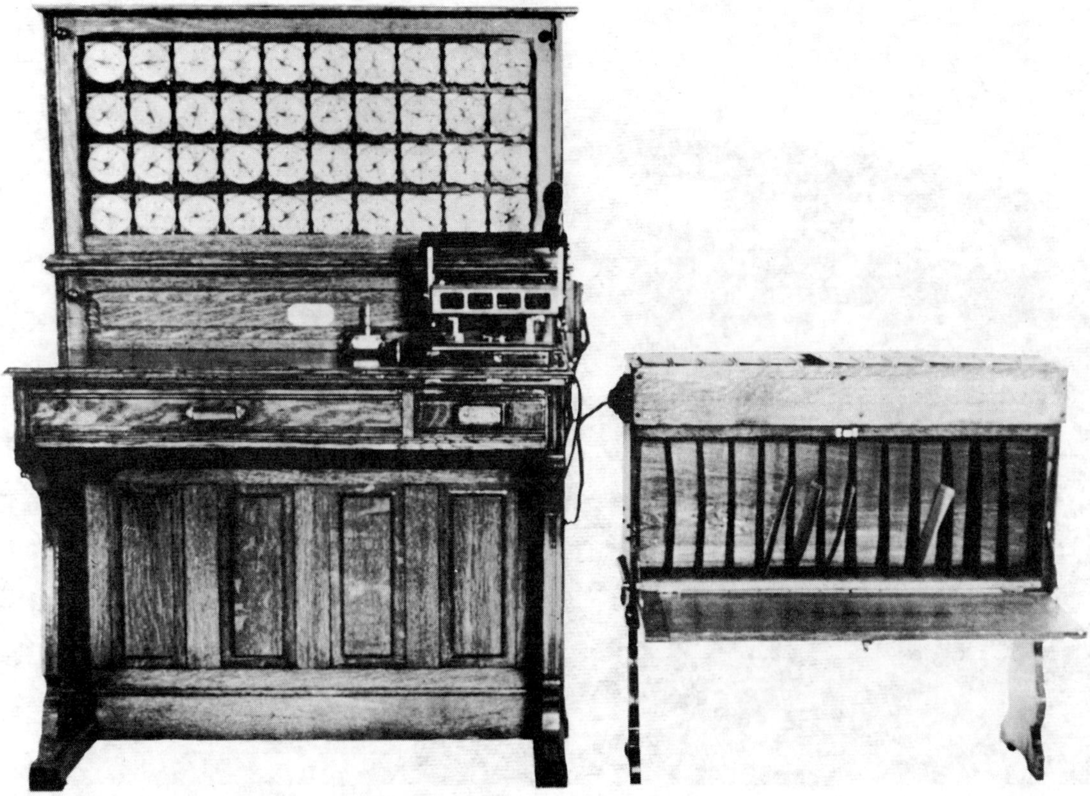

Diagram 1.6.1 Hollerith's tabulating machine

to be taken in 1890, Census Bureau officials realized that, if the government continued to process the census results manually, no statistics would be obtained before the next census was due, thus making the statistics virtually valueless. Dr. Herman Hollerith, a statistician with the Bureau, worked out a system whereby a person's name, age, sex, address, and so on, could be coded by punched holes in a card. The data on the cards was counted electrically on equipment containing a series of dials to record the totals. The cards could be semi-automatically sorted according to the various characteristics of the information on them. The census of 1890 was completed in one third the time it took for the 1880 census and it was more complete and comprehensive than any of its predecessors.

In 1896 Dr. Hollerith formed a company to develop his machine. This company later merged with two others and eventually became known as International Business Machines or IBM. James Powers, also at one point a statistician at the U.S. Census Bureau, later founded another company that eventually became part of UNIVAC, a division of the Sperry Rand Corporation. Together IBM and UNIVAC produced most of the electromechanical data processing equipment available today.

Punched-card equipment based on Dr. Hollerith's electrical tabulating machine was developed in the first half of the twentieth century and is still used. This type of equipment has limitations, however. Such functions as sorting, collating, calculating, reproducing, interpreting and keypunching require separate pieces of equipment, thereby slowing down the processing of data. Hence scientists continued to search for a design that would incorporate all these operations.

Diagram 1.6.2 Detail of Hollerith's machine

The Early Computers

In 1937 Dr. Howard H. Aiken of Harvard University, using many of Babbage's original ideas together with the punched-hole concept of Jacquard and Hollerith, designed an automatic computing machine that did combine the various operations in one device. He was assisted in his development by IBM, and in 1944 the Automatic Sequence Controlled Calculator or Mark 1 was completed and presented to Harvard University. The Mark 1 had a mass of 5t and consisted of a complex of 78 adding machines and calculators connected by 800 km of wiring. Instructions were punched into a roll of paper tape and, once the machine started on the first instruction, no further human assistance was required.

The Mark 1 was an electromechanical computer, all operations being carried out by a system of electric relays and switches. Though it was a great improvement over previous equipment, it was still restricted by slowness and mechanical operating difficulties. The machine was used extensively by the United States Navy during the Second World War and was used afterwards until it was officially retired in 1959.

Computer development was taking place in Great Britain and Germany as well as in the United States. Most of the German work was lost during the war, but the first electronic computers were produced in the United States and Britain in the forties. ENIAC (Electronic Numerical Integrator and Calculator) was developed at the University of Pennsylvania by Dr. John W. Mauchly and a student, J. Presper Eckert. EDSAC (Electronic Delay Storage Automatic Calculator) was developed at Cambridge University in England by Maurice V. Wilks and was the first

Diagram 1.7 UNIVAC 1

computer to incorporate Dr. John von Neumann's ideas of a stored program (or a stored set of instructions). Until this time there was little flexibility possible in using the computer. Control of the computer had been by removable plug wires or paper tape and, once the processing of data had been started, no modifications were possible even if the need arose. With EDSAC it was possible to have the instructions and the data stored together in the computer storage facility.

The stored program concept allows modification to take place during the execution of instructions. Intermediate calculations can be stored for future use, sets of instructions can be repeated, and different sets of instructions can be executed according to the circumstances. In a definition of a computer, mention should always be made of
(i) its ability to store a program and to modify the program if required
(ii) its incredible speed.
These two characteristics distinguish a computer from any other calculator.

As technology advanced in all areas, research in the area of computers became more widespread and the results more commercially practical in size and cost. UNIVAC 1 (UNIVersal Automatic Computer), installed at the United States Bureau of Census in 1951, was the first commercially produced computer. It contained many of the features found in present day computers and was marketed by Remington Rand. Commercial use of the UNIVAC machine began in 1954 and from this start the data processing industry has grown to its present size. Most of the improvements in computers since then have been in the area of size reduction, to the point of miniaturization of parts, which results in increased speed of operation. Computers are now designed and manufactured in many countries of the world including Russia, Japan, the United States, Great Britain,Germany and China.

Parallel Technological Development

It is very interesting to parallel the development carried out in the field of mechanized calculators with the advancement of techniques in other fields. What was the impact on civilization of, for example, the printing press, the steam engine, and the telephone? Information was exchanged via the written word, travel became easier, communication was instantaneous over telephone lines. *Communication* perhaps is the key word. Because man was able to communicate more easily, his knowledge increased and technology advanced as more and more information became available.

Information pollution is now a problem. What information is important? What shall we keep? What statistics are available? How can we improve our health, our education, our housing? We need facts and figures reduced to a meaningful and manageable size so that we can make decisions based on accurate calculations. Leibniz's requirement has certainly been fulfilled—the computer does indeed remove man from the drudgery of massive and continual calculations and allow him to apply his brain to interesting and stimulating tasks.

Computer Uses

The computer is more than just a rapid calculator. It has become man's tool in a vast variety of tasks:

–providing doctors and nurses with up-to-date information about a patient's health

–plotting weather patterns and producing airline flight plans accordingly

–providing travel information

–assisting in oceanographical research and aiding navigation

–keeping the records and calculating the statistics at the Olympic Games

–designing bridges and testing them theoretically before construction

–setting newspaper type

–controlling aircraft simulators to give a pilot initial training on the ground

Diagram 1.8.2 Computer in use at a nursing station in a hospital.

Diagram 1.8.1 Computer-controlled scoreboard at the Montreal Olympics

Diagram 1.8.3 Lab technician making use of a sensor- based computer to analyze samples

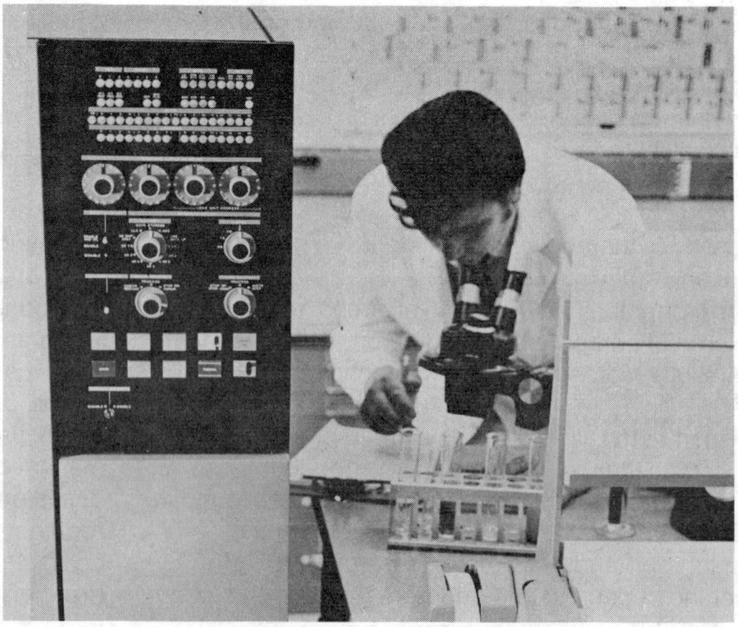

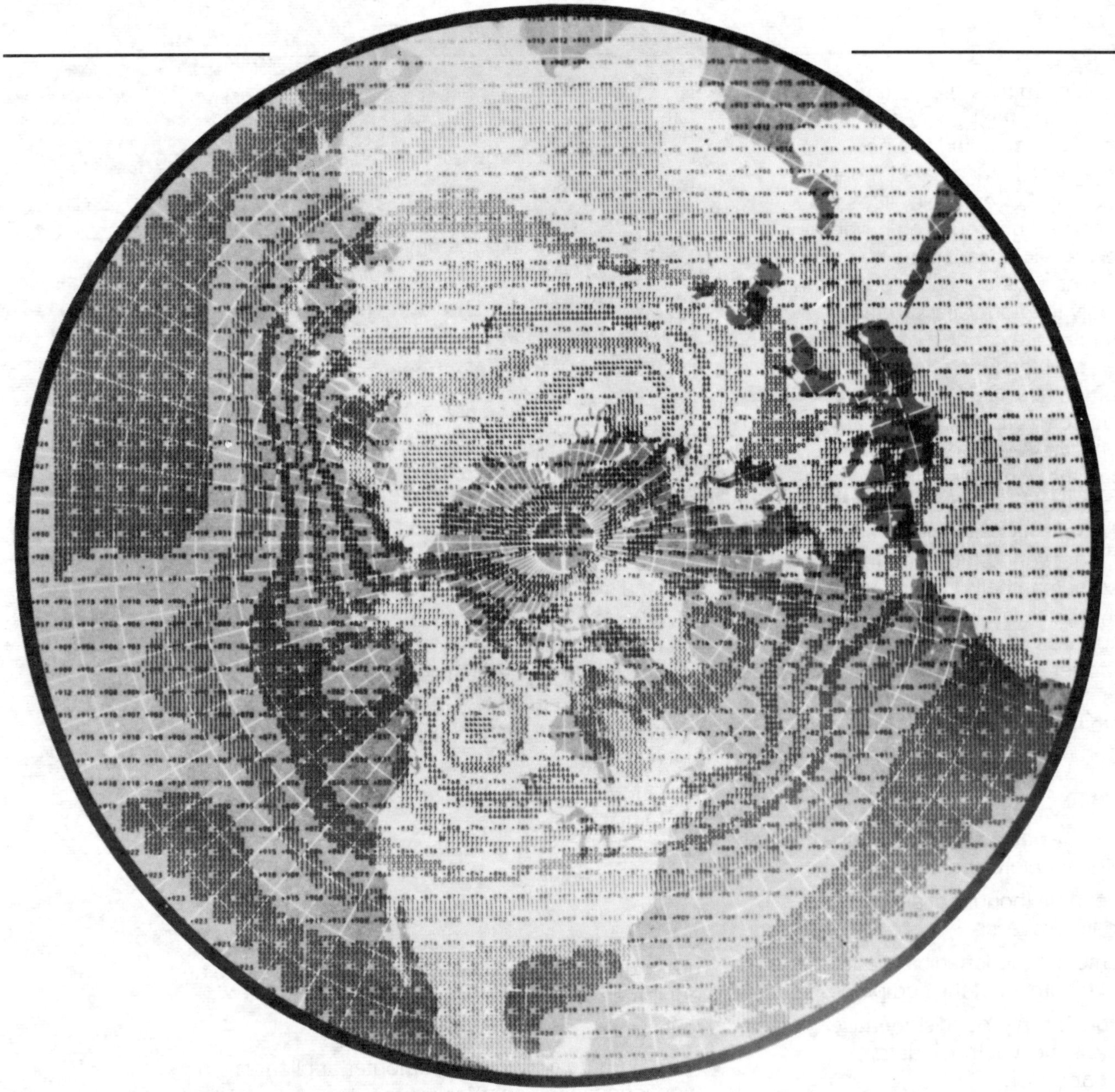

Diagram 1.8.4 Circular section of polar projection map

The Computer in Society

Much has been said about the computer taking over our lives, putting people out of jobs and invading our privacy. These topics cannot be discussed intelligently without knowing more about the computer, but they should be given some thought as your knowledge and understanding increase. Remember that the computer cannot do anything unless it is told what to do by human beings. We should control the computer—it should not control us.

One question we should ask is, "Is the computer being used efficiently for the right tasks?" In using it to solve the problem of providing fast accurate information we may well have created more problems to be solved. For example, does the manager read the four hundred page report he now gets on time every week? In fact does he need a full report at all? Perhaps an exception report—that is, a report showing only the abnormal situations—will do. The computer is quite capable of exception reporting; however, which type of report is best is a problem for a human to solve. We must give instructions to the computer to produce an exception report if this is what we need.

Have we tapped the computer's full potential? The computer has contributed a great deal so far to research in such areas as medicine, space projects and archeology, uncovering facts and figures that would have taken human beings many years to arrive at. In today's society can we do without it? As we learn more about its capabilities and limitations, we can probably offer a better judgement about its place in our lives. Let us try and find out how it works and then return to these questions.

Points to Review

(1) The computer is a valuable tool because it is able to perform functions rapidly and accurately.

(2) The abacus can be thought of as the first "mechanized" data processor.

(3) The development of punched card equipment paralleled the development of the computer.

(4) Many inventors throughout history have contributed towards the electronic data processor—the computer.

(5) Computer development has expanded rapidly since the forties.

(6) The computer is used in a variety of ways in today's society.

What Do You Know?

(1) What advantages has the computer over human beings? What disadvantages?

(2) Give three examples of data being processed without any mechanical or electronic help.

(3) Why did Babbage fail to get his difference engine to run successfully?

(4) Who would you consider made the greatest contribution towards the development of the computer? Give reasons for your choice.

(5) Why is punched-card equipment not fully satisfactory for data processing?

(6) What makes the electronic computer superior to its predecessors?

(7) What contribution did Dr. Hollerith make in the development of punched-card equipment? Did his work also help in the development of the computer?

(8) Research further the work done by the following in the development of the computer:

(a) Dr. Howard Aiken
(b) Dr. John Mauchly
(c) Dr. J. Presper Eckert
(d) Dr. John von Neumann

(9) Who were the following people and what contribution, if any, did they make towards computer development?

(a) George Boole
(b) Lady Lovelace
(c) Alan Turing
(d) James Powers

(10) Prepare a chart showing in parallel the development of data processing equipment and communication facilities. Give the dates, people and equipment involved.

(11) Define a computer.

(12) Prepare a list of ten computer applications not mentioned in the chapter.

(13) List any uses of the computer that personally affect you.

2 Feeding the Computer a Problem

This chapter introduces the computer as a problem solving tool. We shall investigate how the computer receives the problem to be solved.

Probably a better name than computer is **computing system**, since very few computers consist of a single 'box'. Generally, a computer is several boxes linked by cables. Any computing system is composed of three main parts: the **input unit**, the **processor**, and the **output unit**.

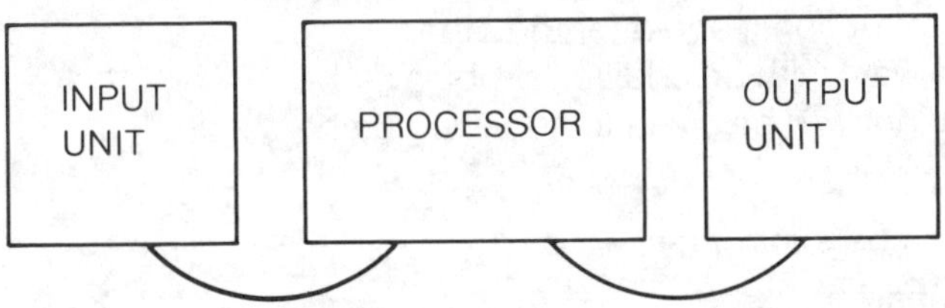

Diagram 2.1 Computing system

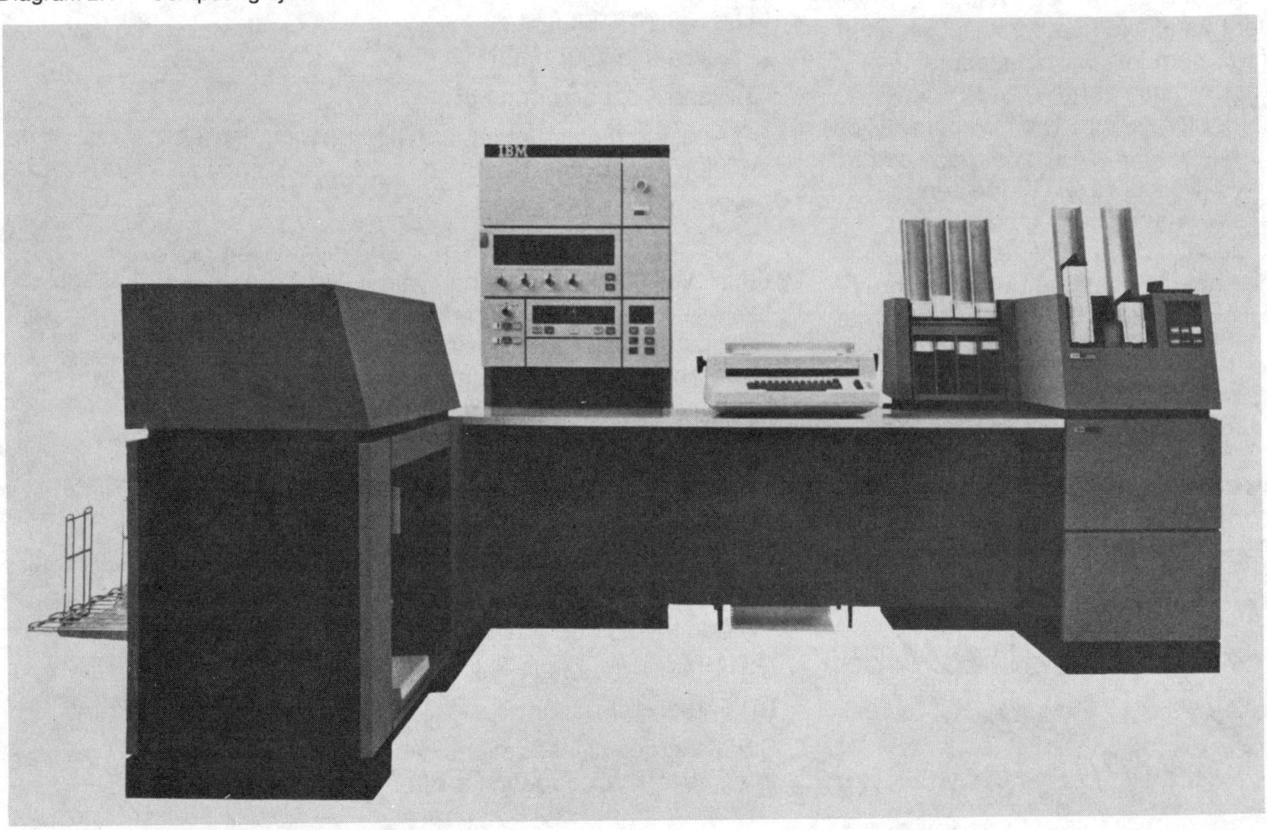

The Computing System

It is interesting to note that the three boxes above could apply to a variety of 'computers' that are not necessarily electronic. Consider the calculation of the average of exam marks:

	Input Unit	*Processor*	*Output Unit*
	eyes	brain	typewriter
	Input	*Processing*	*Output*
(1)	exam marks	calculation	average mark
(2)	average marks	calculation of class average	report cards

Notice that the **output** from example 1 becomes the **input** to example 2. Our brain, the processing unit, requires help on occasion from a pencil and paper. We shall discover later that the computer often needs a scratch pad too. There are many more instances of the input-processing-output cycle connected with problem solving and data processing.

If we are to use a computer to solve a problem, then there must be a means of feeding information into the computer, so the processor can work on it. We also need the results in a form we can read and understand. In a computer we have an input unit, an output unit, and a processor that is called the **central processing unit**. Assuming that we do have these three units, we can use our simple computing system to solve an easy problem such as adding two numbers together.

First we must establish how to tell the computer what we want it to do, since yelling at it does not have quite the required effect!

Instructions

Using the input unit we can give the computer the **instructions** it needs to solve our problem. The instructions first are stored in the central processing unit. Then they are carried out. Our instructions will tell the computer to add two numbers. But what numbers? Any two numbers will be acceptable providing they are within a certain range that will vary with the computer design. The numbers will be the data to be processed and must be ready at the input unit. They will be stored within the central processing unit so that they can be added.

Suppose you need to drive from here to Seeville. You have no idea how to get there but someone gives you the following instructions which you write down:

1) Take Main St. to Hwy. 609
2) Right on Hwy. 609
3) Drive east on 609 app. 10 mi. to Hwy. 10A.
4) Left on Hwy 10A for 2 blocks
5) Turn right for 5 blocks (Seeville P.O. on corner)

Feeding the Computer a Problem

In this set of instructions several assumptions are made: First, you know you must put your key in the ignition and start the car. Second, you know how to get to Main Street and which direction to go for Highway 609. Third, you realize you must follow the instructions in the sequence given. (If you follow instruction 5 before instruction 4, you might get lost!) Fourth, you understand that instruction 5 is the last instruction because it tells you that you are at Seeville.

Having written down and understood the instructions, you will then return to the first step and *execute* the instructions, one after the other.

In the same way, with an addition problem, what instructions might you be given to add two numbers?

(1) Read two numbers

(2) Add the numbers together

(3) Write the answer

If you analyze more closely what you do when adding, it would probably be something like this:

(1) Read one number

(2) Store it in your brain

(3) Read a second number

(4) Add it to the first number using the method of addition already learned

(5) Write down the answer

The computer, however, must be given even more detail. We must tell it the equivalent kinds of things to 'put your key in the ignition', and so on. Also, we shall have to give it the instructions in the correct order and to indicate when the last instruction has been received. Consider the following instructions:

(1) Read a number and store it

(2) Read a second number and store it

(3) Move the numbers to the special part of the central processing unit where arithmetic is performed

(4) Add the two numbers

(5) Give out the result

(6) End of instructions

Such a series of instructions, which are precise and in some logical sequence is often referred to as an

algorithm. The term algorithm is often used in mathematics to describe a systematic procedure, and is probably used in computer science because computer science relates closely to mathematics. The solution of problems in a commercial data processing environment involves an algorithmic approach but the term algorithm is not as frequently used.

In communicating with the computer we first develop an algorithm for the solution. The algorithm provides a logical sequence of events described in English or mathematical terms. When these instructions are written in a form the computer can interpret, they are called a **program**, and the person who writes them is called a **programmer**.

Once we have a set of instructions for our problem, we will feed the instructions into the computer using the input unit. When the last instruction is read, the computer returns to instruction 1 and executes the instructions in sequence. In order for the computer to execute the instructions we may be required to provide data. For the example above we must provide the two numbers that are to be added.

At this point we must take a closer look at the following:

Input

What does our *input* look like?
What does our *input unit* look like?
How is the information (instructions and data) getting from the input unit to the central processing unit?
How are the numbers added?
In what form is the output?

Input

One of the most common forms of input to a computing system is the **punched card**. The most common size of punched card is about 83 mm by 187 mm. The reason why it is this size is interesting—it happens to be the original size of an American dollar bill. The colour of the card is not significant—input units are colour blind! What is most important is the position and number of holes punched in the card.

Notice that the card is divided into 80 vertical columns and 12 horizontal rows. Each column can be used to represent any single letter of the alphabet, number or special character. By special character,

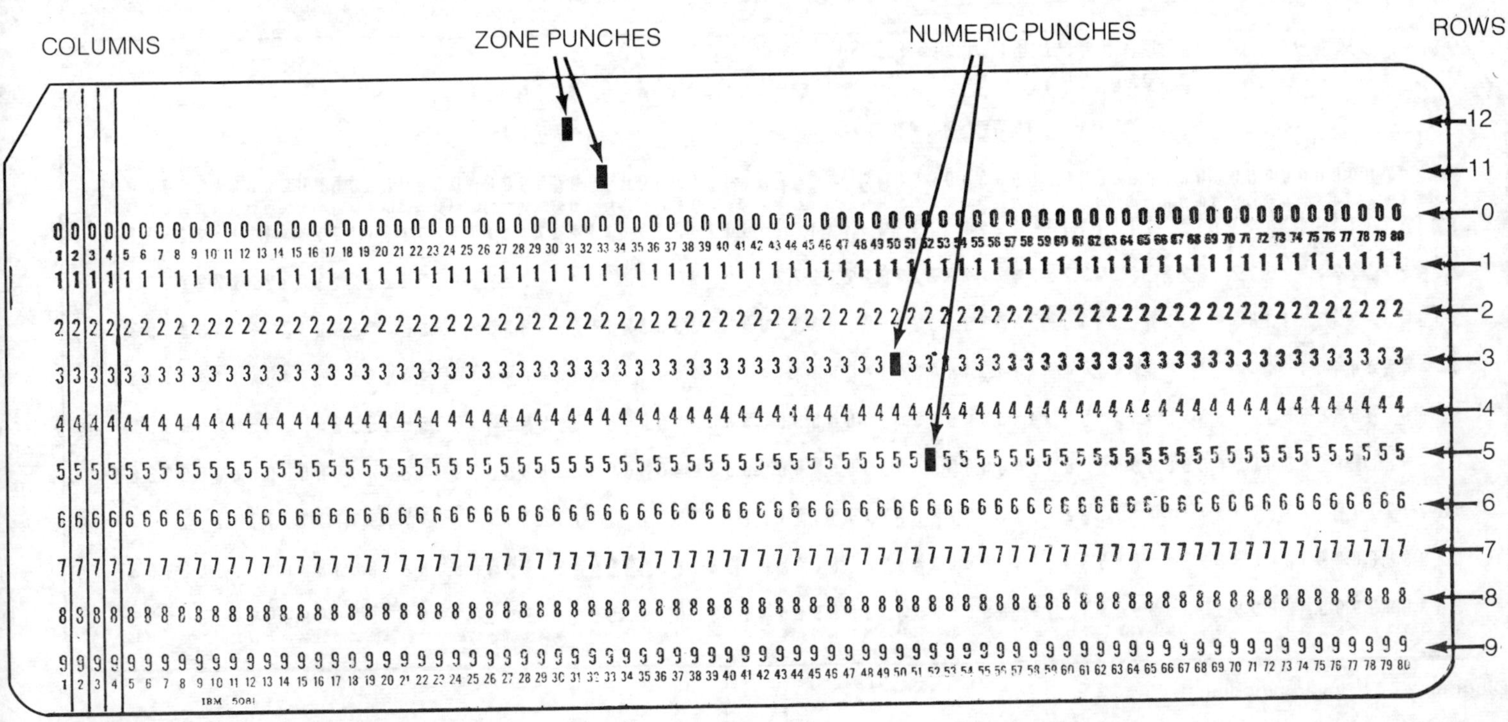

Diagram 2.2 Punched card

we mean such symbols as *,$,(,). The top two rows are not numbered but, together with row zero, are called **zones**.

Top row	12 zone
Second row	11 zone
Third row	0 zone

Row zero is also considered a number position.

The numerals from 0 to 9 can be represented in each column by a single punch. To represent a number greater than 9, more than one column must be used. Thus, to punch 3621 takes 4 columns with a single punch in each column.

We have used up almost all the single punches to represent the numbers. In order to represent letters and special characters, we shall have to use more than one punch per column. To represent the alphabet requires two punches in a column, one punch being a zone punch, the other a numerical punch.

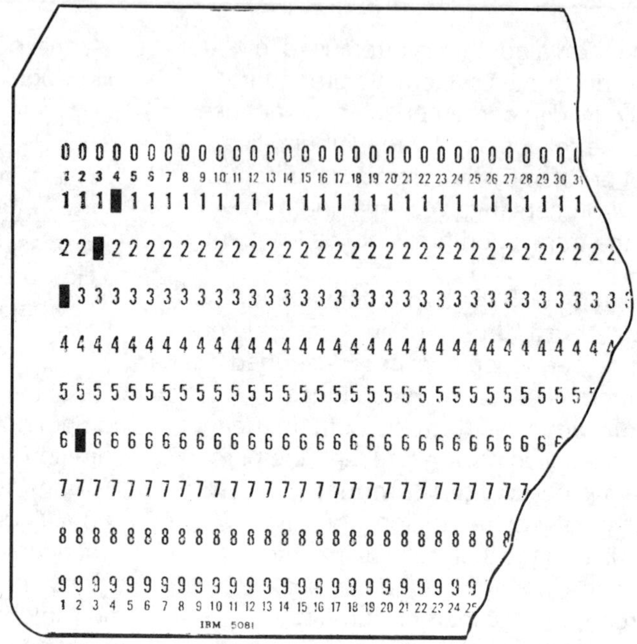

Diagram 2.3 The number 3621 punched into a card

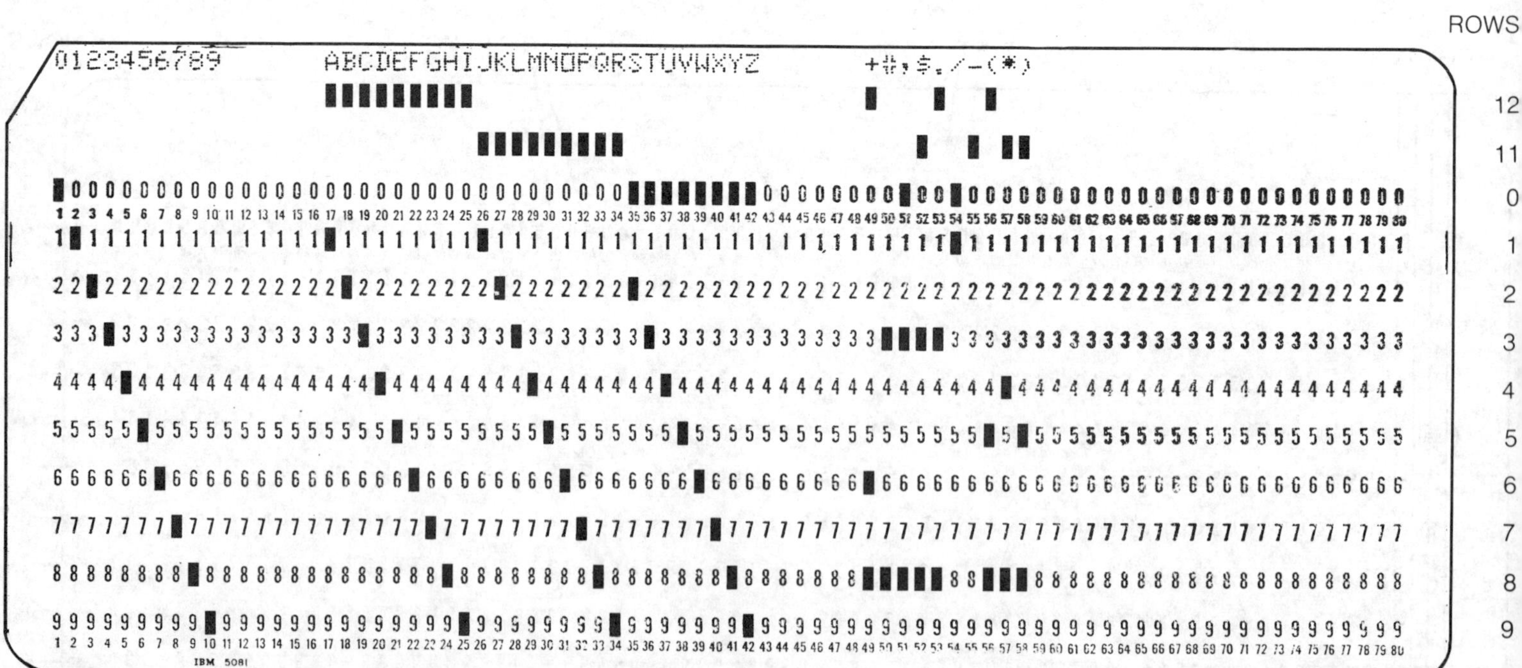

Diagram 2.4 Hollerith coding

The letters A,B,C,D,E,F,G,H,I need a 12 zone and the numbers 1-9.

The letters J,K,L,M,N,O,P,Q,R need an 11 zone and the numbers 1-9.

The letters S,T,U,V,W,X,Y,Z need a 0 zone and the numbers 2-9.

Special characters usually require three punches. For example,

$	11 zone, 3 and 8 punches
(	0 zone, 4 and 8 punches
)	12 zone, 4 and 8 punches

Plus and minus signs are represented by single punches.

+	12 zone
–	11 zone

This coding structure, called **Hollerith coding** after the inventor, Dr. Herman Hollerith, is the most common coding structure used in a punched card but it is not the only one. The card in diagram 2.5 employs a different coding structure, known as Binary Coded Decimal (BCD). The card is a different size and uses 3 levels to contain 96 characters of information.

Letters and numbers are collectively called **characters**. We have shown that characters and special characters can be represented on a card by punching holes. There now arise three more questions:

(1) How do we get the holes into the cards?
(2) How does the input unit 'read' the information?
(3) How does the information get to the central processing unit?

Diagram 2.5 BCD punched card

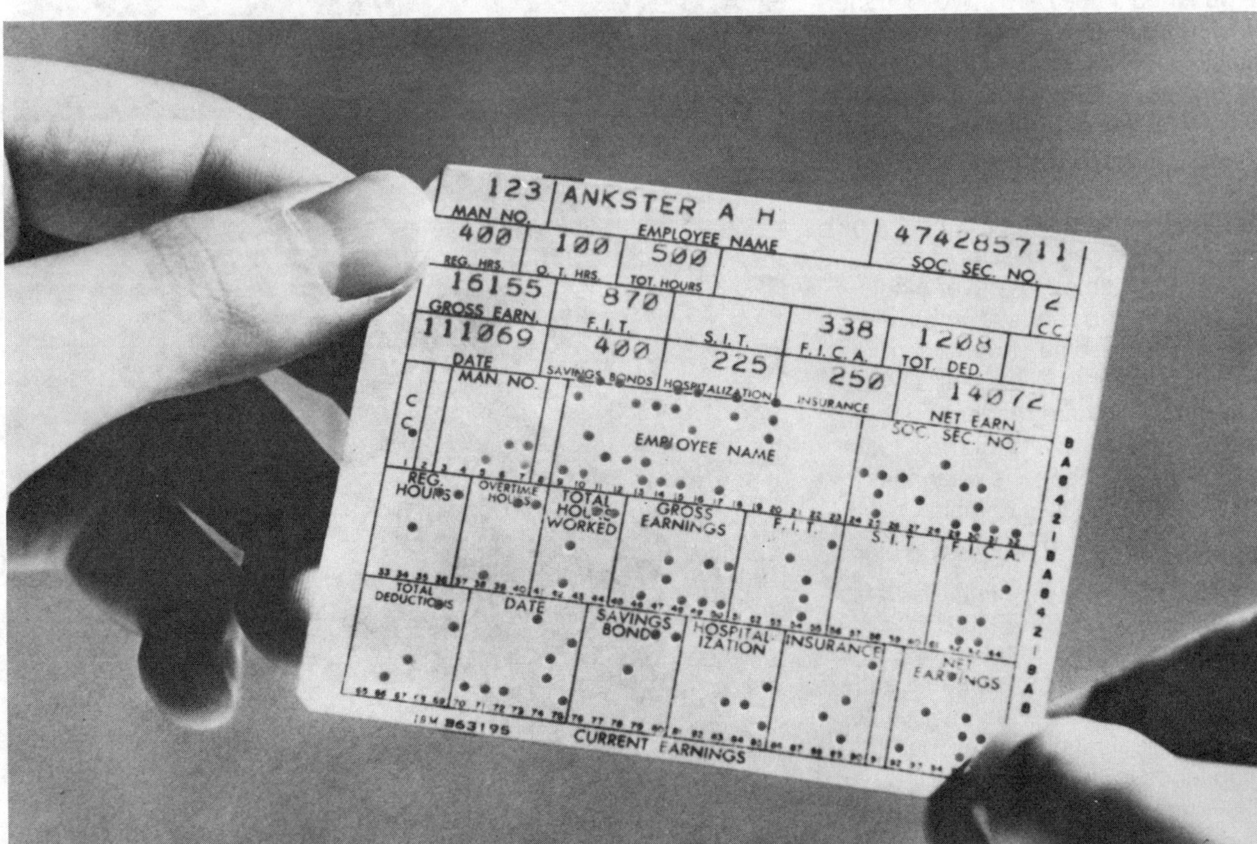

(1) *Punching the holes in the card.*
The holes are punched in the card by using a device called a **keypunch** or a **data recorder.** The keyboard of a keypunch, as you can see, basically resembles a typewriter keyboard. When the keys are depressed, the appropriate holes are punched in the card and automatically converted by the keypunch to Hollerith code. If we wish to punch another type of coding structure into the cards, then we must either have a special keypunch for it or punch each hole singly. The latter method is very tedious and slow. As well as punching holes, keypunches optionally will print the characters punched across the top of the card. This makes it easier for us to understand exactly what we have punched.

(2) *Reading the information*
To answer question two let us take a closer look at our input unit. One of the most common input units is a **card reader**. This is a device capable of sensing the holes we have punched in the cards. We feed the cards in via the **card hopper**. One card at a time slides through a small gap at the base of the hopper and follows a path through the reader. As it follows this path it passes through the various stations of the card reader. The 'reading' of the card—in fact, electronic sensing of the position of the holes—is done at the read station by a series of 12 lights—one for each row on the card. The card passes across these lights, one column at a time. Wherever a hole occurs, the light penetrates and sends an impulse to the central processing unit. In some card readers brushes are used instead of lights to sense the holes. The card is routed through the card reader and drops into a **stacker** unchanged by its journey. Later on we shall take a look at what happens when these impulses arrive at the central processing unit.

(3) *Communication with the central processing unit*
Communication by electronic impulses implies that the card reader is attached physically to the central processing unit. In fact the two are attached by a cable. In many computer installations this cable and others are covered by a false floor, for safety's sake, and therefore are not visible. In these cases the computer installation tends to give the misleading impression that all the units or boxes are separate and independent.

Diagram 2.6 Keypunch

Diagram 2.7 Card reader

To sum up the procedure so far:
The problem: to add together two numbers
(1) Write the instructions in the required sequence
(2) Punch the instructions into cards using a keypunch
(3) Punch the data into cards
(4) Feed the instructions into the card reader
(5) Make sure the data is behind the instructions in the card reader

In the next chapter, we shall see what happens to the electronic impulses when they leave the card reader.

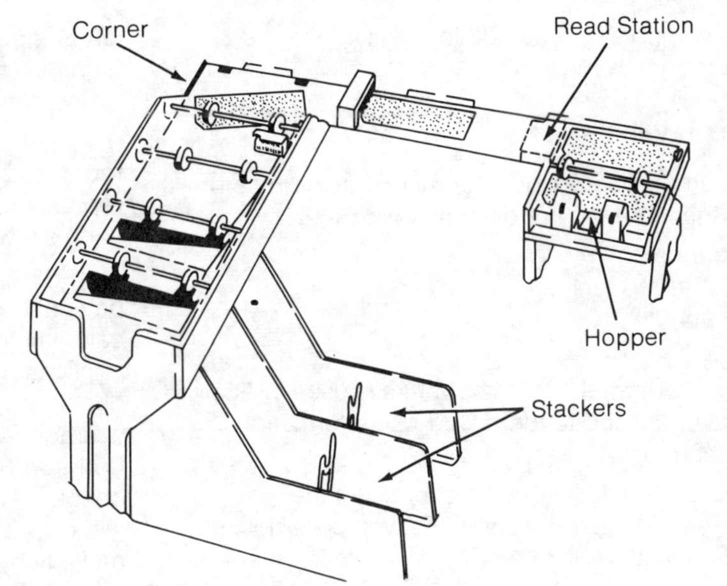

Diagram 2.8 Inside a card reader

Buzz Words

Input unit
Processor
Central processing unit
Output unit
Punched card
Zone
Character
Hollerith coding
Stacker
Algorithm
Input
Output
Instructions
Program
Programmer
Keypunch
Card reader
Card hopper
Computing system
Data recorder

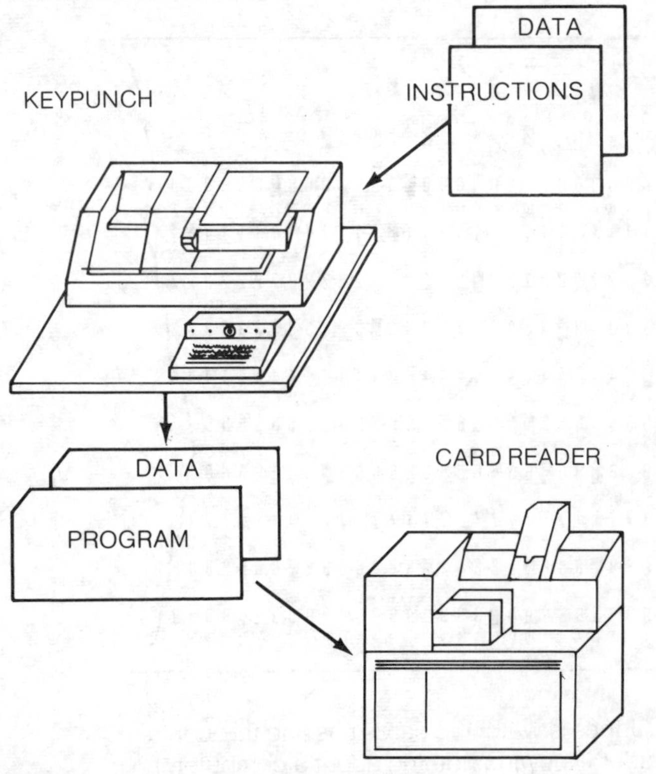

Diagram 2.9 Processing data: the initial steps

Points to Review

(1) Every computing system consists of an input unit—a processor—an output unit.

(2) Input must be in a form readable by the input device used. For example, a card reader can 'read' the holes in a punched card.

(3) Coding structures exist so that information may be represented by holes in a punched card.

(4) One commonly used coding structure was invented by Dr. Hermann Hollerith.

(5) The description of the problem solution, in logical sequence, is sometimes called an algorithm.

(6) Instructions to solve a problem form a program. These instructions must be detailed, exact and in logical sequence.

(7) A computer will do nothing until it receives instructions.

What Do You Know?

(1) Using a diagram or an actual 80-column card, code the following in Hollerith coding:

(a) Your name
(b) Montreal, Quebec
(c) $69.41
(d) 3 + 7 = 10

(2) Find out what coding structure is used in ASCII code (American Standard Code for Information Interchange).

(3) Give detailed instructions for using the telephone, suitable for someone who does not know how to use it.

(4) Can the output from one processing system be the input to another system? Give two examples.

(5) Interpret what is punched into the card.

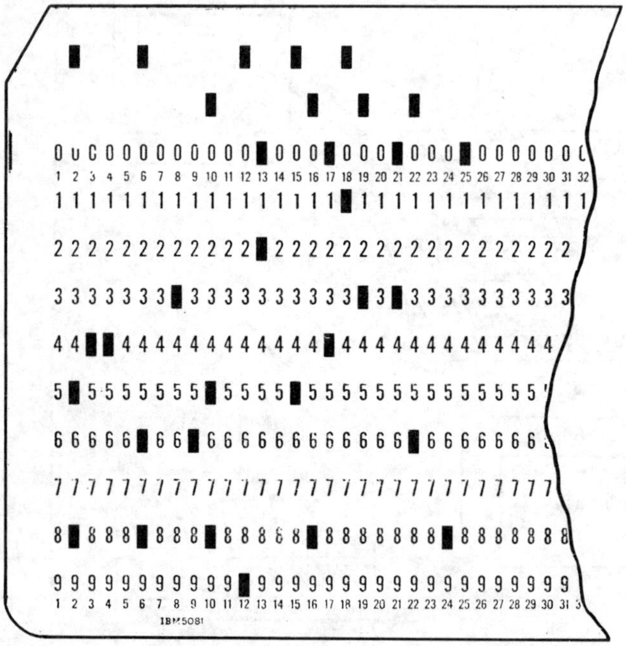

(6) Mr. Jones is watching cards passing through a card reader. Knowing nothing about a computer, he is puzzled. Explain to him exactly what is happening.

(7) Suggest three data processing systems not mentioned in the chapter, specifying input, processing and output in each case.

(8) Unscramble the following list so that there are four sets of input, processing and output, each representing a data processing system. Indicate for each set what or who does the processing:

money
pay cheque
calculation of average
application form
check & update bank balance
average monthly sales
hours worked
check for number of credits
withdrawal slip
multiply by rate of pay
acceptance at college
monthly sales figures

3 Getting the Answer Out

In this chapter we shall see how the computer is able to solve the problem it has been given and output the answer in a form we can understand.

The Central Processing Unit

The central processing unit, or *CPU* as it is often referred to, really consists of three sections. The term *central* is applied to this unit since all information that moves through a computing system must pass through the unit one or more times.

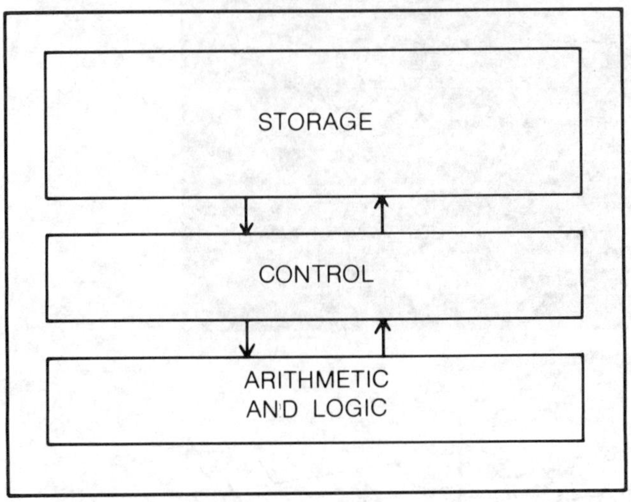

The **control unit** is responsible for directing and co-ordinating the entire computer system and is comparable to a telephone exchange. In our problem a number will be read from the card reader when the appropriate instruction is issued. The control unit will check that the card reader has a card in the hopper to be read and will supervise the transfer of the number to storage. Both the control unit and the arithmetic/logic unit are a mass of electronic circuitry and we are concerned not with their make-up but only with their functions.

The **arithmetic/logic unit** performs such operations as addition, subtraction, multiplication, division, comparing and testing. In the arithmetic/logic unit there is circuitry that is capable of adding two numbers together in much the same way as does an adding machine. Similarly, there is circuitry to perform the other functions. These

Diagram 3.1 Computer circuitry

capabilities of the computer are called *hardware* features. The number of functions provided as hardware circuitry varies with the computer design. Multiplication is sometimes not included as a hardware feature and special instructions or a multiplication program must be provided. This program would form part of the computer *software*.

The **main storage** of computers takes many forms all of which have in common the conservation of space. This storage area is the place where our instructions and data will be stored. Information is moved into and out of storage, and from place to place within storage, and therefore the smaller the area the faster information can be moved. A single tiny storage unit can be used to represent a **bit**—from the words **bi**nary digi**t**. Physically the unit can have only two states that we shall call on or off. The 'on' state is represented by a one and the 'off' state a zero. Three common types of storage are **monolithic storage, core storage** and **MOSFET** (**M**etal **O**xide **S**emi-conductor **F**ield **E**ffect **T**ransistors.)

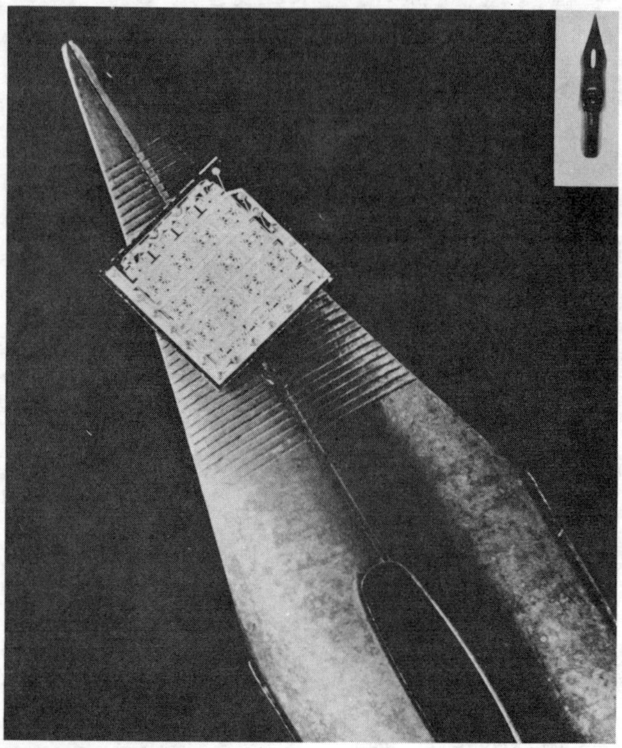

Diagram 3.2 Monolithic circuit

Diagram 3.3 Core storage

Monolithic storage is manufactured by concentrating, on a single chip measuring 2.9 mm by 3.1 mm, 128 bits and the required circuitry to enable them to be turned on or off and accessed. Thus in an area no bigger than your thumbnail could easily be stored the names of all the students in your school. Research in this area has produced even denser storage called MOSFET.

Core storage consists of a large number of tiny doughnut-shaped cores with wires passing through them. Core storage is seldom used in today's computers but its structure lends itself to a simple explanation of how storage works, so we shall use it for just that.

The group of bits which represent a character are referred to as a **word** or **byte**. One core can store one bit, and a word or byte would be stored on a group of cores.

In core storage the wires passing through the cores enable them to be magnetized positively or negatively—'on' or 'off', if you like. The hundreds of cores in core storage are arranged in core planes.

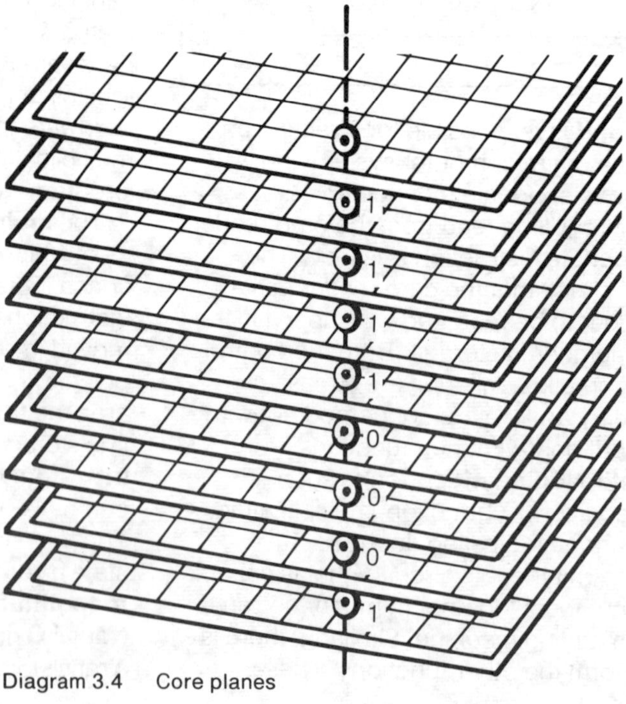

Diagram 3.4 Core planes

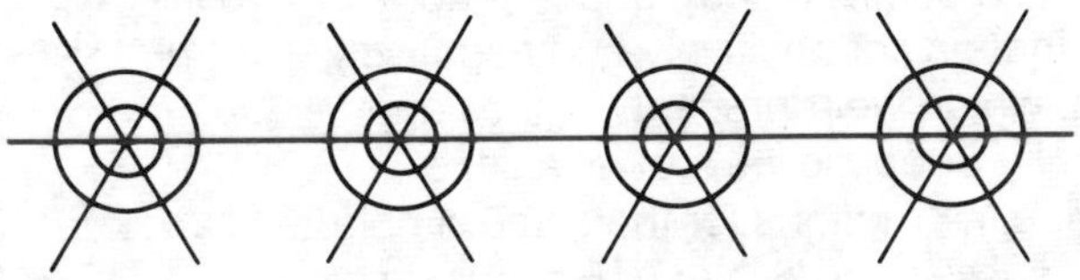

Diagram 3.5.1

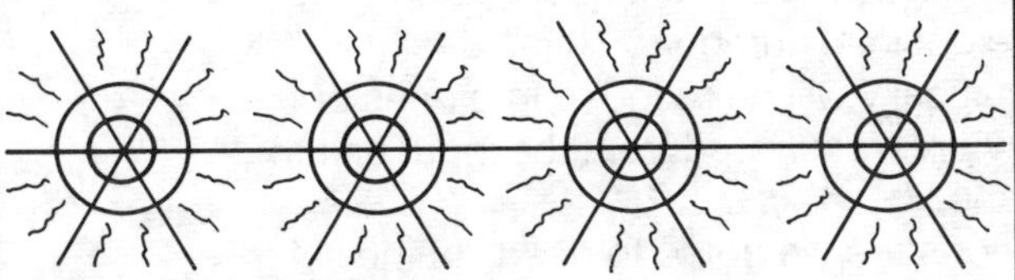

Diagram 3.5.2

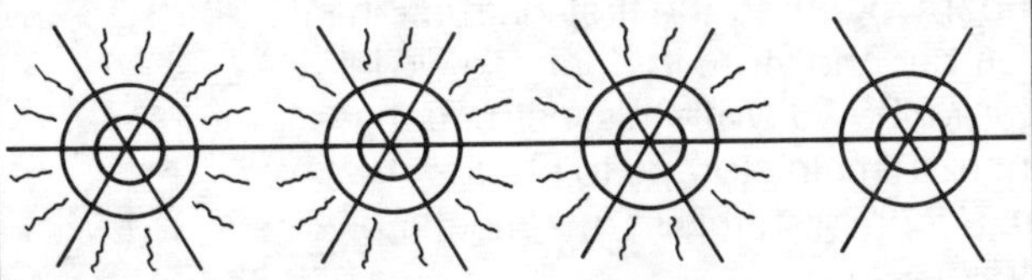

Diagram 3.5.3

How can we use the cores to store information? Suppose we group the cores together in fours and use them to represent characters (see diagram 3.5.1). We could represent the letter A by having all four cores turned 'on' (see diagram 3.5.2). Three turned 'on' and one 'off' could represent the letter B (see diagram 3.5.3). Drawing cores in this manner is a little tedious so we will use 1 for 'on' and 0 for 'off'.

1111	represents A
1110	represents B
1100	represents C
1000	represents D
0000	represents E
0100	represents F

The possible different combinations with four cores are limited to sixteen and thus only 16 different letters can be represented in this way. We have not represented the entire alphabet, let alone the numbers and special characters. It would seem that grouping four cores together was not too smart a choice. Suppose we try eight? If we experiment with the number of combinations possible here, we see that it is quite enough to cover all the letters, numbers and special characters, as well as many different instructions that we shall need—in fact, there are 256 possible combinations.

Whether the group of bits representing a character is referred to as a word or as a byte depends upon the manufacturer. The number of bits grouped together to form a word or byte also varies with the computer and is an integral part of the design of the computer. The IBM 370 computer was designed with one byte, composed of eight bits. Four bytes form a word in this computer. In an IBM 1130 computer sixteen bits form a word and there is no unit called a byte. The Honeywell 1200 has eight bits in a word, two of which are used for punctuation. In all computers there are also one or more extra bits associated with each byte or word and used for checking purposes.

You may have heard the expression 'Their computer is 64K'. This term refers to the size or capacity of storage and the 'K' stands for 1000. Thus a 64K computer has approximately 64 000 positions of main storage, specified as bytes or words according to the machine design. In fact, because of the way storage is constructed, that is, in powers of 2, the actual number of positions is 65 536. In referring to a particular computer it would be more meaningful to say 'Their computer has 64K bytes of main storage' or 'Their computer has 64K words....' The term **main storage** refers to that storage we have been discussing, namely core storage or, in the latest computers, monolithic storage. Although main storage is sometimes called computer memory, we shall see later that this is a somewhat misleading term.

The positions of storage are all 'addressable' that is, they all have a numeric address associated with them. Each addressable position is a byte or word depending upon the computer design. Main storage can be compared to a giant array of post office boxes. The numbers on the boxes uniquely identify the locations. Similarly, all locations of storage are uniquely identified. (See diagram 3.6.) Each storage position is capable of storing a piece of data or an instruction. Thus, storage location 105 may contain

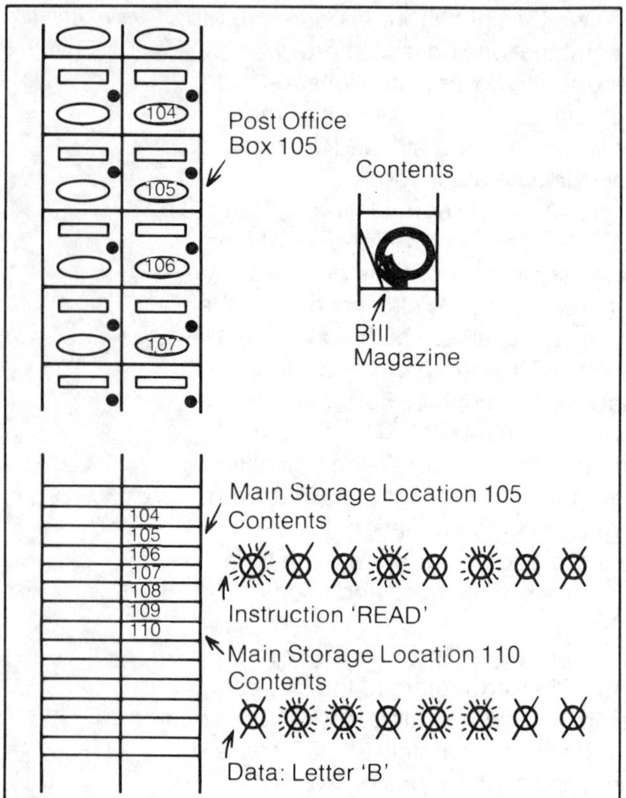

Diagram 3.6 Storage: Post office and computer

the instruction READ. Storage location 110 may contain the letter B. (Actually they would be represented by ones and zeros, not by English letters.)

In our addition problem we had reached the point where impulses from the card reader were being sent to the CPU. The control unit makes sure that the arriving instructions are stored in main storage. How do our Hollerith coded punches become bytes or words? Fortunately, hardware circuitry is built in as part of the CPU or software is provided to make sure that the correct change of coding takes place.

Machine Language Instructions

Our instructions to the computer have been written in English sentences. Unfortunately the computer does not understand English. The only language a computer understands is its own **machine language**, each machine having a unique language. The instructions a computer can understand consist of combinations of positively and negatively magnetized bits, which we represent as ones and zeros, respectively. Suppose we look at a set of machine language instructions for the same simple computer we discussed in Chapter 2. For our simple hypothetical machine the instructions we punch into the cards will be decimal numbers. These decimal numbers automatically will be recoded into ones or zeros when they are transferred from the input unit to the processor unit.

What instructions are we going to need? In the set of instructions we drew up for solving the problem of adding two numbers together, the first instruction was to read a number and store it. Suppose we let the instruction 'read' be 30. With this instruction we must specify where in main storage to put the number. We can accomplish this in one machine language instruction.

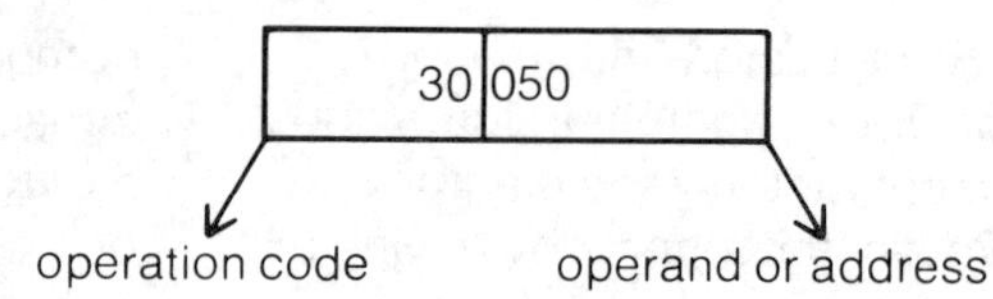

In other words every instruction consists of two parts:

(1) The **operation code** telling the computer what operation is to be performed. In the example above, 30 will tell the computer to read.

(2) The **operand** or **address** qualifying the operation code, that is, providing additional information. In the example, 050 is the storage address where we shall store the number.

The size of main storage varies from one system to another. For ease of illustration, let us assume we have a main storage of 1000 positions.

As well as main storage a computer has other special storage positions called **registers**. The number of registers varies with the design of the computer and most of their locations are independent of the positions of main storage. There is always a register called the instruction address register that stores the address of the next

Machine Language Instructions

instruction to be executed. As well, there is always at least one register used in arithmetic and logic operations. This register is sometimes called the **accumulator register** or just the accumulator. When arithmetic is being performed one factor (number) must be in the accumulator. At that time other factors (numbers) can then be added to the number in the accumulator—similarly with subtraction, multiplication and division. All logic operations are accomplished using the accumulator register. There are other special purpose registers and usually some general purpose registers connected with the control and operation of the computer but we shall concern ourselves only with the accumulator register.

Many of the instruction capabilities of a computer exist as hardware features. Almost all general purpose computers have the following instructions:

Load	Store	Add
Subtract	Multiply	Divide
Branch	Input	Output

Very often there are several different instructions in each type. For example, the branch instructions for the IBM 1130 are

	Operation Code
Branch and store IAR	01000
Branch and skip on condition	01001
Modify index and skip	01110

Although these actual instructions do not make a lot of sense to you, one fact that should be obvious from them is that the operation code could be considered a binary number.

What about our simple computer? It has fifteen instructions altogether, of which we are presently interested in the following six: (XXX is a location between 000 and 999.)

0000030XXX	Read a number and store at XXX
0000031XXX	Write the number stored at XXX
0000010XXX	Load the contents of location XXX into the accumulator register
0000011XXX	Store the contents of the accumulator register at location XXX.
0000020XXX	Add the contents of location XXX to the accumulator register
0000040000	Stop

Now we are in a position to *code* our instructions in machine language. By coding we mean writing the English instructions we understand in the language the computer understands.

	Oper. Code Address
Read a number and store in main storage	0000030050
Read a second number and store in main storage	0000030051
Load the first number into the accumulator register	0000010050
Add the second number to the accumulator register	0000020051
Move the number in the accumulator register to storage	0000011052
Write out the answer	0000031052
Stop	0000040000

Some points to note:

(1) The instructions must be punched into specific card columns.

(2) Information remains in a storage position or in the accumulator register until replaced with another number by executing instructions such as read or store. Consider the following example:

Read a number (456) and store it at 050
before executing instruction 050 [147]
after executing instruction 050 [456]

Write the number stored at 050
before executing instruction 050 [456]
after executing instruction 050 [456]

Read a number (123) and store it at 050
before executing instruction 050 [456]
after executing instruction 050 [123]

If we issue a read instruction ten times using the same storage address, the only number remaining in storage is the last one. Thus the use of the word 'memory' in connection with computer storage is debatable. Memory is widely used, however, as a term for main storage. If we issue a write instruction ten times using the same storage address, the original number still remains in storage. Before we feed in our instructions or data the computer has garbage (whatever was left by the last user, which is garbage as far as we are concerned) in main storage. It is possible to make every position of storage zero or blank but this is not really necessary since our instructions wipe out the previous contents of main storage.

For simplicity we will refer to the accumulator register from now on as the register.

(3) Loading a number into the register destroys what was previously in the register. The *add* instruction adds to the number in the register, whatever it might be.

(4) The numbers read by the computer can be any that we choose. The first number might be 123, and second, 479. It is all *data* and the computer is completely indifferent to what number it is reading. The only restriction on the data is that the number must be within the range of the computer. Our computer accepts any ten-digit number, which gives us plenty of choice!

(5) We cannot read directly into the register and we cannot write directly from the register. Reading and writing can be done only into and from storage.

(6) Stop does not require an address.

(7) We must indicate to the computer that the last physical instruction has been received. Otherwise the computer tries to read the data that follows as instructions—with resulting chaos! We have to give the computer an indication of when it has finished reading instructions so that it can return to the beginning of the instructions and start to execute them. This is usually done by following the instructions with a special card.

The seven points above represent some of the 'rules' under which our particular computer can operate. Every computer has such 'rules'.

In Chapter 2 we discussed how to feed the problem into the computer. One of our instructions is a write instruction, so we will take a look at an output unit.

Diagram 3.7 Line printer

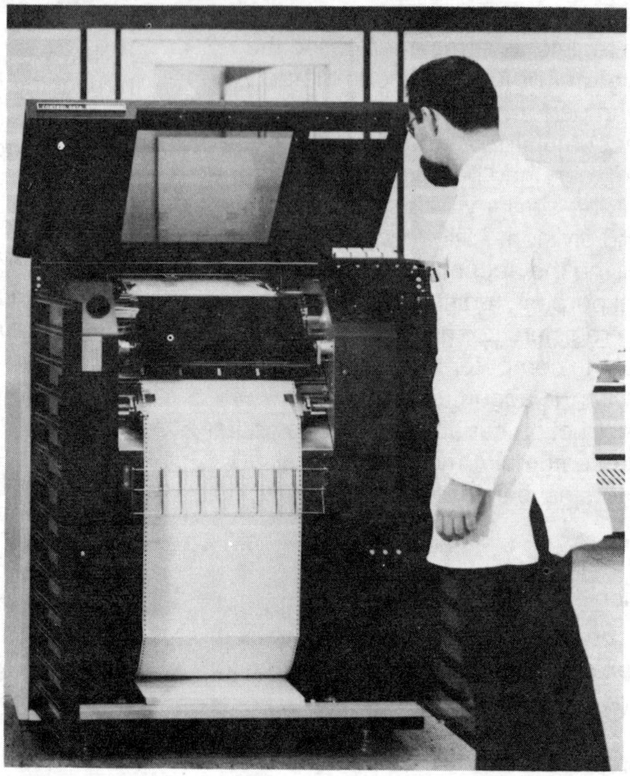

Output Unit and Output

Perhaps the most common form of output unit is a line **printer** producing printed output. The printer receives electronic impulses from the CPU. These impulses cause the appropriate print elements to print the letter or character. There are various types of printing devices, including the print wheel, the chain printer, the bar printer, and the matrix printer. The chain printer, for example, has the required print characters, repeated several times, on a chain. The chain moves horizontally and as the characters reach the position where they are required to print, a hammer presses the character against the paper and inked ribbon. The printer is controlled by impulses from the CPU. The chain moves very fast and hundreds of lines can be printed in one minute.

Output Units and Output

Diagram 3.8 Print chain

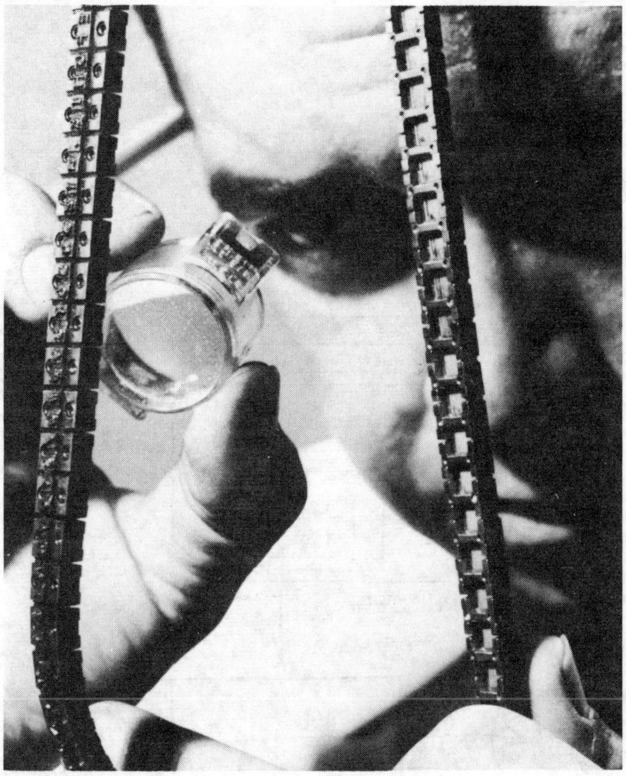

We are now in a position to completely follow through how the computer can be used to solve our problem to add two numbers.

(1) Write out the steps required, remembering that the computer requires detailed instructions.

(2) Code in the language of the computer.

(3) Punch the instructions into cards using a keypunch. (These instructions form a program.)

(4) Punch the data into cards.

(5) Make sure the data is following the program.

(6) Feed the cards, via the hopper, through the card reader.

(7) Check the output to see if the numbers were correctly added! We may have, inadvertently, issued incorrect instructions.

As instructions are read, they occupy consecutive positions in storage starting at location zero. When the last instruction is received, control returns to location zero and the CPU starts analyzing the instructions and executing them. It will execute the instructions in sequence, unless directed otherwise, until the last instruction has been completed.

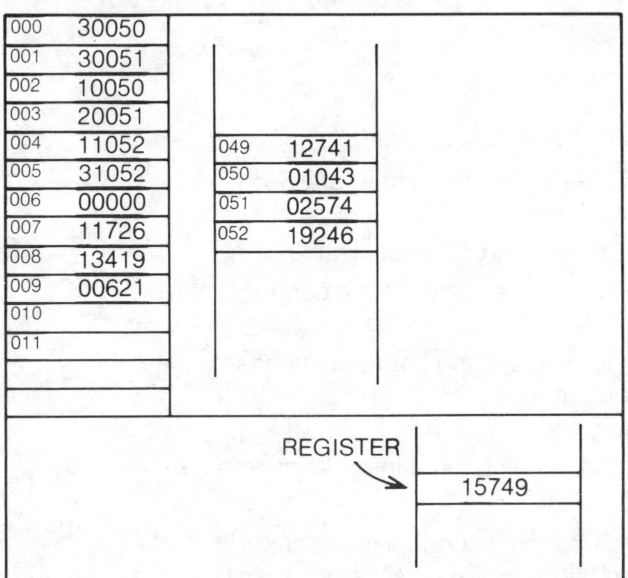

Diagram 3.9 Contents of storage before execution

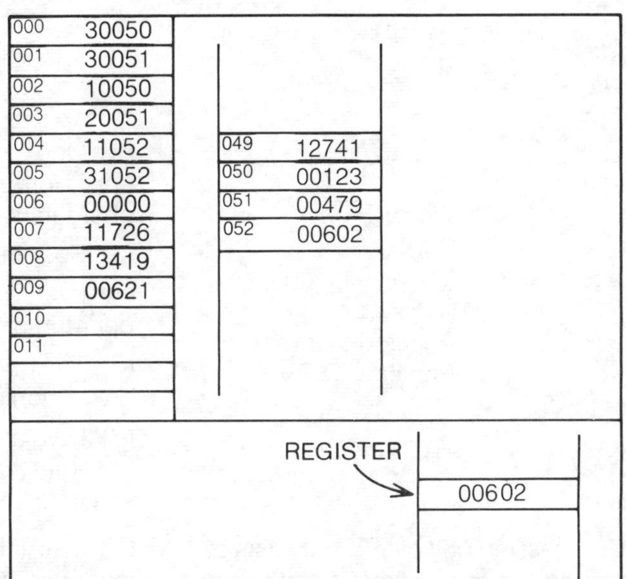

Diagram 3.10 Contents of storage after execution

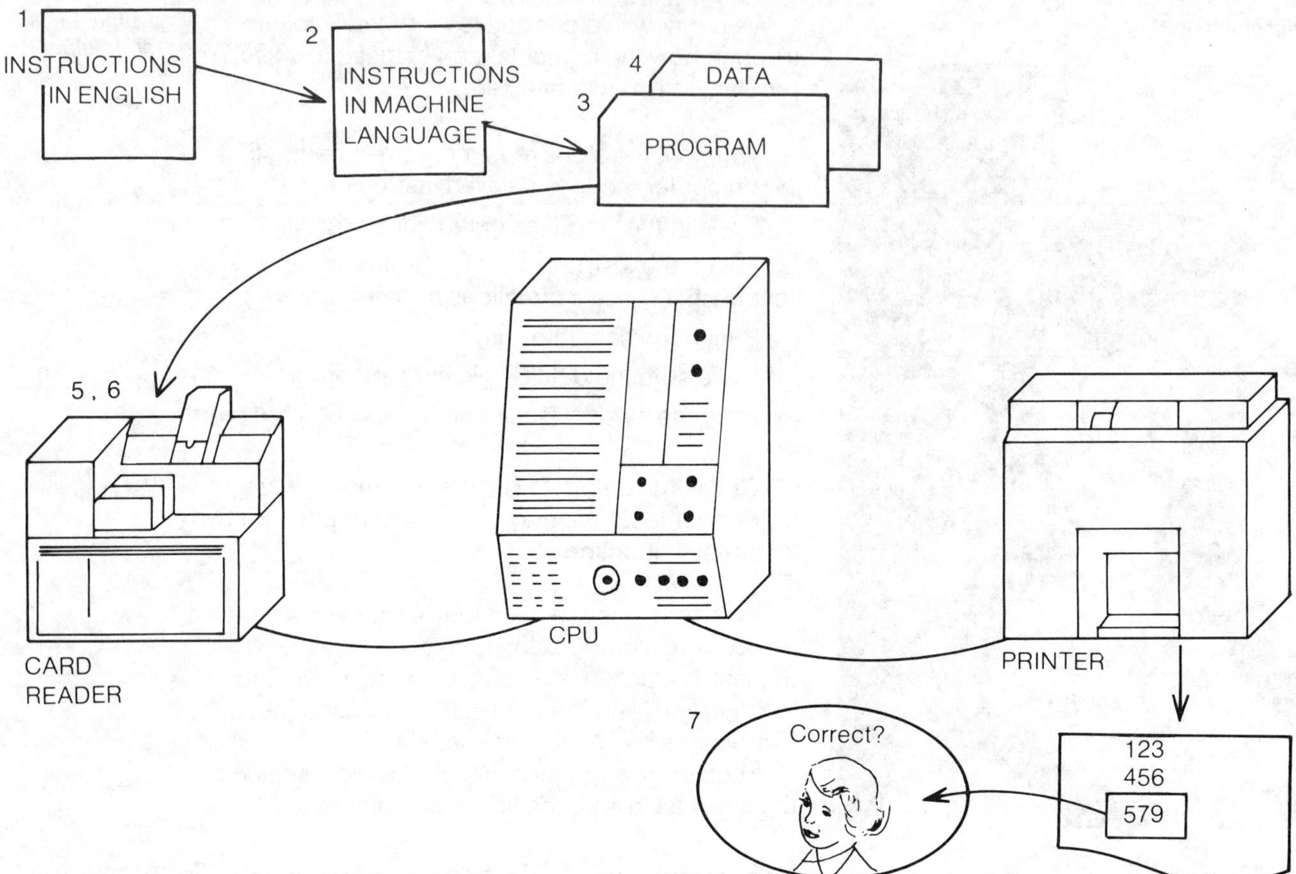

Diagram 3.11 Processing data: the complete procedure

Buzz Words

Control unit
Arithmetic/logic unit
Main storage
Core storage
Monolithic storage
MOSFET
Operation code
Operand
Storage address
Output unit
Bit
Word
Byte
Machine language
Register
Accumulator register
Printer

Points to Review

(1) The central processing unit or CPU consists of control, main storage and the arithmetic and logic unit.

(2) One easy to understand form of main storage is core storage. Cores grouped together enable characters to be stored.

(3) Positions of storage are all addressable.

(4) Instructions consist of an operation code and an operand or address.

(5) The only language a computer understands is its own machine language.

(6) Data and instructions remain in main storage until 'destroyed' by reading more information into the same location.

(7) Instructions are stored sequentially in storage locations, starting at zero. We must keep track of where data is stored.

(8) Special storage locations, called registers, are needed for control and operation of the computer.

(9) A printer is the most common output unit of a computing system.

What Do You Know?

(1) Write a program to read two numbers and write them out, using the instructions from the chapter.

(2) How many main storage positions has a 4K computer? A 48K computer?

(3) Is there a limit to the number of instructions in any one program? Explain your answer.

(4) What happens to Joe's program when Sue feeds hers in directly afterwards?

(5) What is the least practical number of 'bits' in a word to represent uniquely all numbers, letters, special characters and twelve instructions? Show proof.

(6) Explain why calling main storage the computer 'memory' is not accurate. (Take a look at the dictionary definition of memory.)

(7) How many times can we use data that has been punched into cards? Can we use data punched for one program with another program? Explain.

(8) The following six instructions represent a program to read and write three numbers. It does not work! Why? Correct the program.

```
0000031020
0000030020
0000030021
0000030022
0000031022
0000040000
```

(9) Explain briefly the functions of the main parts of a computing system.

(10) Can instructions and data be punched into the same card? Explain.

(11) Explain the difference between a bit, a byte and a word.

(12) Write instructions for adding two numbers stored at locations 200 and 201 and storing the answer at 202.

(13) Rewrite the problem in the chapter so that it will write out the two numbers and the answer to their addition.

4 Flowcharting

Before proceeding to solve more difficult problems using the computer, we need to understand the technique of flowcharting, which is a means of diagrammatically representing the solution to a problem. This chapter introduces program and systems flowcharts.

Program Flowcharting

The problem we considered in Chapter 2 was relatively simple. However, the logic involved in problems solved by a computer can become very complex. In order that we can follow clearly this logic, a method of diagrammatically representing the steps involved in solving a problem has been evolved. This method is called **flowcharting**. Suppose we flowchart the problem in Chapter 2.

Notice that different shapes or *symbols* are used for different operations: a parallelogram for input and output functions, a rectangle for processing functions, an oval for terminating functions (stop and start). What is contained in the symbols is in English. We put our logical solution to the problem in a compact visual form and from this we will code in the appropriate computer language. This type of flowchart is called a **program flowchart**. In this instance each item in our flowchart is translated into an instruction but this does not always happen. There may be more or less instructions according to the language being used. However, when we draw a flowchart we are usually aware of the computer language to be used. A flowchart should be general enough that the programmer can code from it in any language. In fact, a flowchart does not have to be connected with a computer at all!

Suppose we flowchart cooking bacon and eggs. (See diagram 4.2.) In doing this we have used two new symbols: a diamond for decisions and a small circle for connections. Flowcharts normally 'flow' down the page and from left to right across the page. Sometimes we run out of page before we run out of flowchart! At such times the connector symbol becomes useful. Lines with arrows sometimes occur, indicating that the normal flow is to be altered in some way; for instance, several instructions are to be repeated. At certain points decisions have to be

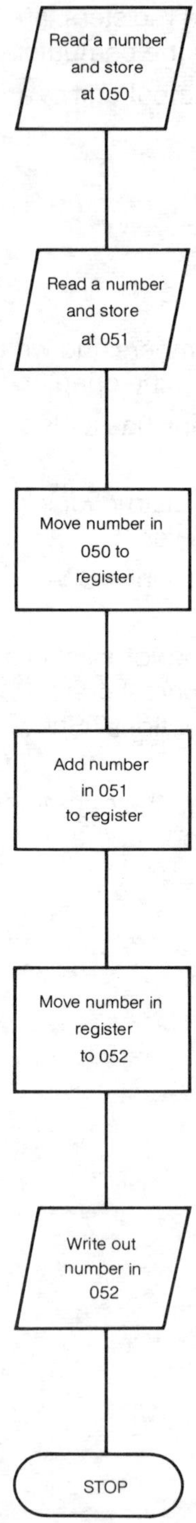

Diagram 4.1 Flowchart: to add together two numbers and write out the result

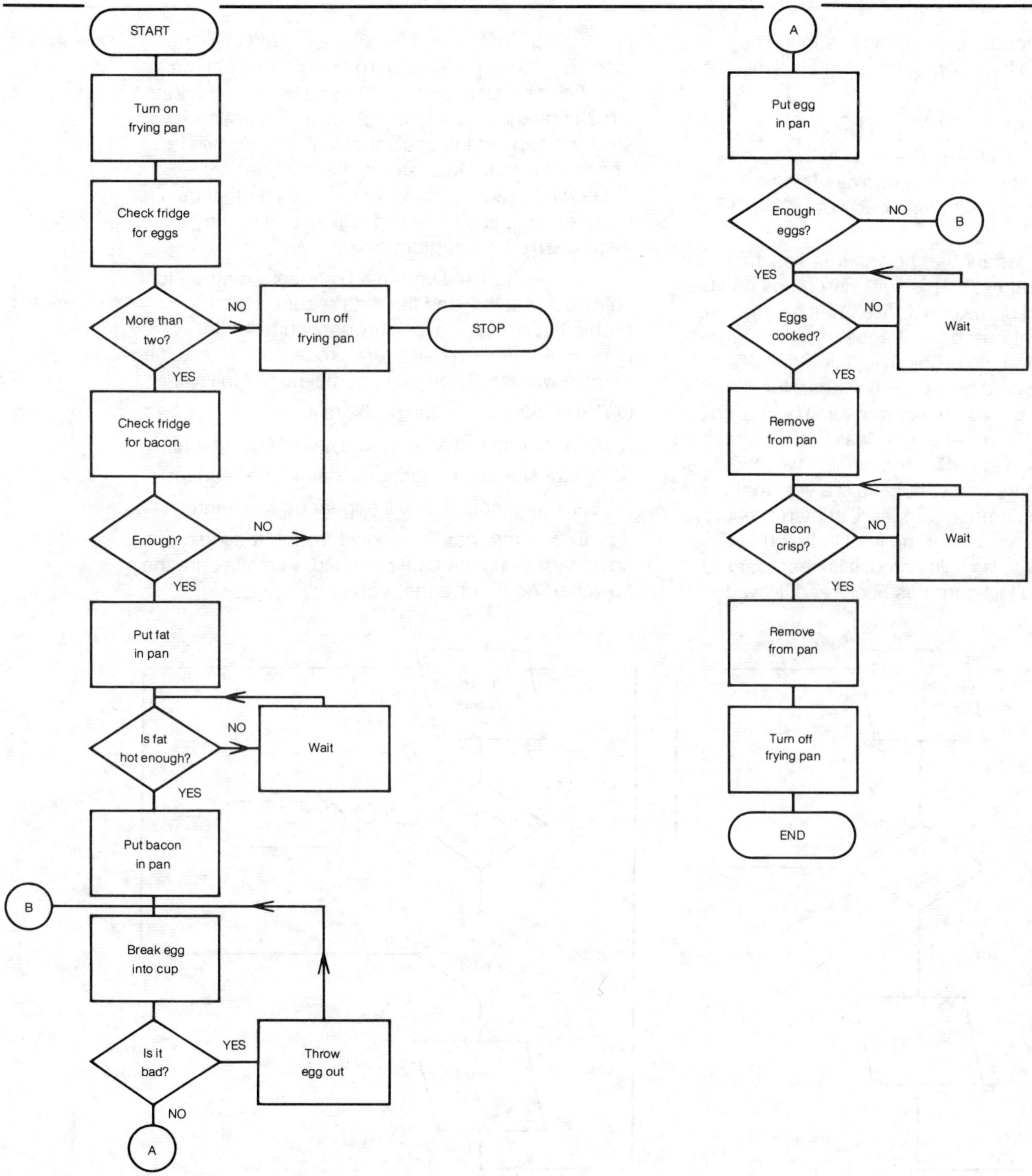

Diagram 4.2 **Flowchart: cooking bacon and eggs**

made and a decision block indicates this. The decisions made by a computer are quite simple:

(1) YES or NO
(2) NEGATIVE, POSITIVE, ZERO
(3) HIGH, LOW, EQUAL

The diamond can indicate a choice of paths according to the result of the decision.

Let us consider another flowcharting example as shown in diagram 4.3. This flowchart reads numbers from cards and prints only those numbers that are positive. One interesting fact appears. Although we have flowcharted the problem solution quite accurately, it would be a poor flowchart for a problem to be solved on a computer. There is no symbol to say STOP—neither does there seem to be any logical place to put it! Presumably we stop when there are no more cards, but this is a very inefficient way of using a computer. Indeed, in many cases, for example when we ask for the total to be printed or some statistics to be calculated, it is necessary to know when the last card has been read. How do we know when we have got to the last card? In many instances there is a hardward feature that can be checked or a blank card at the end of the data. Since we do not know how many cards there are, and we wish to keep repeating a set of instructions, we must check *every* card in case it is the last one.

Let us redraw our flowchart, assuming that the last card is blank, and include a logical end to our flow of instructions (see diagram 4.4).

The flowchart in diagram 4.5 shows a method for solving a problem and the data required for the problem. Carefully follow through what would happen if the given data were processed as specified in the flowchart. Then try to complete the following:

(1) Write down what the problem is.

(2) Give another 'rule' for the hypothetical machine.

(3) Suggest more instructions that will be required.

(4) List any output that will appear on the printer.

It is always important to follow through the logic of a flowchart, using the data provided, to make sure the flowchart does solve the problem.

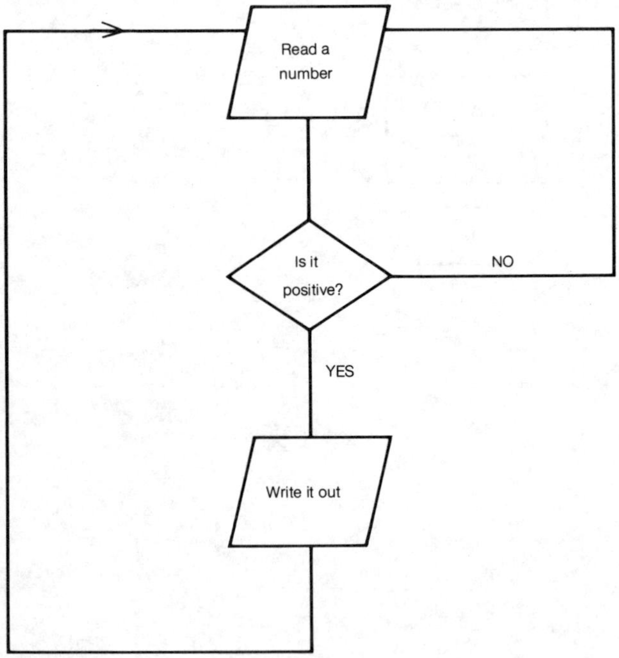

Diagram 4.3

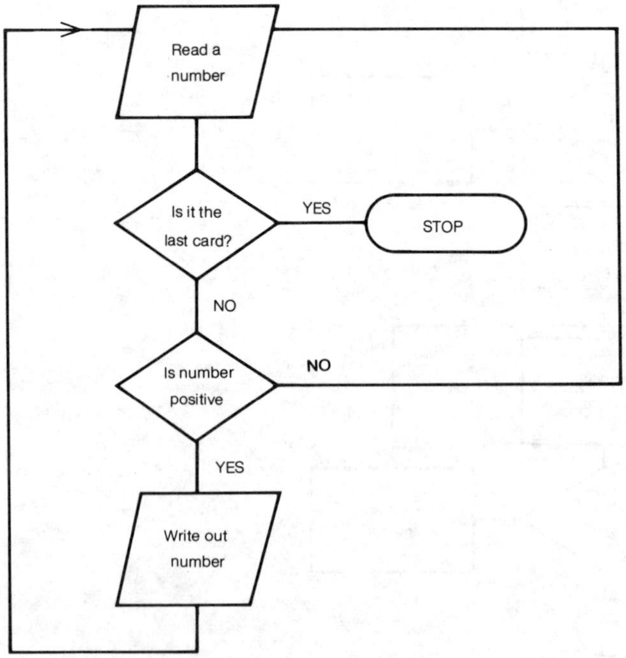

Diagram 4.4

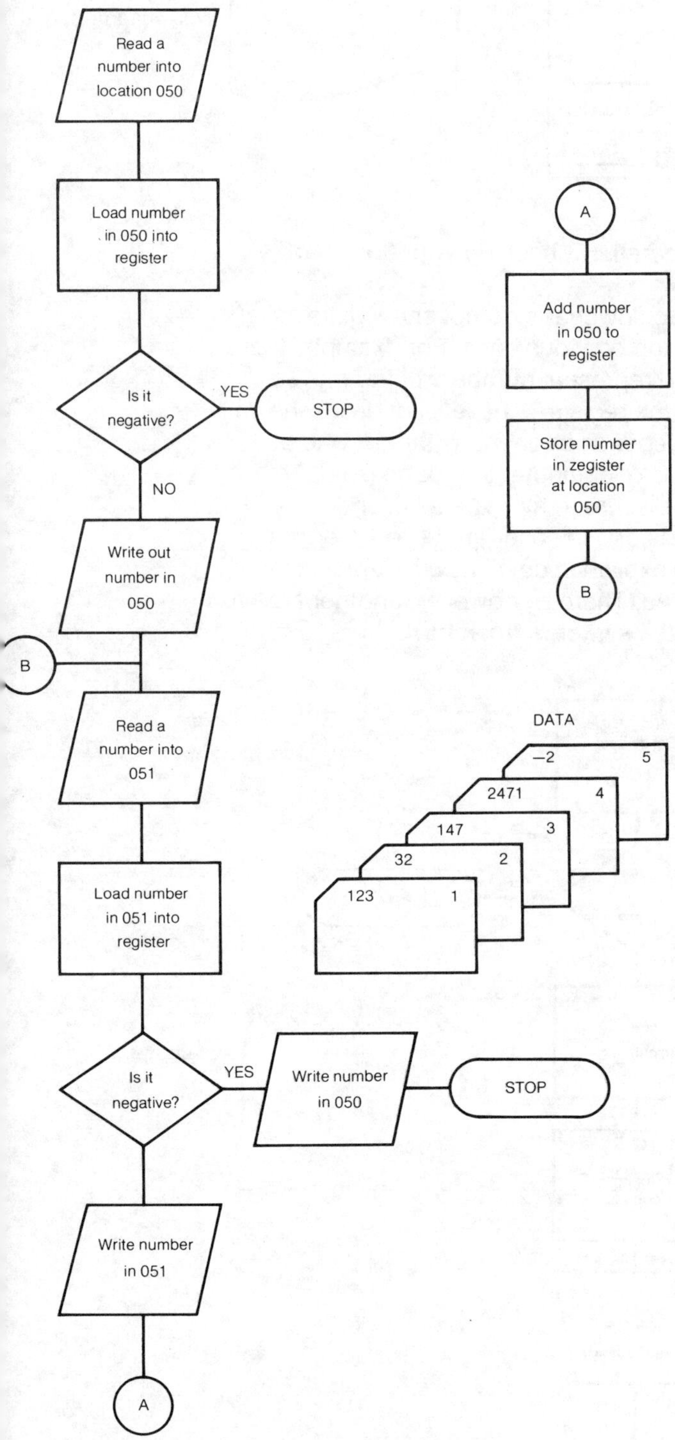

Diagram 4.5

Let us discuss the answers to the above problems:

(1) The problem is to read and write positive numbers, to find their total and to write it out. The negative number is a 'dummy' card indicating the last card and thus causing the program to come to a logical end. Although there are only four positive numbers given, the program would work for any number of positive numbers. Most programs for computers are made as general as possible in order to be flexible. For example, if a program were written to print pay cheques and it were written for only twenty employees, then every time there was a new employee the program would have to be altered!

(2) Another 'rule' for our hypothetical machine is that numbers to be tested must be in the register. Only in the register can we check to see if a number is negative, positive or zero. Once the number is in the register and an instruction is issued to do the testing, then the actual testing is a built-in hardware function.

(3) If we are to code the problem, we need an instruction to test for a negative number. Also we need to instruct the computer to branch and repeat some instructions. When the connector B is reached, we branch to the other connector B and *loop* through several instructions many times. You will notice that the program is not in a permanent loop. A negative number causes the number stored at location 050 to be written out and the program to end.

(4) The printer output should be

123
32
147
2471
2773

In following through a flowchart you will find it helps to draw a rough diagram of the CPU showing only the locations used and the register. Then fill these according to the directions in the flowchart. For example, the situation within storage at block 5 of the flowchart, the first time through, is shown in diagram 4.6. The situation after reading three data cards is shown in diagram 4.7.

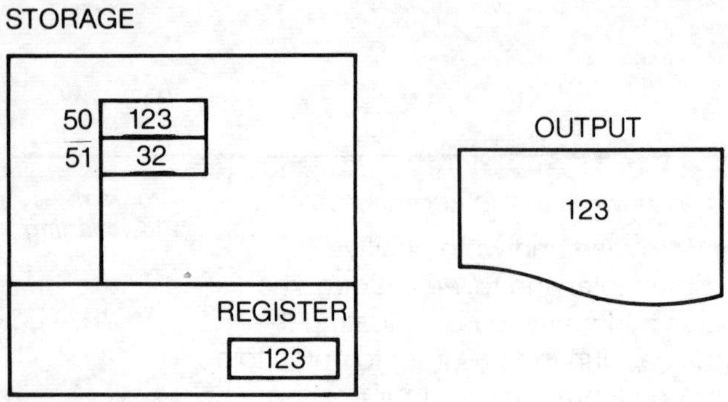

Diagram 4.6

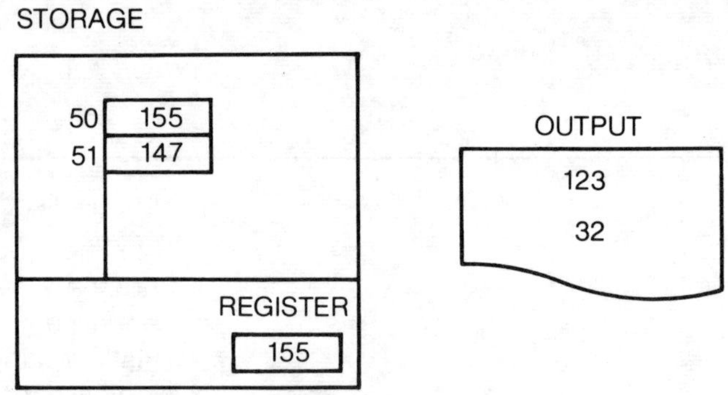

Diagram 4.7

The flowchart in diagram 4.8 refers to the problem: Print the numbers from 1 to 25 and also print their squares. We are not using our hypothetical machine and you will see that the flowchart is not as detailed. The use of the register for arithmetic has not been shown.

Something is wrong with the flowchart shown in diagram 4.8. Can you find the problem and can you correct it? In this flowchart the square of 25 would never be calculated and written. Diagram 4.9 shows one correct version. Altering 25 to 26 in the decision block also corrects the error. An error like this is a very easy error to make and emphasizes the importance of carefully checking your flowchart logic.

These last two flowcharts do not show quite as much detail as the previous ones. For example, there are no blocks to represent numbers being moved into and out of the register. The level of detail shown in a flowchart depends upon many things, one of which is the type of computer language used. This factor we shall discuss in more detail later.

The flowcharts drawn so far are called *program* flowcharts and explain in detail how a particular problem is solved. There is, however, another type of flowchart called a **systems flowchart.**

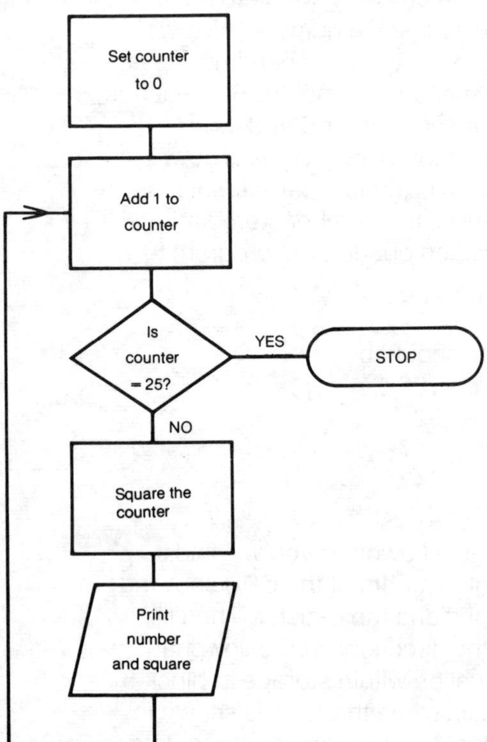

Diagram 4.8

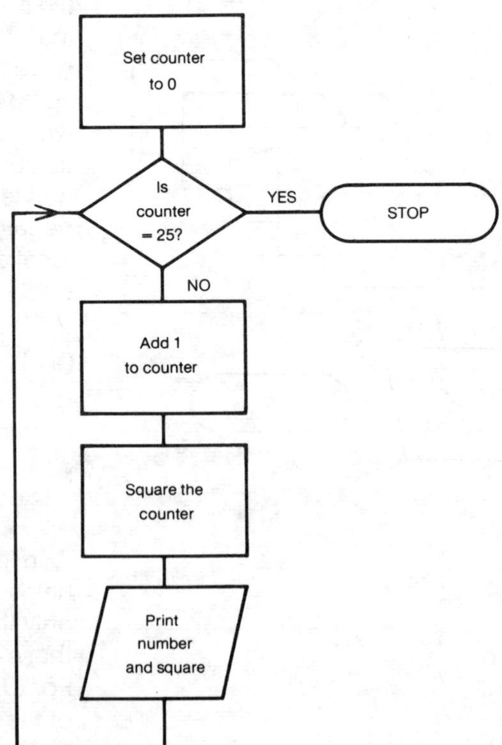

Diagram 4.9

Systems Flowcharting

Study the flowchart in diagram 4.10. You will notice that some of the symbols used here are different from any we have used before.

Symbol	*Meaning*	*Example*
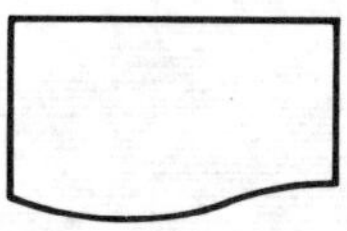	Document	Data required for input or computer output
	Auxiliary operation (off-line)	Keypunching, verifying (not under control of the computer)
	Collection of punched cards	Deck of data cards
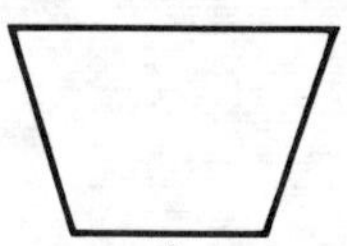	Manual operation	Visual checking—an operation done at 'human' speed
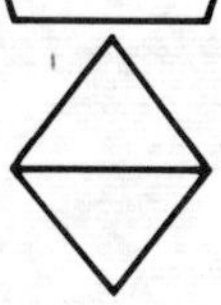	Sorting operation	Putting items into some sequence
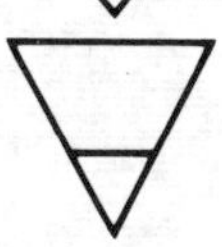	Store off-line	A card file stored in a drawer, that is, not stored in any part of a computer system

There are no *program* details, the only reference to the program being the block

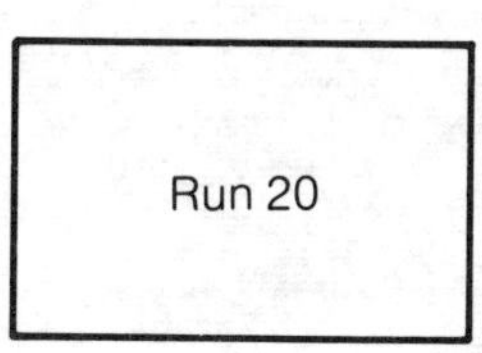

Run 20 represents a computer job and would be expanded into a *program* flowchart on a separate sheet.

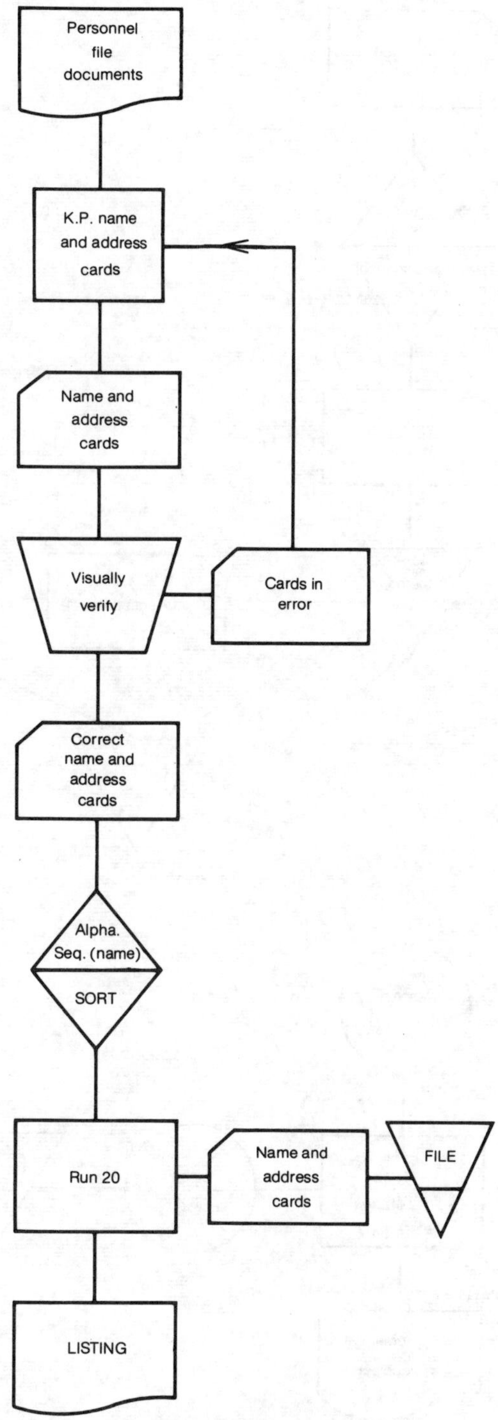

Diagram 4.10 Systems flowchart: creation of name and address file

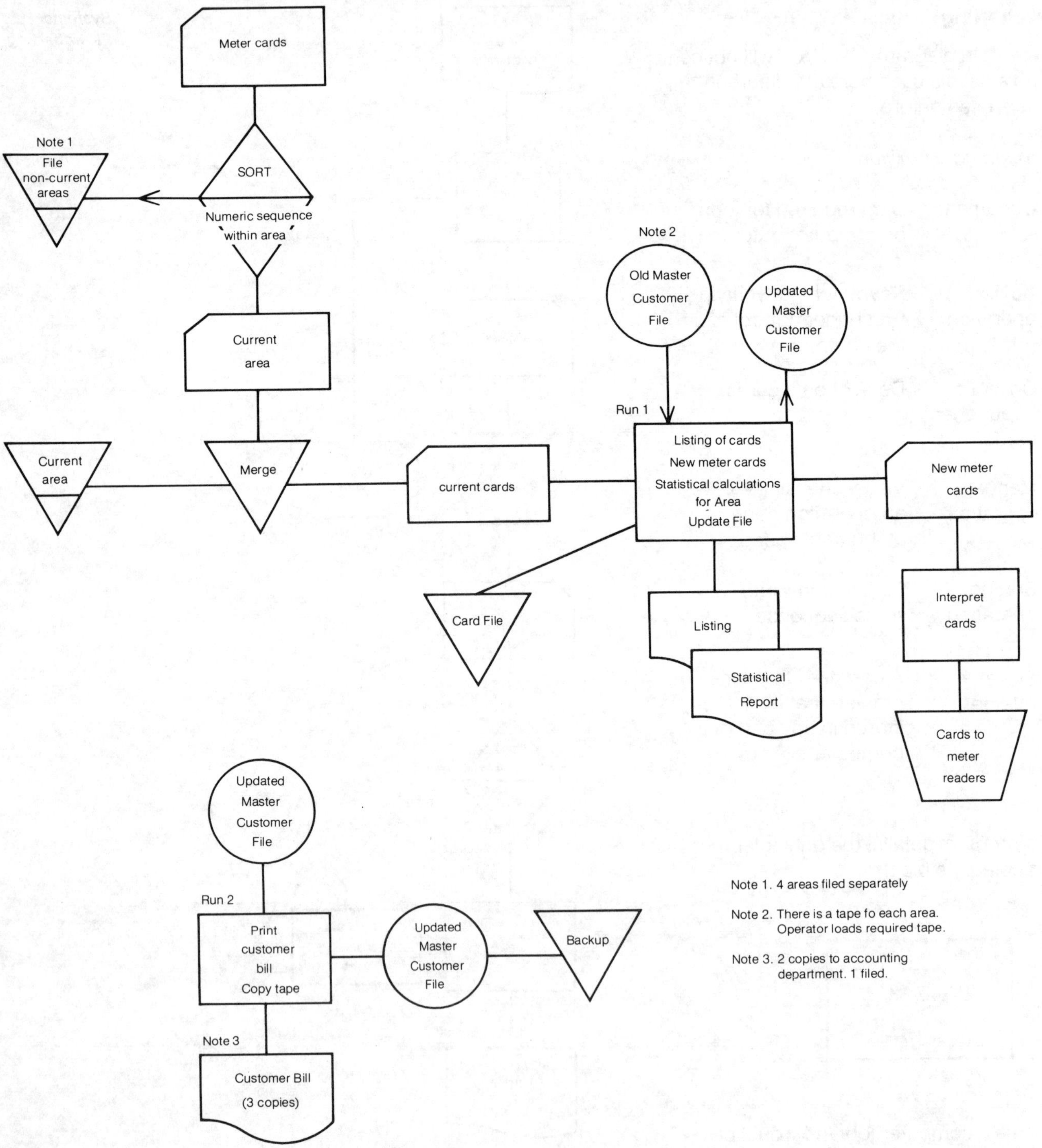

Diagram 4.11 Systems flowchart: meter billing

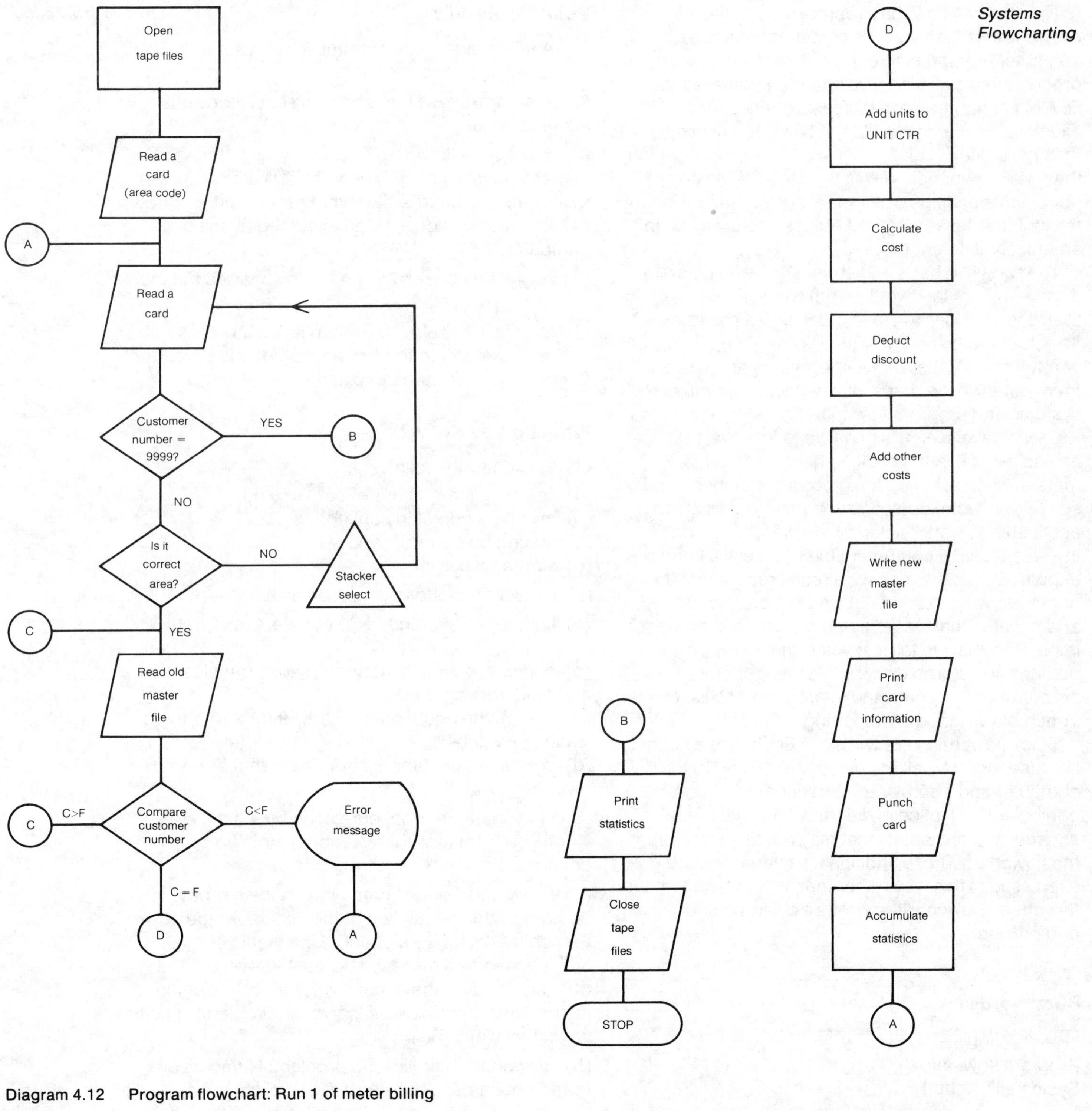

Diagram 4.12 Program flowchart: Run 1 of meter billing

The systems flowchart represents a series of *events* rather than a series of instructions to a computer. For the efficient running of a data processing installation, it is important to have the flow of events shown in logical sequence. For example, the cards should not be sorted until after they have been visually checked. The order in which they were keypunched was the order of the original documents and this order makes checking easier at this point. After sorting, the entries could well be in an entirely different order.

The two flowcharts in diagram 4.11 and diagram 4.12 represent the two different types of flowchart. Diagram 4.12 is Run 1 expanded into a program flowchart. Since both flowcharts are quite complex, you will quickly realize the importance and value of them both. Notice that some symbols occur in both systems and program flowcharting.

As we have seen it is possible to flowchart almost any series of events: cooking bacon and eggs, a meter billing system, adding positive numbers, and so on. The technique of flowcharting is particularly applicable to work related to the computer. The inefficient use of computer time is usually a very expensive waste. Since we already realize that the computer will do *only* what we tell it and *no more*, and *exactly* what we tell it and *no different*, then it is imperative that we tell it exactly what we want it to do. Most logic problems, both in the general organization of events and in program details, can be ironed out by good flowcharting.

Since flowcharts are written in English, they can be understood by all the personnel related to the computer and also by new personnel taking over a particular job. Notice in diagram 4.11 that notes expand on a few points that may not be clear from the flowchart. These additional explanations are expressed in this way rather than by cluttering up the flowchart. Flowcharts should be clear, neat, orderly and precise.

Buzz Words

Flowcharting
Program flowchart
Systems flowchart

Points to Review

(1) A flowchart is a diagrammatic representation of a logical solution to a problem.

(2) A *systems* flowchart shows a series of events in a logical order.

(3) A *program* flowchart shows a series of detailed steps to be followed in solving a particular section of a systems flowchart—often that part which is coded in a computer language and executed by the computer.

(4) Any series of events can be flowcharted but the method is particularly related to a computer.

(5) Special symbols are used in flowcharting. Most of these conform to the standards of the International Organization for Standardization.

What Do You Know?

(1) Flowchart the following:

(a) counting the number of balls in a box
(b) making a cup of instant coffee
(c) putting on ski boots and skis
(d) starting a car

(2) Flowchart the following problems:

(a) finding the average of 50 numbers read from cards.
(b) computing simple interest (read in principal, rate and time from cards)
(c) solving the equation $y = x^2 + 9$ for $x = 1$ to 10 (read in x values)
(d) counting the numbers from a set that are divisable by 7

(3) Flowchart the procedure used by a bank clerk when you want to withdraw money from your account.

(4) Flowchart (for programming on the hypothetical computer) the calculation of the class average of French marks for 25 students. The marks are keypunched and the last card contains zero. Print out only the average. If new hypothetical machine instructions are needed to solve the problem, specify what they would be.

(5) Flowchart the following problem: Numbers are read from cards, one per card, and processed

What Do You Know?

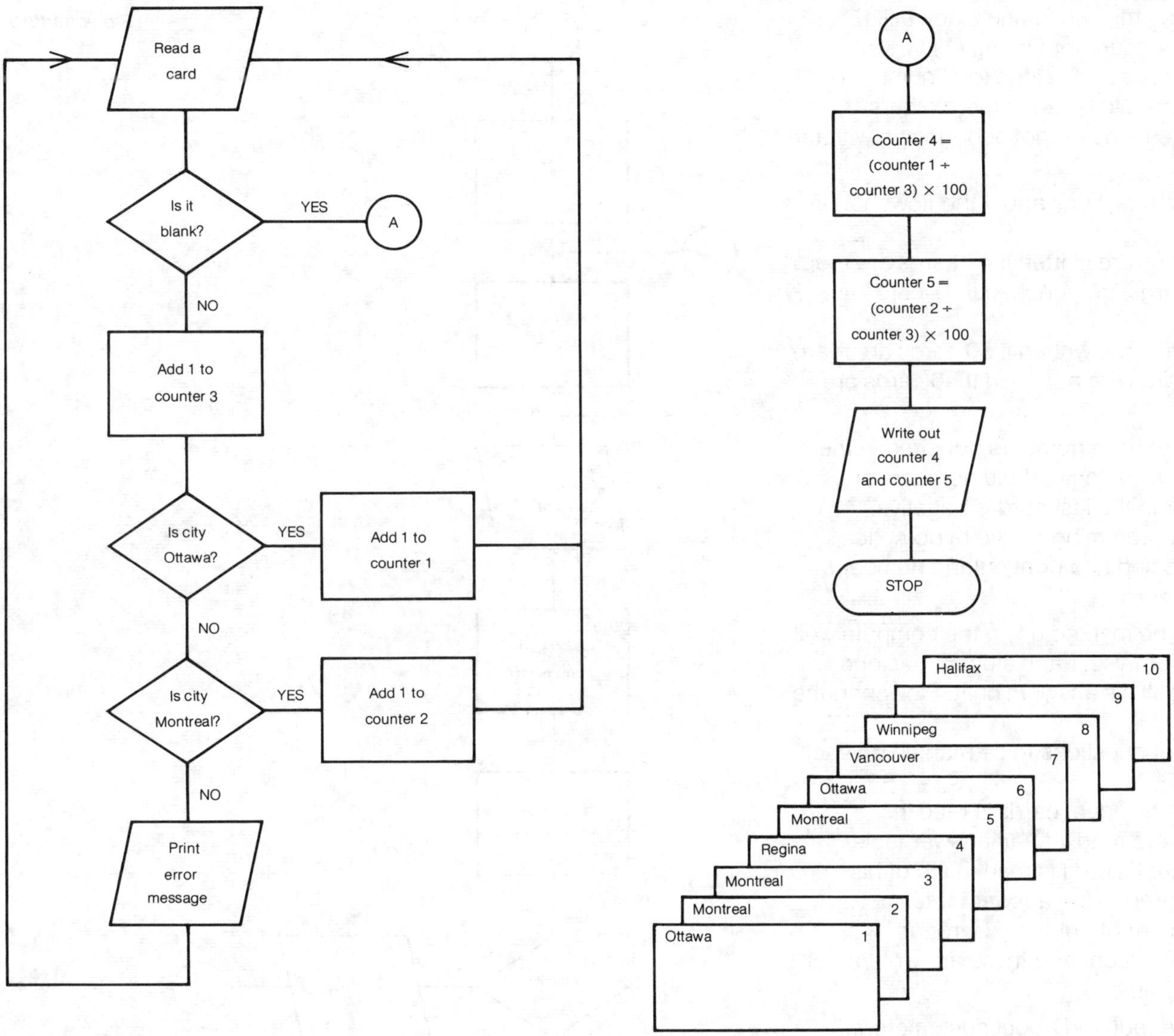

Diagram 4.13

according to their signs, using the following criteria:
(i) Zero is ignored.
(ii) Positive numbers are doubled and the result printed out.
(iii) Negative numbers are squared and the results accumulated, only the total being printed. After processing each number, another number is read. The last card is blank.

(6) Flowchart how to calculate and print the square root of all even numbers less than 100.

(7) Answer the following questions about the flowchart in diagram 4.13.
(a) How many error messages will be printed?
(b) What is the value of counter 3 at the end of processing data?
(c) What do counters 4 and 5 represent and what is their value when they are printed out?
(d) Does the processing come to a logical end? Explain.
(e) How many cards are processed? Explain.

(8) A box contains red, white and black balls. Flowchart the procedure for finding (1) how many of each colour there are and (2) the total number of balls. If there happen to be any other colours present, reject them and do not add them in with the total.

(9) Answer these questions about the flowchart in diagram 4.14:
(a) How many lines are written if 47 cards are read?
(b) How many cards are punched if 47 cards are read?
(c) How many lines are written if 50 cards are read?
(d) How many cards are punched if 50 cards are read?

(10) Cards in a set have numbers punched in them, one number per card. Some of the numbers are zero. The number in the last card is negative. Flowchart (for programming on the hypothetical computer) how to find and print out the number of cards containing zero.

(11) Tests are to be marked using the computer. All answers are true or false. Each student has one answer card with all his answers on it. Flowchart the operation.
(i) The number of questions to be marked on each card is read in.
(ii) The number of student cards is read in.
(iii) The answers are read into an answer table.
(iv) As each student's card is read, each of his answers is compared to the answer table.
(v) The total number of rights and wrongs is required for each student and these are written out together with his name.

(12) Statistics are required about customers with over $100 owing. The cards of these customers, containing area codes and other customer information, are processed to find the total number of customers owing over $100 in each of three areas. The area codes on the cards are one, two or three. The results are to be printed out. Flowchart the problem. (Use a blank card to indicate the end of the deck.)

(13) Explain the difference between a program flowchart and a systems flowchart. Illustrate your answer with examples of each type.

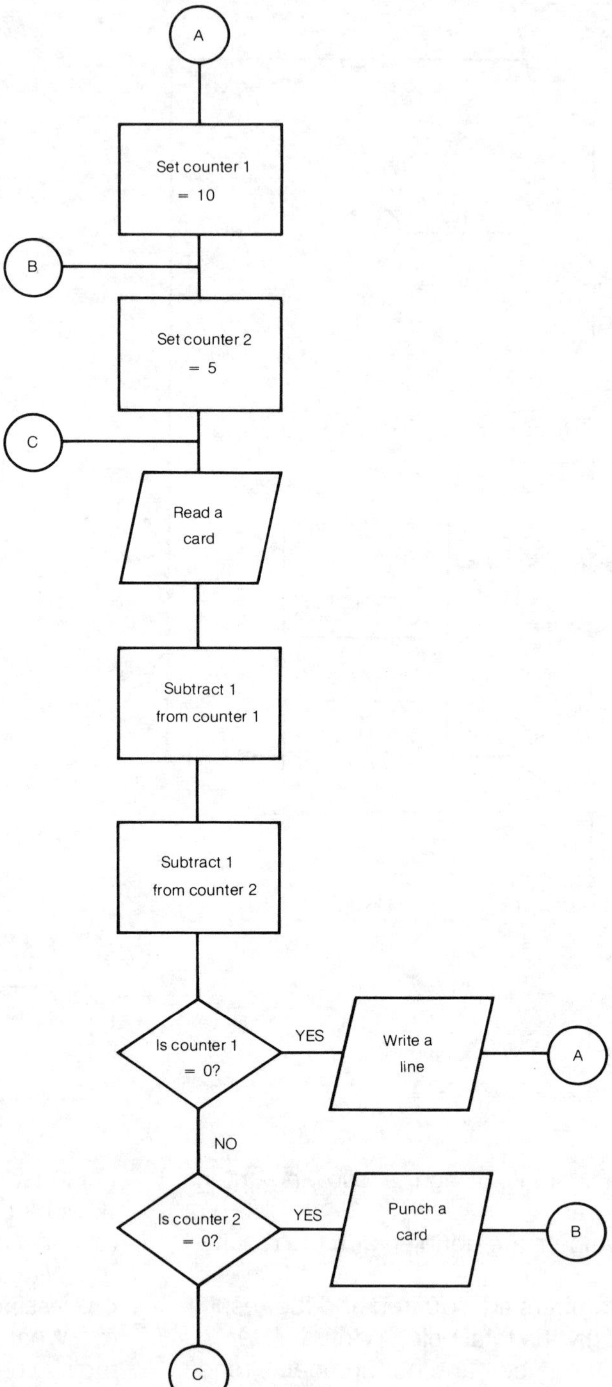

Diagram 4.14

(14) Draw systems flowchart segments to illustrate the following events:
(i) Payroll data is to be keypunched and key verified and then the cards are to be sorted into three areas: A, B and C.
(ii) Customer name and address cards are merged with payment cards and an edit run is performed on the computer.
(iii) The student file on cards is sorted by grade. Grades 9 and 10 are filed, Grades 11 and 12 are listed on the computer and Grade 13 is sent to the guidance department for review.

(15) Flowchart the following procedures that take place when a customer order is received at the Smith Drug Company.
(i) Price and item numbers are checked against a catalogue.
(ii) Valid item numbers have the price extended (number of items multiplied by unit price).
(iii) Total is obtained.
(iv) Tax is added.
(v) Discount is applied.
(vi) Credit check is made on the customer.
If order is less than $100 and balance owing is less than $500, order is marked to be shipped. If order is greater than or equal to $100 and credit rating is greater than $100, order is marked to be shipped. All rejected orders go to the manager for review.
(vii) Ordered quantities are checked against the stock on hand. If there is sufficient on hand, the entire order or part of it is shipped. Quantities out of stock are back ordered (out of stock written on order). One copy of order is filed in partial shipment file.
(viii) Packing slips are prepared: one with order, one with bill, one filed.
(ix) Bill is prepared: one copy mailed with copy of packing slip, one filed, one to accounts receivable.

(16) Flowchart the following office procedure for processing customer payments made by cheque: The stub returned with the cheque is marked with the amount paid if only a partial payment is made. The cheques are totalled on a calculator and sent, together with the adding machine list, to the bank. The stub is sent to the data processing keypunch department where the contained information is keypunched onto cards. The cards are sorted in customer number sequence and then listed on the computer. The listing and stubs are filed in case there are any problems.

5 Machine Language

We will study some more machine language instructions for our hypothetical machine in order to gain a greater understanding of how a computer works.

More Hypothetical Machine Language Instructions

In Chapter 4 we studied a flowchart that related to our hypothetical machine and we found that sometimes certain instructions needed to be repeated continually. In order to show this in our flowchart we used either a connector or a line looping back to the first repeated instruction. Diagram 5.1 and diagram 5.2 illustrate the two ways of flowcharting the looping.

In the flowcharts, after step 4 we are directed back to step 1 by means of a line with an arrow on it or a connector that indicates we must transfer to another instruction. We must be sure the computer knows when we want to repeat instructions and where to go to find the next instruction at all times. The instruction

0000050XXX

changes the logical sequence of instruction execution, causing the computer to branch to an address represented by XXX. The next instruction the computer executes is the one stored at XXX. When you use the instruction 0000050XXX, be quite sure that XXX is the correct address. Otherwise, you may get some unpredictable results!

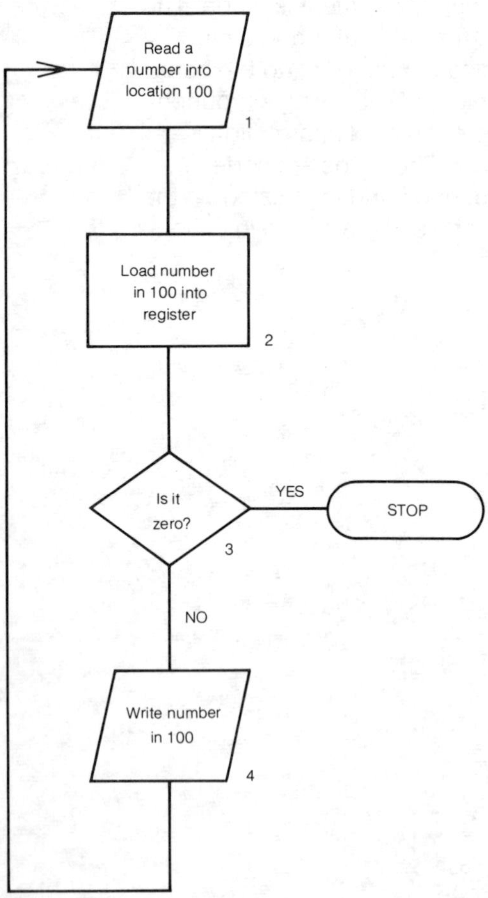

Diagram 5.1

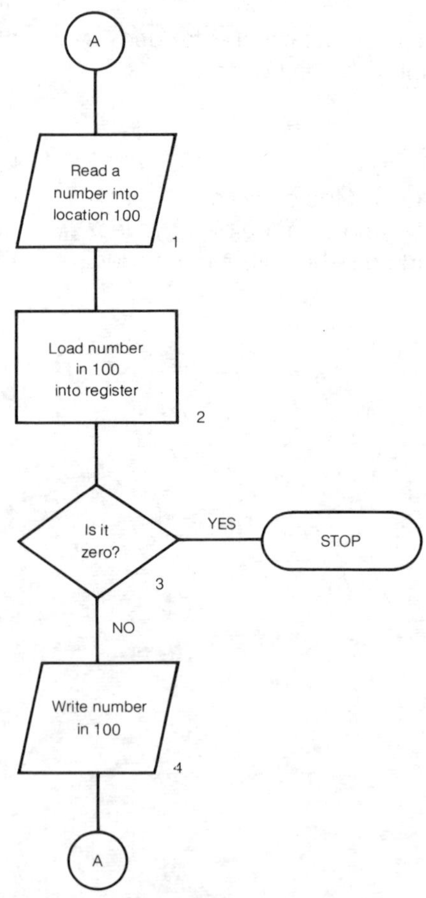

Diagram 5.2

Example 1:

0000030070	Read a number into 070
0000031070	Write the number stored at 070
0000050001	Transfer to the instruction stored at location 001

Example 2:

0000030070	Read a number into 070
0000031070	Write the number stored at 070
0000050070	Transfer to the instruction stored at location 070

Example 1 is a small looping program. It is not a practical program but it could be executed.

Example 2 could give very odd results! 0000050070 causes a transfer to the instruction stored at location 070. At location 070 is stored a number read from the card reader and it could be anything. It may happen to be an instruction but most likely it is a number that the CPU cannot possibly interpret as an instruction!

In Chapter 3 we found that testing a number to see if it is negative, positive or zero can be carried out only in the register. We already know the instruction for loading or moving a number into the register (0000010XXX). But, once it is there, how is it tested? The instruction to test whether a number is negative is

0000051XXX

This instruction also can cause a change in the logical sequence of instruction execution. The transfer to the address XXX takes place only if the number in the register is negative. Otherwise the next sequential instruction is executed. For example:

```
011   0000051019
012   0000031060
013                         Register     060
014                         [124]        [175]
015
016
017
018
019   0000040000
```

Instruction 011 tests the number in the register to see if it is negative. Since it is not, the number in location 060 (175) is printed. Consider another example:

```
011   0000051019
012   0000031060
013                         Register     060
014                         [ – 1]       [175]
015
016
017
018
019   0000040000
```

Since this time the number in the register is negative, a transfer to the instruction in location 019 takes place and the program halts.

Other branch or transfer instructions in our hypothetical machine are:

0000052XXX	Transfer to location XXX if the content of the register is zero
0000053XXX	Transfer to location XXX if the content of the register is positive

We have now discussed almost all of the instructions for our hypothetical machine. A complete listing follows:

0000010XXX	Load the number in location XXX into the register
0000011XXX	Store the number in the register at location XXX
0000020XXX	Add the number stored at XXX to the content of the register
0000021XXX	Subtract the number stored at XXX from the content of the register
0000022XXX	Multiply the content of the register by the number stored at XXX
0000023XXX	Divide the content of the register by the number stored at XXX
0000030XXX	Read a number and store it at location XXX
0000031XXX	Write out the number stored at location XXX
0000040000	Stop or halt

0000050XXX Branch or transfer to location XXX

0000051XXX Branch to location XXX if the content of the register is negative

0000052XXX Branch to location XXX if the content of the register is zero

0000053XXX Branch to location XXX if the content of the register is positive

Since integer arithmetic is performed, any remainder in division is lost. For example,

$$10 \div 3 \rightarrow 3$$
$$2 \div 3 \rightarrow 0$$

Using the Hypothetical Machine Language

We now are able to solve many problems using our hypothetical computer and its instruction set. Study carefully the following examples:

Problem 1: Given a series of numbers punched into cards, write a program that will read the cards and print out the numbers and their squares. Zero is punched into the last card. (See diagram 5.3.)

Notice that the third instruction is a transfer instruction to location 008 if the content of the register is zero. How did we know to transfer to location 008? When we were coding the third instruction, we did not. The coding of the instructions must be vertical and cannot have horizontal arms as the flowchart can. Therefore we usually complete the main routine first and put any other routines after that, making sure there is a correct branch to reach these instructions. Suppose we had coded the first three instructions as

```
000    0000030050
001    0000010050
002    0000052012
```

According to this coding, the STOP instruction is to be found in location 012.

```
000    0000030050
001    0000010050
002    0000052012
003    0000022050
004    0000031050
```

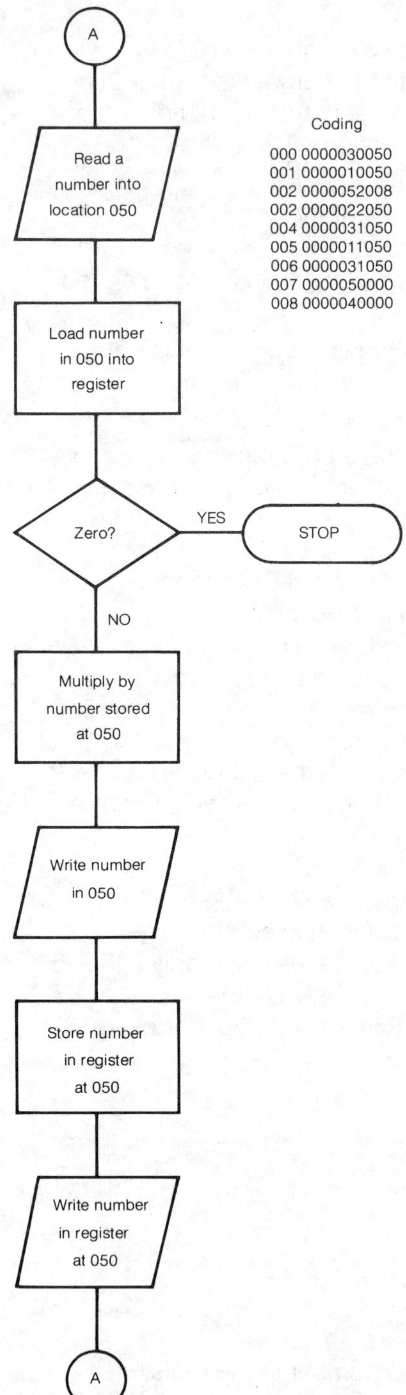

Diagram 5.3

```
005    0000011050
006    0000031050
007    0000050000
008
009
010
011
012    0000040000
```

We would have a real problem getting the STOP instruction stored at location 012 since the instructions are punched into cards and stored *sequentially* in main storage. The STOP instruction would go into storage position 008 and our branch to location 012 could give very unexpected results! Consider the problem following to see how we find the proper address.

Problem 2: Given a series of numbers punched into cards, write a program that will read the cards and print only those numbers that are positive. (See diagram 5.4.)

You will notice in this example that we have to be very careful with branch or transfer addresses. Our coding is done in steps as follows:

Step 1: Code one complete loop (0-4 on the flowchart)

000	0000030060	Read a number into location 060
001	0000010060	Load number in location 060 into register.
002	0000053 ?	Transfer to ? if register is positive. If number is *not* positive, that is, branch is not taken, the next sequential instruction is executed.
003	0000052 ?	Transfer to ? if register is zero. If number is *not* zero, that is, branch is not taken, the next sequential instruction is executed.
004	0000050000	Branch to location 000.

Step 2: We are now in a position to fill in the first branch address (the alternate path from block 2), immediately following the last instruction coded, and complete the other loop (5,6 on the flowchart).

```
000    0000030060
001    0000010060
002    0000053005  ⎫
003    0000052 ?   ⎬ if positive
004    0000050000  ⎪
005    0000031060  ⎭
006    0000050000
```

Step 3: The last missing address now can be filled in and our program is complete.

```
       000    0000030060
       001    0000010060
       002    0000053005  ⎫
       003    0000052007  ⎬ if positive
if     004    0000050000  ⎪
zero   005    0000031060  ⎭
       006    0000050000
       007    0000040000
```

(if zero: 003 → 007)

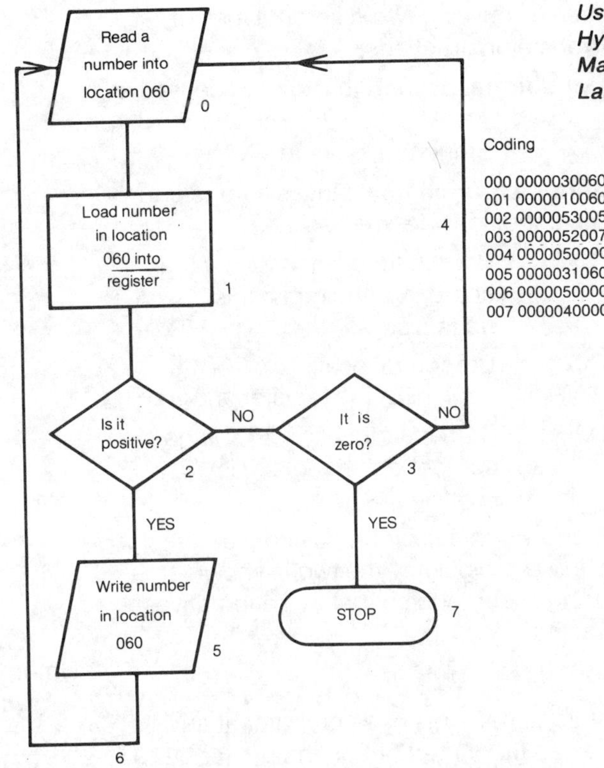

Diagram 5.4

We have been discussing two different types of branch or transfer instructions:

(1) An **Unconditional branch** that always causes a transfer:

0000050XXX	Branch to location XXX

(2) A **conditional branch** that causes a transfer only when certain conditions are met:

0000051XXX	Branch to location XXX *if* the content of the register is negative
0000052XXX	Branch to location XXX *if* the content of the register is zero
0000053XXX	Branch to location XXX *if* the content of the register is positive

Type one is shown on a flowchart using a connector or a line linking two blocks. Type two is shown on a flowchart using a diamond so that two alternatives can be indicated.

Storage Contents

The main storage contents of a computer at any point in time can be printed out on the printer by using a special set of instructions. This process is known as taking a **storage dump** or taking a **core dump** if main storage is composed of cores. Since the main storage of a computer usually occupies thousands of positions, the contents,when printed, occupy many pages. In order to conserve paper, the numbers are printed sixteen or more to a line. Each number represents an operation code plus address, or a piece of data. Take a look at part of a storage dump in diagram 5.5. The numbers seem to have some letters scattered through them! The reason for this is that the storage dump has been printed in **hexadecimal**, instead of decimal, numbers. The hexadecimal number system has a base of 16, which means that we run out of numerals before all the hexadecimal digits can be represented. The first six letters of the alphabet are used to make up the deficit.

Decimal Digits Base 10	*Hexadecimal Digits* Base 16
0	0
1	1
2	2
3	3
4	4
5	5
6	6
7	7
8	8
9	9
10	A
11	B
12	C
13	D
14	E
15	F

You can see that C in hexadecimal is 12 in decimal and F in hexadecimal is 15 in decimal. One reason for dumping storage in hexadecimal is that writing numbers in hexadecimal takes less room than writing in decimal or binary.

In order to read a storage dump we need to know
(1) what computer it was from
(2) the instruction set for the machine
(3) where the dump started

Usually only part of the contents of main storage, that part containing the program or data to be studied, need be dumped.

There are many similarities between the machine language of a real computer and that of our hypothetical machine. Diagram 5.5 illustrates a storage dump from the IBM 370. A storage dump of our hypothetical machine might look like diagram 5.6. The storage dump starts at location zero. Can you recognize the program? If you can, check and see if the data is in the correct location.

From the work we have done with the machine language of our hypothetical machine, it is obvious that it would be a horrifying prospect to write a payroll program or a program to produce student report cards in machine language! This thought obviously struck many other people and thus other computer languages were invented. However, machine language is still very important because it is the only language the computer understands. All other languages must be translated to machine language. The study of a storage dump is the only way of finding any translation errors.

0868E0	58A0B054	D507A010	B0804740	C2529180	B07847E0	C28C947F	B07858A0	B054D207
086900	A018B098	D207B080	A010D207	B068A018	D207B070	A01098EF	B0685EF0	B07447C0
086920	C2844110	00011EE1	5EE0B070	90EFB090	1FAA50A0	B1184110	B0804100	B10441E0
086940	002389E0	0018160E	0A2F58A0	B0545880	A0241288	4780C2C0	5800A020	18184110
086960	10000A0A	58A0B054	5880A00C	41F00002	5EF0800C	8BF00002	BEF7A021	5800A020
086980	4510C2E0	0A0A58A0	B0545010	A0245880	B0545880	802458A0	A02850A0	800041A0
0869A0	B11850A0	B00458A0	B05458A0	A00C58A0	A00450A0	B0584120	000347F0	C34418A2
0869C0	8BA00002	5880B054	58808024	5830B058	41F03014	5E80C654	50FA8000	58A03000
0869E0	50A0B058	5E20C648	58A0B058	12AA4770	C31A18A2	8BA00002	5880B054	58808024
086A00	1EA35EA0	C6509680	A0001818	41101000	41000001	13110780	BF08C373	0A0158A0
086A20	B05458A0	A0289140	A00047E0	C3BE4110	B0F441E0	B05C50E1	00000A28	58A0B05C
086A40	5820A004	95402004	4770C3B0	9680B088	47F0C3BE	12224780	C3BE5820	200047F0
086A60	C3A058A0	B05458A0	A00C5880	A0045080	B0584130	A00447F0	C47658A0	B0584180
086A80	00141E8A	91408000	47E0C468	58808000	41808000	12884780	C40A58A0	A0205880
086AA0	B05455A0	802C47D0	C40A50A0	802C58A0	B05858A0	A01050A0	B0604110	B0600A3E
086AC0	58A0B054	58A0A00C	D503B058	A0084770	C4325030	A00858A0	B05458A0	A00C5880
086AE0	A00C0680	5080A00C	5880B058	58808000	50803000	5800A010	18285810	B0584110
086B00	10000A0A	5020B058	47F0C476	58A0B058	183A58A0	A00050A0	B05858A0	B05812AA
086B20	4770C3D6	41A0B118	9140A000	4710C494	9180B088	47E0C302	41F0000E	0A6D182F
086B40	18811222	4780C4E0	1832D203	B064C64C	47F0C618	58A0B054	58A0A008	9101A013
086B60	47E0C4C8	9102A013	4780C4E0	58A0B054	58A0A008	9102A013	47E0C5C0	9101A013
086B80	4770C5C0	58A0B054	58A0A00C	5800A010	4510C4F0	0A0A5010	B05858A0	B05858F0
086BA0	B05458E0	F00850E0	A0185080	A01C58E0	F03450E0	A0205EE0	C64850E0	F034D207
086BC0	A024B0A0	58E0F038	50E0A030	1FEE50E0	A0149200	A02F50A0	A00441E0	F02C50E0
086BE0	A00858F0	F00450F0	A00C4130	A0141878	5E70C654	1F224320	70004110	A00441F0
086C00	B0A841EF	001C50EF	0000D207	F01CC570	47F0C578	C9D9C2D4	C6D9C7D4	BE37F009
086C20	9606F008	502F000C	9620F014	923CF037	0A2A58A0	B0585010	A0101F88	5080A000
086C40	5880B054	5880800C	58108008	50A01000	50A08008	41A00001	5EA0800C	50A0800C
086C60	47F0C606	41200001	47F0C5EC	18A28BA0	000258AA	800012AA	4780C5E8	5EA0C654
086C80	5800A000	181A4110	10000A0A	5E20C648	59208000	47D0C5C8	18A85EA0	C6545800
086CA0	A000181A	41101000	0A0A58A0	B054D207	A018B090	47F0C122	47F0C302	BF1FB064
086CC0	18F31811	41000080	89000018	16100A0D	47F0C15E	003CC240	00086CEC	00086CE8
086CE0	00086CE8	00086CE8	00000000	00000001	000004B1	FFFFFFF8	FFFFFFFC	0000011C
086D00	400C5CE0	C23C4AF0	C00E5AF0	C16850F0	00005810	C16418E1	4820400C	0620183F
086D20	18A34420	C01A4780	B1F61BFF	59F0C23C	4780B1EA	58F0C23C	06F050F0	C23C47F0

Diagram 5.5 Storage dump: actual computer

000	0000030050	0000010050	0000052000	0000022050	0000031050	0000011050
006	0000031050	0000050000	0000040000	0000028156	0000021069	0000031074
012	0000011910	0000000000	0000026121	0000010060	0000017109	0000021746
018	0000018119	0000027001	0000000400	0000001210	0000010090	0000021473
024	0000012471	0000003210	0000000510	0000004691	0000021479	0000030060
030	0000031060	0000009001	0000011214	0000023417	0000009126	0000011245
036	0000025112	0000000000	0000000000	0000011210	0000001235	0000002194
042	0000007219	0000001327	0000011101	0000007210	0000031245	0000011924
048	0000006214	0000019821	0000000002	0000030419	0000010132	0000032767

Diagram 5.6 Storage dump: hypothetical computer

The machine language for each computer is different. If we code a program in IBM 1130 machine language, it will run only on the IBM 1130. If we code a program in Honeywell 120 machine language, it will run only on a Honeywell 120. We say that machine language is *machine dependent.*

Buzz Words

Conditional branch
Unconditional branch
Hexadecimal
Core dump
Storage dump

Points to Review

(1) Instructions exist that can alter the normal sequential execution of a program.

(2) Conditional branching causes the computer to execute a certain instruction *only if certain conditions are met.*

(3) Unconditional branching causes a transfer to another instruction *always.*

(4) When branch instructions are used, addresses must be carefully checked.

(5) There can be no 'gaps' between instructions—the computer stores them in sequential storage slots.

(6) A storage dump is a print-out of the contents of the main storage of a computer.

(7) Machine language is the only language a computer understands and any other languages invented for communication with the computer must be translated to machine language.

What Do You Know?

(1) Flowchart and code the segment of a program to square a number stored at location 107 and write out the square.

(2) Flowchart and code the segment of a program to test the number stored at location 200 to determine whether it is positive. If it is positive, stop; otherwise, write out the number.

(3) It is required to find which is the larger of two numbers stored at locations 110 and 111, to write it out and then to stop. Flowchart and code the segment of a program to do this.

(4) Flowchart and code the segment of a program to find and write out what percentage the number stored at location 307 is of the number stored at location 308. Location 309 contains 100.

(5) Principal, rate and time are stored at locations 040, 041 and 042. Flowchart and code the segment of a program to calculate and write out the simple interest.

(6) Find and explain the errors in the following program segments:

```
(a)  000   0000030004
     001   0000031004
     002   0000030005
     003   0000031005
     004   0000040000
(b)  000   0000030060
     001   0000031060
     002   0000050001
     003   0000040000
(c)  000   0000030060
     001   0000031060
     002   0000050060
     003   0000040000
```

(7) The initial bank balance is on the first data card. The next three data cards represent withdrawals (punched as positive numbers). Flowchart and code a program to print out the initial and final balances.

(8) Three cards are read per customer. The first contains the customer number, the second, the old meter reading, and the third, the new meter reading. Flowchart and code a program to print out the customer number and the consumption for one customer.

(9) Flowchart and code a program to check a set of numbers to see if any are negative. If a negative number is found, write it out and stop. Otherwise write out zero (0) when the end of the deck is reached. Only the last card contains zero.

(10) Code the problem flowcharted in Chapter 4, question 4.

(11) Code the problem flowcharted in Chapter 4, question 10.

(12) Flowchart and code the following problem. The item cost and number of items are punched on successive cards. There are several pairs. Calculate the total cost by multiplying the item cost by the following number of items and then print the answer out. The last card contains zero.

(13) Flowchart and code the calculation of the class average of Chemistry marks for a class of twenty students. Print out only the average. The last card is negative.

(14) Flowchart and code the calculation of the class average of French marks for an unknown number of students. Print out only the average. The last card is negative.

(15) Flowchart and code the following problem. Read in two data cards with the numbers one and twenty punched in them and print out all the integers from one to twenty.

(16) Flowchart and code a program to find the total cost of articles. The total cost is found by adding five percent tax to the cost punched on the cards. Write out the initial cost for each article, the cost with tax added and the total cost for all articles (with tax added).

6 Low Level Languages

This chapter deals with low level languages, discussing their general characteristics and their advantages. The instructions for a low level language for the hypothetical computer are studied in order that some programs may be written in a language at this level.

Structure of a Low Level Language

We have already briefly mentioned the existence of languages other than machine languages. There are, in fact, a great variety of computer languages in existence and these can be divided roughly into three sections:

(1) machine languages
(2) low level languages
(3) high level languages

In Chapters 3 and 5 we discussed machine languages. In this chapter we shall take a look at **low level languages**.

Low level languages can be considered the first step in the sophistication of computer languages. They make it easier for us to communicate with the computer. Consider some of our difficulties in coding machine language problems. First of all, we were required to remember, or look up, numbers for instructions. Human beings remember much more easily if there is some meaning attached to what they are trying to remember. For instance, R is easier to remember for 'read' than is 30; similarly, W is easier for 'write', A for 'add', B for 'branch', and so on. We can list the instructions of our hypothetical machine and choose suitable letters to represent them, but we have to be careful not only to choose meaningful letters, known as **mnemonics**, but also not to duplicate their meanings. For example, S could represent subtract, stop or store. Study the following list of suggested names.

Machine Language	*Assembler Language*	
10	L	(Load Register)
11	ST	(Store Register)
20	A	(Add)
21	S	(Subtract)
22	M	(Multiply
23	D	(Divide)
30	R	(Read)
31	W	(Write)
40	H	(Stop or Halt)
50	B	(Branch)
51	BN	(Branch if Negative)
52	BZ	(Branch if Zero)
53	BP	(Branch if Positive)

Why have we restricted ourselves to one or two letters and not used the whole word, for example, the word READ? Then there would be no doubt at all about the meaning! However, there is one important consideration that we must always bear in mind. Whatever we choose has to be translated to machine language. The less letters we use for the instructions, the less checking the translator has to do. Remember, machine language is the only language the computer understands.

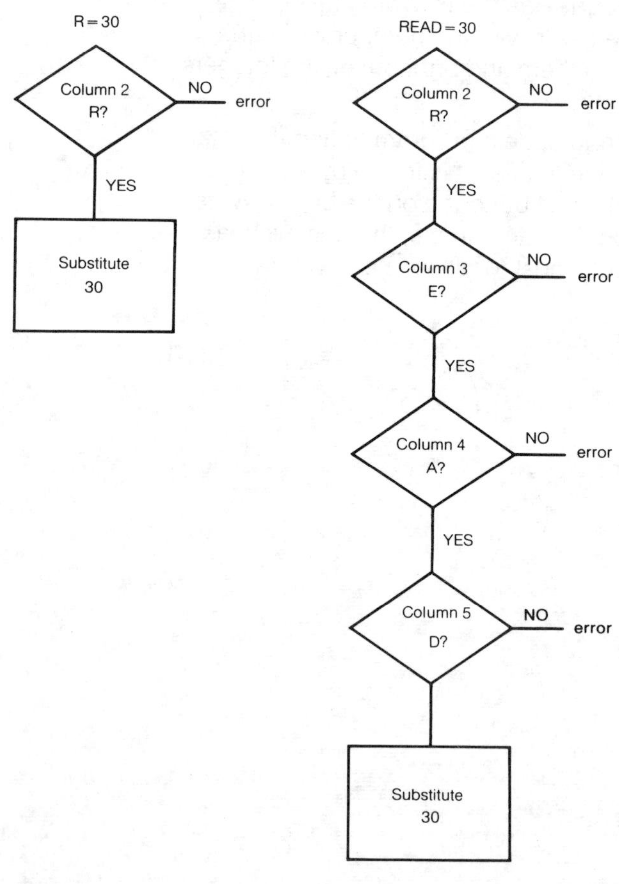

Diagram 6.1 Flowchart: checking card columns

The type of language we are developing is sometimes called an **assembler language**. Some examples of assembler or low level languages are

IBM 1130 Assembler
IBM System/370 Assembler
Easycoder
Neat

If we choose to code our instructions in Assembler, Easycoder, and so on, before the computer can execute these instructions, they must be translated to machine language.

The **translator** program is a computer program capable of analyzing our mnemonic instructions and substituting the machine language version. The translator program is sometimes referred to as an assem*bly* program, but we will not use this term because it can very easily be confused with assem*bler*. The simpler we keep our assembler language, the easier the translator program is to write. For example, suppose an assembler language allowed instructions to be punched into any card column. The translator program would then have to provide a series of instructions that would search a card for assembler language instructions. To eliminate this need, we will require that all instructions in our assembler language be punched into specific card columns. The translator will have a built-in table of letters for operation codes and their machine language substitutes. It will search the table for a match. If it can find no match, then an error message will be printed out to help the programmer in finding the errors or **bugs** in his program, that is, in **debugging** his program. Most low level language translators are capable of distinguishing between different types of errors, a feature that is very useful to the programmer but one that requires more work of the person writing the translator program. The error messages are not very sophisticated but they are of considerable help in debugging.

Another desirable feature in our assembler language would be to be able to eliminate the actual storage address in a branch instruction. Details like this are very tedious to keep track of and to code in machine language and the coding is very susceptible to errors. Study the following program segment:

```
019    STRT    R    060     0000030060
020            W    060     0000031060
021            B    STRT    0000050019
```

The location 019 has been replaced in our program by a **label** STRT. We are labelling a statement rather than referring to it by giving its actual location. As the translator program reads the assembler language program, it will form a **table of labels** and their actual addresses. It also will tell you if you have tried to branch to a label that does not exist!

The translator is now checking for
(1) the validity of the operation code
(2) the existence of a label
(3) addresses or label references
in each instruction.

In our example the translator would form a very short table:

Label	*Address*
STRT	001

Suppose we add instructions to our program and rerun it.

```
019    STRT    R     060     0000030060
020            L     060     0000010060
021            BN    STOP    0000051024
022            W     060     0000031060
023            B     STRT    0000050019
024    STOP    H     000     0000040000
```

The table now would be

Label	*Address*
STRT	019
STOP	024

Notice that we do not have to wait until the coding of the main loop is completed before filling in the branch-if-register-negative address. We say BN STOP and put the label STOP on the H instruction. Each time we run our program the label table is reformed. Therefore we can choose, within certain predetermined size limits, any word or group of letters for our labels. The translator matches the letter combinations ocurring in the address columns against those occurring in the label columns. In choosing labels it is a good idea to avoid letter combinations that are already used as operation codes. This can cause confusion to the programmer when debugging. Remember that the operation code table within the translator is permanent, whereas the label table can change each time the instructions are translated.

If we add an instruction to our program,

019	STRT	R	060	0000030060
020		L	060	0000010060
021		BN	STOP	0000051025
022		BZ	STOP	0000052025
023		W	060	0000031060
024		B	STOP	0000050019
025	STOP	H	000	0000040000

Label	*Address*
STRT	019
STOP	025

we notice that the machine address for STOP is now 025. This change of *actual* location is taken care of by the translator.

So far we have had to specify with a number address, exactly the storage location where data is to be stored. It would be much easier to keep track of the numbers if we named them I,J,K, and so on, and let the translator take care of their actual addresses.

```
R     I     0000030060
R     J     0000030061
L     I     0000010060
A     J     0000020061
ST    K     0000011062
```

In the examples above, the translator has assigned location 060 for I, 061 for J and 062 for K. It does not matter to us where I and J are stored providing they can be accessed when required.

The translator builds a table to keep track of the actual location so that, any time an instruction refers to I, the translator knows exactly where I is stored. *We* are concerned now only with the *value* of I. The translator is concerned with the location where I is stored.

Also programming would be much easier if we did not have to read in constants that we wish to use in processing. For example, frequently we require the number one for counting. In our assembler language we can generate required numbers.

```
L     =1
```

loads the number 1 into the register and if we wish to use it continually or refer to it later, we can name it N. Then

```
ST    N
```

causes the number one to be stored at a location determined by the translator. We can use it continually by referring to it as N.

The use of the '=' sign implies a single value that we may or may not wish to store for future use. in the first example where we read in numbers and called them I and J, the values of the numbers the translator stores at I and J could vary. We might well loop back and repeat the instructions

```
STRT    R    I
        R    J
        –
        –
        –
        B    STRT
```

and two new numbers are read and stored at I and J. Names of this type are called **variable names**. In our assembler we can only use single letters for variable names. Labels can have from two to four letters, which means they can be made more meaningful and the readability of the program can be increased.

We shall require a translator with at least four tables:

(1) operation code table (always the same)
(2) label table (varies in each program)
(3) variable name table (varies in each program)
(4) error message table (always the same)

Using assembler language let us code a problem which we studied in machine language in Chapter 5.

000	STRT	R	F	0000030008
001		L	F	0000010008
002		BP	POS	0000053005
003		BZ	FIN	0000052007
004		B	STRT	0000050000
005	POS	W	F	0000031008
006		B	STRT	0000050000
007	FIN	H		0000040000

The machine language version would be generated by the translator, not coded by us. You will notice that the translator has assigned the next available storage location for the variable F. Where tables and data are stored is a function of the translator design and will vary. The storage addresses are only listed for reference.

What will tables (2) and (3) look like for this example?

Label	*Address*	*Variable Name*	*Address*
STRT	000	F	008
POS	005		
FIN	007		

Translation to Machine Language

How is the low level language program translated? Our instructions, written in an assembler language, are punched into cards. Before our program can be translated, the translator program must be present in the main storage of the computer. Consider how this will work using a computer with a reader, a CPU and a printer as before.

(1) Translator program is read by card reader.
(2)Translator program is present in main storage.
(3) Assembler language instructions are read by card reader.
(4) Each statement is analyzed and translated.

Now what happens? We want the translated machine language version to replace the translator program in storage and to process our data. One way this could be achieved is to have the translated version (in machine language) punched into cards. Then we can feed the machine language version back into the computer and things will proceed as they did with machine language programs before.

In order to have the computer punch cards, we must introduce a new output unit, a **card punch**. When a card punch receives impulses from the CPU, it punches holes in cards in the indicated columns. Blank cards are fed into the card hopper. The cards pass along a path much the same as that in a card reader and are stacked in the stacker.

Some card punches are combined with card readers into one unit, either with two separate hoppers and two card paths or with one hopper and one card path. In the latter case the program would decide whether the card is read or punched or both.

Diagram 6.2 Card reader/punch

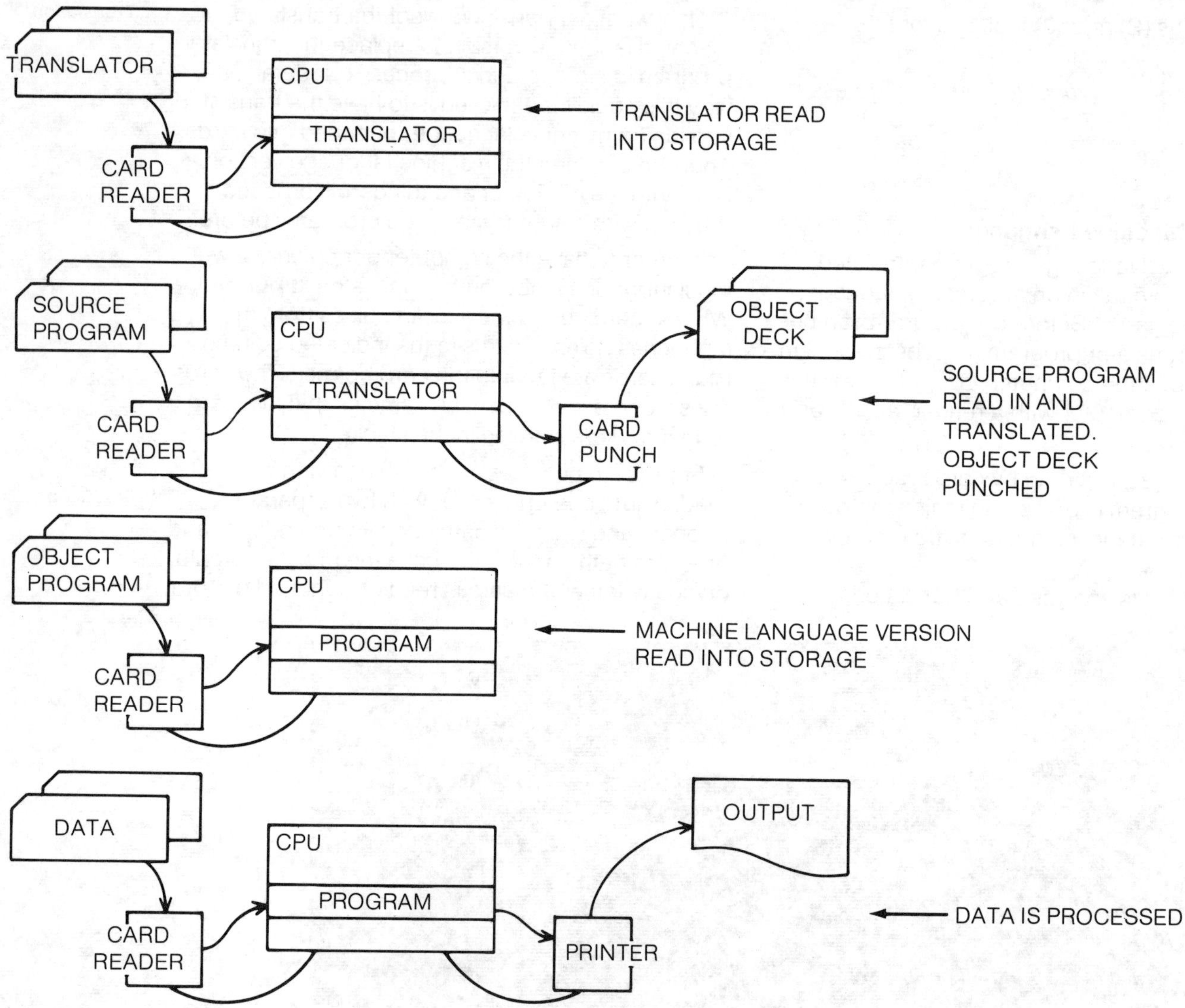

Diagram 6.3 Processing data using a low level language program

Punching the translated program into cards is not the only way of eventually having it replace the translator in storage, as we shall see later. In diagram 6.3 we can follow the entire solution process when a low level language is used to communicate with the computer.

Some new terms are used in diagram 6.3 that may require some explanation. All programs written by the programmer and requiring translation are called **source programs**. The machine language version is called an **object program**. The computer understands only the object program. In order to have the computer follow a series of instructions written in low level language, two main steps are necessary:

(1) translation from the source program to the object program
(2) execution of the object program to process the data

Who writes translator programs? Usually these programs are provided by the computer manufacturer and form part of the software available with a computer. Since every computer has its own machine language, a low level language translator program must be written for each computer. The low level languages are, to a certain extent, **machine independent**, but they do tend to be associated with a particular machine series. You may hear the phrase, ''Language A is **implemented** on computer XYZ and computer PQR.'' This means that two different translator programs have been written to translate language A for computer XYZ and for computer PQR. It is not economical to write translators for all languages for all computers.

The programmer coding in a low level language will receive as output a listing of his coded statements and a corresponding list of the machine language version. The output also contains a list of the labels used and their actual addresses. Study the diagrams of actual computer output from low level languages. The programmer may have several translation computer runs before his program is 'clean', that is, until he has no keypunch or language errors.

You will notice that diagram 6.5 shows a listing with both keypunch and language errors. *Using incorrect card columns* means the translator program cannot find the information it is looking for. *Using mispelled operation codes* means the translator program is unable to find the code in its table. The translator program is doing very much the same job as you would in translating from English to French. If the word does not make sense in English, how can you possibly translate it into French!

Characteristics of Low Level Languages and Their Translators

One characteristic of a low level language is that it translates one for one, that is, one low level language instruction becomes one machine language instruction. In many cases the object card deck contains several machine language instructions per card. The translator also can number the cards for us. Although relatively unsophisticated, the translator is capable of performing many tasks to improve the lot of a programmer writing in that language. As we have discussed, the translator program can

(1) check for correct operation codes in a table

(2) build a label table (often referred to as a symbol table)

(3) specifically indicate errors

(4) assign actual addresses

(5) pack machine language instructions (several to an object deck card)

(6) number the object card deck or object deck

There are many more functions that the translator program is able to perform, but no translator can find logic errors. Thus a flowchart is still very important. Coding sheets for the different languages are provided, making it easier for the programmer to fit operation codes, labels and addresses in the correct card columns.

The advantages to the programmer of writing in a low level language rather than a machine language are obvious. In order to justify the economic existence of the computer, it must be kept working as much as possible. It is much more economical to have a programmer writing three programs a day in assembler language than one a day in machine language. The translator has to be written only once.

But where do high level languages fit in? Once we have discussed high level languages, we shall be able to compare the various language types.

Buzz Words

Low level language	Source program
Mnemonics	Object program
Translator	Bug
Assembler language	Debugging
Card punch	Label or symbol table
Card reader/punch	Machine independent language
Implemented language	
Variable names	

```
0000FC 0700                       176          CNOP  2,4
0000FE 58F0 20FA          00144   177 SUBERSE  L     15,=V(ERSE)                  LOAD ENTRY POINT IN MONITOR
000102 4110 2042          0008C   178          LA    R1,PARMLIST+8                LOAD ADDRES OF PARM. LIST
000106 05EF                       179          BALR  R14,R15                      BRANCH AND LINK TO MONITOR
000108 07FA                       180          BR    R10                          RETURN TO CALLER

                                  182 *                                          *********************************
                                  183 *                                          *                               *
                                  184 *                                          * DUCS WRIT                     *
                                  185 *                                          *                               *
                                  186 *                                          *********************************

00010A                            188          CNOP  2,4
00010A 58F0 20FE          00148   189 SUBWRIT  L     R15,=V(WRIT)                 LOAD ENTRY POINT IN MONITOR
00010E 4110 203A          00084   190          LA    R1,PARMLIST                  LOAD ADDRES OF PARM. LIST
000112 05EF                       191          BALR  R14,R15                      BRANCH AND LINK TO MONITOR
000114 07FA                       192          BR    R10                          RETURN TO CALLER

                                  194 *                                          *********************************
                                  195 *                                          *                               *
                                  196 *                                          * READ SCREENS FILE             *
                                  197 *                                          *                               *
                                  198 *                                          *********************************

000116 5814 0000          00000   200 SUBREAD  L     R1,0(R4)                     GET SCREENS DTF ADDRESS
                                  201          READ  (1),ID                       READ SCREEN FORMAT
                                  202+* 360N-CL-453 READ      CHANGE LEVEL 3-0
00011A                            203+         DC    0H'0'
00011A 58F1 0010          00010   204+         L     15,16(1) GET LOGIC MODULE ADDRESS
00011E 45EF 001C          0001C   205+         BAL   14,28(15) BR TO READID
                                  206          WAITF (1)                          WAIT FOR COMPLETION
                                  207+* 360N-CL-453 WAITF  CHANGE LEVEL 3-3                                      3-3
000122 58F1 0010          00010   208+         L     15,16(1) GET LOGIC MODULE ADDRESS
000126 45EF 0004          00004   209+         BAL   14,4(15) BRANCH TO WAITF ROUTINE
00012A 07FA                       210          BR    R10                          RETURN TO CALLER
```

Diagram 6.4 Part of a low level language program

```
000048 0520                          65 START    BALR  R2,0                     ESTABLISH BASE REGISTER
00004A                               66          USING *,R2,R3
00004A 4122 0000          00000      67          LA    R2,0(R2)                 STORE RELOCATION FACTOR IN BASE
00004E 4132 0FFF          00FFF      68          LA    R3,4095(R2)
000052 4133 0001          00001      69          LA    R3,1(R3)

000056 18BE                          71          LR    R11,R14                  SAVE RETUTRN ADDRESS

000058 184C                          73          LR    R4,R12                   GET ADDRESS TABLE ADDRESS
00005A 5884 0008          00008      74          L     R8,8(R4)                 GET SCREEN INPUT ADDRESS
00005E 0000 0000          00000      75          L     R7,(8,R4)                GET SCREEN INPUT ADDRESS
         *** ERROR ***
000062 5854 000C          0000C      76          L     R5,12(R4)                GET ADDRESS OF TERMINAL#

000066 4167 0000          00000      78          LA    R6,0(R7)
00006A 5060 203A          00084      79          ST    R6,PARMLIST              STORE I/O START
00006E 4167 01DE          001DE      80          LA    R6,478(R7)
                                     81          OT    R6,PARMLIST+4            STORE I/O END
         *** ERROR ***
000072 4165 0000          00000      82          LA    R6,0(R5)
000076 5060 2042          0008C      83          ST    R6,PARMLIST+8            STORE TERMINAL NUMBER
00007A 9280 2042     0008C           84          MVI   PARMLIST+8,X'80'         TURN ON HI ORDER BIT IN LIST
00007E 47F0 2052          0009C      85          B     ENTRY1

                                  DIAGNOSTICS

STMT  ERROR CODE   MESSAGE

  75  IJY039       NEAR OPERAND COLUMN   6--INVALID DELIMITER
  81  IJY088       UNDEFINED OPERATION CODE

   2 STATEMENTS FLAGGED IN THIS ASSEMBLY
```

Diagram 6.5 Part of a low level language program with errors

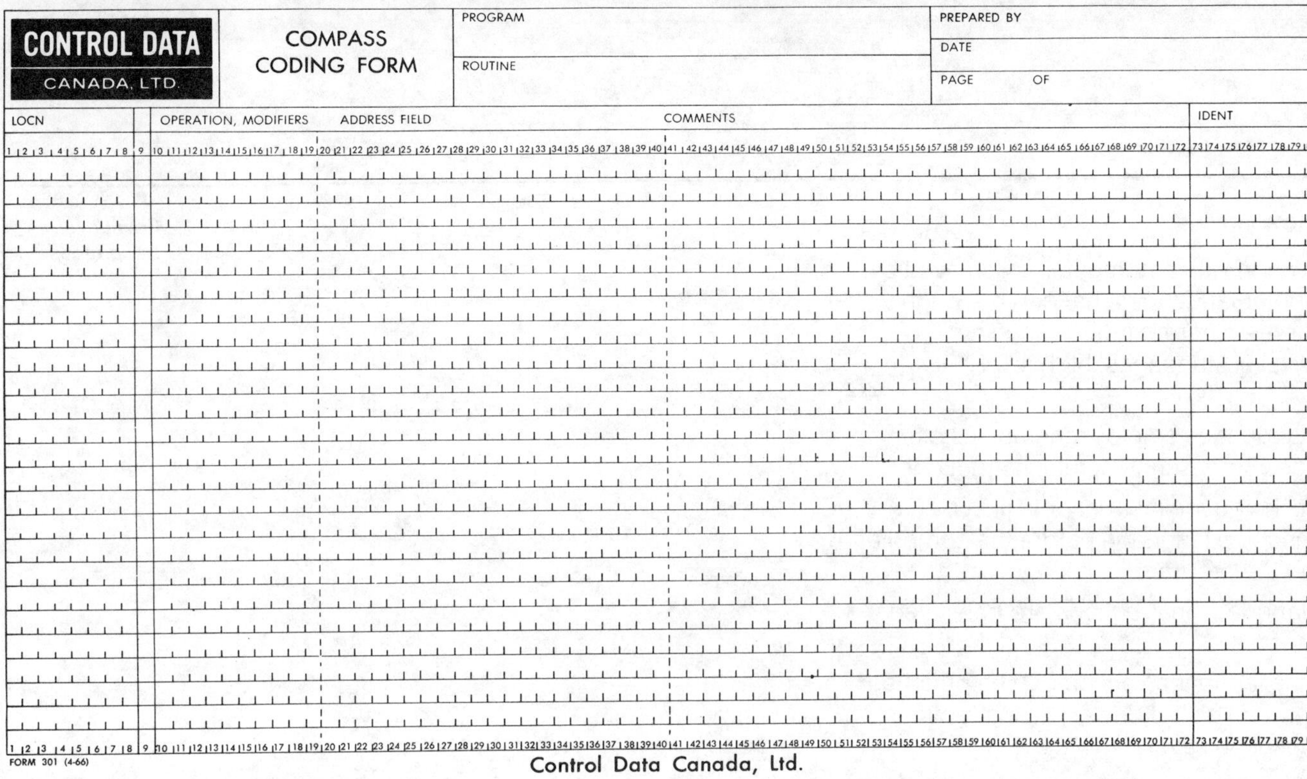

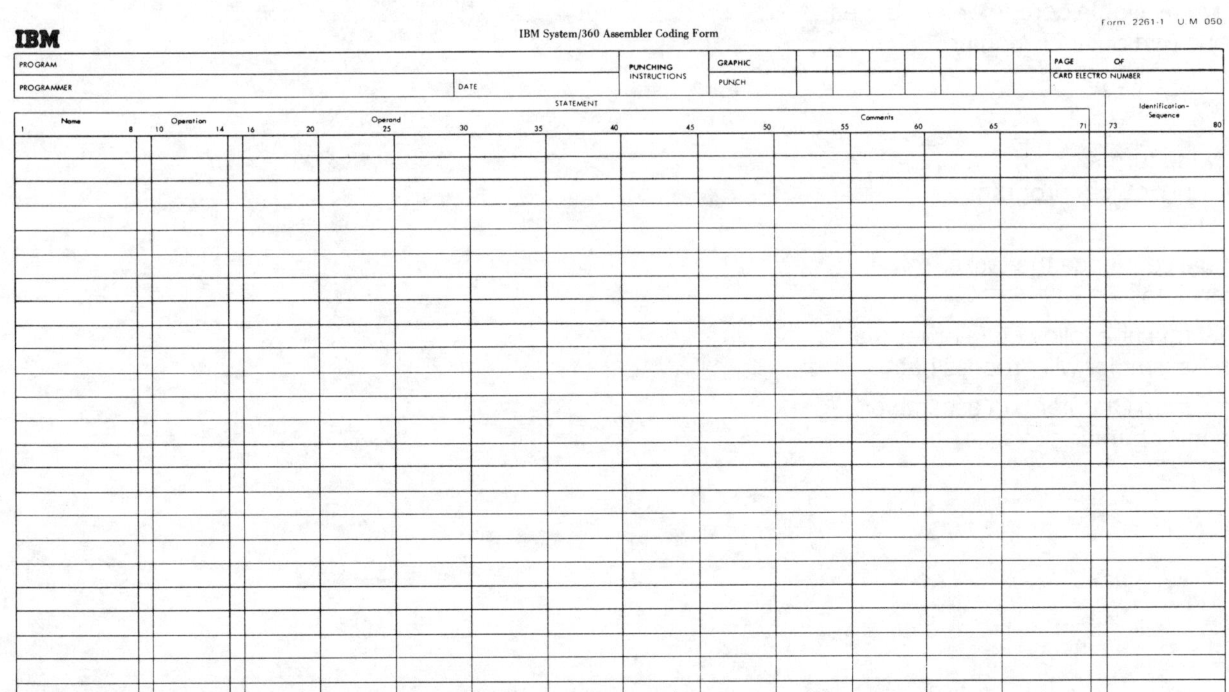

* A standard card form, IBM electro 6509, is available for punching source statements from this form.

Diagram 6.6 CDC and IBM coding forms

Points to Review

(1) Communication with a computer is achieved by means of computer languages that can be roughly classified into three different types: machine languages, low level languages, high level languages.

(2) Low level languages employ mnemonics or 'shorthand codes' to describe actual instructions.

(3) All low level language instructions must be translated to machine language before the computer can understand the program.

(4) Low level language instructions are translated one for one.

(5) The machine language version can be punched into cards to form an object deck. The instructions are frequently packed several to a card.

(6) The translator program takes care of many tasks the programmer would have to perform if he were programming in machine language.

(7) The translator program provides the programmer with helpful information for debugging his program.

(8) Only a selection of available computer languages is implemented on one particular computer.

What Do You Know?

(1) Explain the following terms:
(i) source program (ii) object program
(iii) translator program

(2) List in some logical sequence the tasks performed by the translator.

(3) List the steps that must be followed in order that a program written in Assembler will process data.

(4) Rewrite problems from Chapter 5 in assembler language as used in this chapter.

7 High Level Languages

High level languages are now reviewed, thus completing an overview of all types of computer languages.

Characteristics

High level languages represent the ultimate in the sophistication of computer languages. Economically, it is beneficial to have the programmer solving problems with ease and speed. In order to achieve ease and speed, the language of communication with the computer must be flexible, easy to learn and easy to debug. With these needs in mind high level languages were developed.

Suppose we improve upon low level languages by removing some of their restrictions and limitations. For one thing we can use whole words or accepted symbols, instead of letters, for operation codes:

READ WRITE ADD(+) SUBTRACT(−)...

We can also allow the programmer to be more flexible in keypunching the instructions.

Restricting certain items to specific card columns can lead to more errors. Perhaps clearer error messages would help as well. Such messages are often called **diagnostics**.

As we evolved an assembler type language, we saw that the easier the programmer's job, the harder the job of the translator writer. With just the improvements suggested above, you can imagine what the translator program will become!

Take a look at the following segment from a program written in a high level language called PL/1.

```
STRT..GET LIST (PRINC,RATE),.          1
IF PRINC=0 THEN STOP,.                 2
INT = PRINC * RATE,.                   3
AMT = PRINC + INT,.                    4
   PUT LIST (PRINC,INT,AMT),.          5
GO TO STRT,.                           6
```

What do you notice?

(1) No card column restrictions
(2) Resemblance to English
(3) Use of accepted algebraic symbols (=, +)

Without any knowledge of the rules of PL/1, it is obvious that the problem is one involving simple interest. A flowchart for the problem is shown in diagram 7.1.

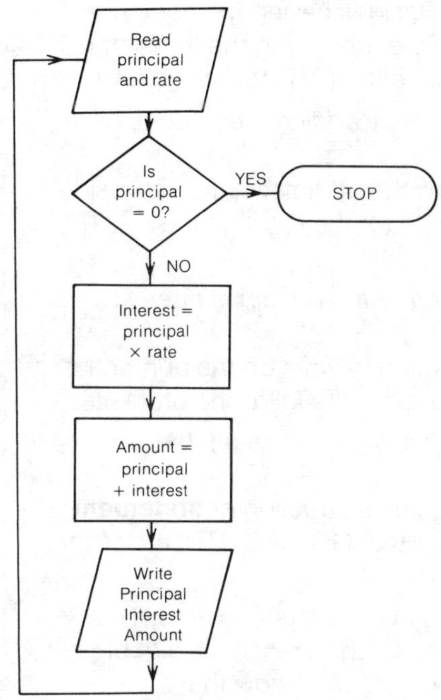

Diagram 7.1

Suppose we write out the steps of the problem in English and see how PL/1 takes care of each one.

(1) *Read, from a card, two numbers representing Principal and Rate*
GET LIST is the instruction to read the information from the data card at the card reader. The storage locations for principal and rate are called PRINC and RATE. PL/1 allows us to choose the names for storage locations and we usually try to make them as meaningful as possible. The translator assigns actual locations for storage and keeps a table of the names and addresses.

(2) *When a card that contains blanks or zeros (the last card) is read, stop!*
If the principal is zero, that is, if the card has a zero punched in it, then stop.

(3) *Multiply the principal by the rate to find the interest.*
We cannot use the conventional 'X' to mean multiplication because the computer would have trouble distinguishing between the letter X and the

multiplication symbol. Besides having the computer perform the arithmetic, we are asking the translator to set aside a storage location (INT) for the result.

(4) *Calculate the amount by adding the principal and the interest.*
The translator performs the arithmetic and sets aside a storage location (AMT) for the result of the addition.

(5) *Write out on the printer the principal, interest and amount.*
PUT LIST is the instruction to write on the printer the list of data items enclosed in the following brackets.

(6) *Go back to the beginning and repeat the instructions.*
The label STRT on the first instruction or **statement** provides a reference so that GO TO STRT causes the process to be repeated.

There are several points of interest to note. The calculation statements (3 and 4) resemble algebraic statements to a great extent. We know that the computer cannot execute a statement such as AMT = PRINC + INT,. in one instruction. There are many much smaller steps involved. Suppose locations 090, 091 and 092 are allocated for AMT, PRINC and INT. Then, as we have seen before, a series of instructions such as the following are involved:

Move number in location 091 to register
Add number in location 092 to register
Store number in register at location 090

In other words the translator has to generate three instructions in machine language for the one instruction we wrote in PL/1. A high level language is obviously not translated one for one as is an assembler language. A translator that generates more than one machine language instruction for each statement is called a **compiler**. Therefore, another advantage of high level languages is that we need fewer instructions to solve our problems. The translation is often done in two steps. First the high level language instructions are translated to a series of low level language instructions. Then the translation to machine language takes place. The compiler assigns storage locations for any variable names that it finds as it reads and translates the instructions. We do not know where they are; neither do we care! The compiler makes sure that these areas do not conflict with the area where the program itself is stored. The programmer has the ability to specify storage areas consisting of more than one location and we shall discuss this later.

An instruction in a high level language is often called a statement. A statement may consist of more than one instruction and, when translated, may result in many machine language instructions. The end of every statement in PL/1 is signified by; or,..Thus we could pack several statements onto one card and cause the compiler no problem because the compiler recognizes ; or ,. as the end of a statement. The compiler also is able to help the programmer by supplying explicit error messages or diagnostics. The statement where the error occurs is indicated and the type of error is often pinpointed. For example, had we coded statement 1 in our PL/1 program as
STRT..GET LIST (PRINC,RATE,.
we might be told that statement 1 has a syntax error, that is, a bracket or comma missing or an error of this type. The statement is not syntactically correct according to the language rules. Obviously, a missing bracket is the exact error.

Although the translator finds all language errors and some logic errors, it is not capable of finding *all* logic errors. If you make the mistake of giving two statements the same label, and then specify a branch to the label, the translator detects this error in your logic.

```
STRT..A=B-C,.
   IF A=0 THEN GO TO STRT,.
   ELSE GET LIST (X,Y),.
STRT..Z=X-Y,.
```

However, coding a statement to add the principal to the rate is perfectly acceptable to the translator although you really want the principal multiplied by the rate. These logic errors can be found only by the programmer.

High level languages have 'rules' just as other languages, such as French, English and Assembler do. The compiler frequently has the capability of making an assumption if the coding is not quite clear. For example, for our incorrect PL/1 statement

STRT..GET LIST (PRINC,RATE,.

we could get the message
STATEMENT 1—RIGHT PARENTHESIS MISSING
—PARENTHESIS ASSUMED.

This facility often saves an extra computer run since the program executes even though it still has a few errors. The programmer might not like the assumptions made by the compiler, but it is now his problem to make all required corrections. The translator has done its best to help!

The various functions capable of being performed by a compiler are not necessarily present in all translators. A compiler is designed to have those functions thought to be most valuable as programming aids. Listed below are the features of high level languages we have mentioned so far and beside them is the compiler capability required.

Language Features	*Compiler Requirements*
English words for operation codes or 'commands'	Table for translation to machine language
Labels	Label table built for each program
Names for storage locations	Assignment of areas and table of matching names
Explicit error message	Table of sentences for printing and ability to analyze the error exactly
Flexibility in keypunching	Search through a maximum of 80 card columns for the instruction
Use of algebraic symbols for arithmetic	Series of instructions to perform required arithmetic using registers
Assumptions for some errors	Series of instructions to logically decide what could be missing or wrong

It would appear that a compiler can be a very complex program! Designing and writing compilers requires a very special talent and is usually carried out by employees of computer manufacturers.

Examples of High Level Languages

Examples

There are several high level languages in existence, the most common of which are FORTRAN,COBOL,PL/1 and RPG. Let us take a brief look at these.

FORTRAN or FORmula TRANslation was originally developed to aid mathematicians and engineers in their problem solving. The mathematical capabilities of the language are highly developed and the arithmetic statements closely resemble algebraic statements.

COBOL or COmmon Business-Oriented Language was originally developed to aid the commercial data processor. It allows the programmer to express his problem in near English statements and provides capabilities for editing the output. For example, it can print leading asterisks on cheques, $ signs immediately preceding dollar amounts and CR or DR where applicable.

PL/1 or Programming Language 1 was developed by IBM at the request of their computer users who required a general purpose language. PL/1 has many of the commercial capabilities of COBOL and many of the mathematical capabilities of FORTRAN.

RPG or Report Program Generator has the capability of producing reports very easily. The programmer fills out a series of forms stating exactly what his data looks like and what the layout and content of his final report is to be.

High level languages are almost completely machine independent. COBOL and FORTRAN have sets of standardized rules laid down by the American National Standards Institute and those of PL/1 are under discussion by a committee. These are adhered to by manufacturers in their implementation of the languages on their computers. Remember that, although the high level language source program can remain the same for a variety of computers, the translator or compiler must have been written for the machine on which the program is to be run. There still exist some variations in the languages since manufacturers add refinements of their own to the basic language features specified by the American National Standards Institute.

```
1070  FORMAT(1H0,10X,'PCT   HRS   YEAR   PCT      ',3('  HRS   PCT   YEAR   PCT
     *  '),1X,'HRS   YEAR   PCT',/,T12,'EFF   UTL    HRS   INC      ',3('  UTL
     *MTH    HRS   ANN      '),1X,'UTL    HRS   INC')
1080  FORMAT(I3,3X,2I2,I1,2I2)
1090  FORMAT(2I2,4(2I3,I4,I3),I3,I4,I3)
1100  FORMAT(1H ,2I3,4X,2(I3,2X),I4,2X,I3,5X,3(I3,2X,I3,2X,I4,2X,I3,5X),
     *I3,2X,I4,2X,I3)
10    READ(8,1080)CTL,MONTH,YEAR,REGEN,SEQMO,SEQYR
      IF(CNTRL-CTL)20,30,20
20    WRITE(MESS,1000)CTL
      PAUSE 1111
      GO TO 10
30    IF(MONTH)40,40,50
40    WRITE(MESS,1010)MONTH
      PAUSE 2222
      GO TO 10
50    IF(MONTH-12)60,60,40
60    IF(YEAR)70,70,80
70    WRITE(MESS,1020)YEAR
      PAUSE 3333
      GO TO 10
80    MONST=MONTH
      M1130=MONST +1
      IF(M1130-13)100,90,100
90    M1130=1
100   YEARS=YEAR-1
      WRITE(3,1050)
      WRITE(3,1060)
      WRITE(3,1070)
110   IF(REGEN)130,120,130
120   READ(1'IRECD)MONTA,YEARA,(INPUT(I),I=1,19)
      GO TO 140
130   READ(8,1090)MONTA,YEARA,(INPUT(I),I=1,19)
140   IF(SEQYR-YEARA)160,180,150
150   WRITE(MESS,1040)YEARA
      PAUSE 4444
      GO TO 110
160   IF(SEQYR-YEARA+1)150,170,150
170   SEQMO=1
180   IF(SEQMO-MONTA)190,200,190
190   WRITE(MESS,1030)MONTA
      PAUSE 5555
      GO TO 110
200   SEQMO=MONTA+1
      SEQYR=YEARA
      IF(YEARA-YEARS)210,240,240
210   GO TO (220,270),SWTCH
220   WRITE(3,1100)MONTA,YEARA,(INPUT(I),I=1,19)
      IF(REGEN)230,120,230
230   WRITE(1'IRECD)MONTA,YEARA,(INPUT(I),I=1,19)
      GO TO 130
```

Diagram 7.2 Part of a sample FORTRAN program

```
       SELECT REPORT-OUT ASSIGN TO PR-1132-C.
   DATA DIVISION.
   FILE SECTION.
   FD CARD-FILE
       LABEL RECORDS ARE OMITTED
       RECORD CONTAINS 80 CHARACTERS
       DATA RECORD IS REC-IN.
   01  REC-IN.
       02 EMPL-NAME                  PICTURE X(30).
       02 DEDUCTIONS                 PICTURE 99.
       02 HOURS-WORKED               PICTURE 99V99.
       02 HOURLY-RATE                PICTURE 99V99.
       02 FILLER                     PICTURE X(40).
   FD  REPORT-OUT
       LABEL RECORDS ARE OMITTED
       RECORD CONTAINS 120 CHARACTERS
       DATA RECORD IS REC-OUT.
   01 REC-OUT.
       02 NAME-FIELD                 PICTURE X(30).
       02 FILLER                     PICTURE X(10).
       02 PAY-FIELD                  PICTURE 999V99.
       02 FILLER                     PICTURE X(10).
       02 NET-PAY-FIELD              PICTURE 999V99.
       02 PAY-MESSAGE                PICTURE X(60).
   WORKING-STORAGE SECTION.
   77  TEMP-PAY                      PICTURE 999V99 VALUE ZERO.
   77  GROSS-PAY                     PICTURE 999V99 VALUE ZERO.
   77  NET-PAY                       PICTURE 999V99 VALUE ZERO.
   PROCEDURE DIVISION.
       OPEN INPUT CARD-FILE, OUTPUT REPORT-OUT.
   BEGIN.
       MOVE SPACES TO REC-OUT.
       READ CARD-FILE AT END GO TO EOJ.
       MOVE EMPL-NAME TO NAME-FIELD.
       IF HOURS-WORKED IS EQUAL TO 0 MOVE 'NO PAY THIS WEEK' TO
       PAY-MESSAGE, GO TO MARGIN.
       MULTIPLY HOURS-WORKED BY HOURLY-RATE GIVING GROSS-PAY.
       MOVE GROSS-PAY TO PAY-FIELD.
       MULTIPLY GROSS-PAY BY .80 GIVING TEMP-PAY.
       IF DEDUCTIONS IS EQUAL TO 50 SUBTRACT 10.00 FROM TEMP-PAY
       GIVING NET-PAY ELSE SUBTRACT 5.00 FROM TEMP-PAY GIVING
       NET-PAY.
       MOVE NET-PAY TO NET-PAY-FIELD.
   MARGIN.
       WRITE REC-OUT AFTER ADVANCING 1 LINES.
       GO TO BEGIN.
   EOJ.
       CLOSE CARD-FILE.
       CLOSE REPORT-OUT.
       STOP RUN.
/*
```

Diagram 7.3 Part of a sample COBOL program

```
   /* PROGRAM TO COMPUTE EMPLOYEE TAX DEDUCTIONS */

   DECLARE EMPNO CHARACTER(7),NAME CHARACTER(15),
           INFO CHARACTER(20),SALTBL(6) DECIMAL FIXED (6),
           (TOTS,TOTN)DECIMAL FIXED(7,2) INITIAL(00000.00),
           TOTT DECIMAL FIXED(6,2) INITIAL(0000.00),
           (FSALY,NET) DECIMAL FIXED(5,2),
           YSALY DECIMAL FIXED(6,2),TAX DECIMAL FIXED(7,2),
           TABLE(6) DECIMAL FIXED (5,2),.
   DECLARE SYSIN FILE INPUT ENV(MEDIUM(SYSIPT,2501) F(80)),.
   ON ENDFILE(SYSIN) GOTO B,.
   PUT EDIT('TAX DEDUCTIONS-EMPLOYEE GROUP 40')(PAGE,X(10),A(32)),.
   PUT EDIT('EMP.NO','NAME','SALARY','TAX','NET')
           (SKIP(2),COLUMN(4),A(6),COLUMN(12),A(4),COLUMN(32),A(6),
            COLUMN(44),A(3),COLUMN(53),A(3)),.
   J=3900,.
   DO I=1 TO 6,.
       J=J+100,.
       SALTBL(I)=J,.
       END,.
   GET FILE(SYSIN) EDIT(TABLE)(F(8,2)),.
 A.,GET FILE(SYSIN) LIST(EMPNO,NAME,INFO,MSALY),.
   YSALY=MSALY*12,.
   IF YSALY GT 4500 THEN GOTO A,.
   DO I=1 TO 6 WHILE(YSALY GE 4000),.
      IF YSALY LE SALTBL(I) THEN DO,.
         FSALY=YSALY/27,.
         TAX=TABLE(I)/27,.
         NET=FSALY-TAX,.
         EMPNO='40-' CAT EMPNO,.
         TOTS=TOTS+FSALY,.
         TOTT=TOTT+TAX,.
         TOTN=TOTN+NET,.
         PUT EDIT(EMPNO,NAME,FSALY,TAX,NET)
                (SKIP(2),COLUMN(4),A(7),COLUMN(12),A(15),
                 COLUMN(30),F(8,2),COLUMN(40),F(8,2),
                 COLUMN(50),F(8,2)),.
         GOTO A,.
         END,.
      END,.
    GO TO A,.
 B.,PUT EDIT('$',TOTS,'$',TOTT,'$',TOTN)(SKIP(3),COLUMN(30),A(1),
            F(7,2),COLUMN(41),A(1),F(6,2),COLUMN(50),A(1),F(7,2)),.
END,.
*
```

Diagram 7.4 Part of a sample PL//1 program

```
SEQ NO  PG LIN    SPECIFICATIONS COL 6 - 74

        01 010    H
        01 020    F*
        01 030    F* UPDATE STUDENT FILE WITH MARKS
        01 040    F*
 0001   01 050    FMARKS   IPE F      80            READ01
 0002   01 060    FSTUDFILEUC  F      98R13KI     1 DISK
 0003   01 070    FSTOUT   O   F     120     OF     PRINTER
 0004   02 010    IMARKS  AA   01
 0005   02 020    I                                        1  13 NAMEC
 0006   02 030    I                                       14  20 C1
 0007   02 040    I                                       21  27 C2
 0008   02 050    I                                       28  34 C3
 0009   02 060    I                                       35  41 C4
 0010   02 070    I                                       42  48 C5
 0011   02 080    I                                       49  55 C6
 0012   02 090    ISTUDFILEBB  02
 0013   02 100    I                                        1  98 RCRD
 0014   03 010    C           NAMEC     CHAINSTUDFILE            1010
 0015   03 020    C   N10     C2        COMP ' '                     21
 0016   03 030    C   N21N10  C3        COMP ' '                     22
 0017   04 010    OSTOUT   H  201   1P
 0018   04 011    O       OR        OF
 0019   04 012    O                                   27 'SELECTIVE STUDENT LIST'
 0020   04 013    O        D  1     01 10
 0021   04 020    O                         NAMEC     15
 0022   04 030    O                                   30 'NO MATCH IN FILE'
 0023   04 040    O        D  1    N10 21
 0024   04 045    O                         NAMEC     15
 0025   04 050    O                                   28 '1 SUBJECT ONLY'
 0026   04 060    O        D  1    N10 22
 0027   04 065    O                         NAMEC     15
 0028   04 070    O                                   29 '2 SUBJECTS ONLY'
 0029   04 120    OSTUDFILED        01
 0030   04 130    O                         C1        63
 0031   04 140    O                         C2        70
 0032   04 150    O                         C3        77
 0033   04 160    O                         C4        84
 0034   04 170    O                         C5        91
 0035   04 180    O                         C6        98
```

Diagram 7.5 Part of a sample RPG program

What Language to Use?

Having studied all levels of computer languages we are now in a much better position to discuss the pros and cons of the various levels. We are faced with the problem of man who talks and thinks in words and sentences trying to communicate with the computer that operates electronically in zeros and ones. If we 'talk' at the computer's level, we are in trouble. We must use tedious, error prone, detailed machine language. If we 'talk' in our own words and sentences, the computer does not understand. If we invent a language similar to our own and provide a translator so that the computer can understand, then the problem would appear to be licked. As far as the programmer is concerned, the nearer the language is to the language he speaks, the easier it is to learn, the less time is involved in programming and the fewer errors are made. That is obviously a big plus for high level languages. The programmer is, however, dependent upon the facilities within the language. There may be special routines he needs that are not in the language. Suppose he needs to find the square root of a number and this instruction is not available in Language A, for instance. In this case the compiler could not translate the instruction. Then the programmer needs to write his program or part of it in an assembler language to break the finding of a square root down into many small steps and, with the use of the register, to achieve the required result. Why does he not use FORTRAN? Maybe FORTRAN is not implemented on his computer. We can see that low level languages have their place—they provide the facility for coding 'off-beat' routines not worth building into a compiler.

The translation of our source program has now become a complex business since there is much checking to be done for each instruction as it is read from the card reader. The compiler, of course, must be present in main storage first. If we had to feed it in from cards before each source program was translated, it would be a very time-wasting process since there may be several hundred cards involved. The aim of high level languages is to make the programmer more productive and to operate the computer at maximum efficiency. We would appear to defeat our object if we waste a considerable amount of computer time reading in a compiler! We overcome this problem by keeping the compiler stored in such a way that it can be read into storage in seconds. In this connection we introduce two more units connected with the computer. Up to this point our computer has consisted of a reader, a CPU and a printer. Chapter 8 deals with disk and tape.

Buzz Words

Diagnostics	FORTRAN
Statement	PL/1
Compiler	COBOL
	RPG

Points to Review

(1) High level languages are more flexible, nearer to English and easier for us to understand than low level languages.

(2) The most common high level languages are FORTRAN, COBOL, RPG and PL/1, each of which has its own rules and area of application.

(3) A compiler is a program that translates high level language statements to one or more machine level instructions.

(4) A compiler can help the programmer by providing explicit diagnostics and by making some assumptions.

(5) Compilers are usually written by employees of computer manufacturers.

(6) High level languages lead to a greater productivity on the part of the programmer.

What Do You Know?

(1) The translators for low level languages and high level languages differ in several ways. Specify some of these.

(2) Distinguish between an instruction and a statement.

(3) Distinguish between a language error and a logic error. Which type can the translator find?

(4) What are diagnostics and who uses them?

(5) What do FORTRAN, COBOL, RPG and PL/1 stand for? Give an example of a suitable problem for

programming in each of the four languages, with reasons for your choice.

(6) Describe in sentences what tasks you think the following program segment perform:

(a)
```
IF AGE>21 AND SEX = 'M'
     THEN MTOTAL = MTOTAL + 1,.
     ELSE IF AGE>21 AND SEX = 'F'
     THEN FTOTAL = FTOTAL + 1,.
     ELSE GO TO ERROR ROUTINE,.
```
(b)
```
TAX = RATE * TOTPY,.
     NTPAY = TOTPY - TAX - DEDN,.
     PUT LIST (NAME,ADDRS,NUMB,NTPAY,
          TAX,DEDN),.
```
(c)
```
READ (RDR,10) A,B
C = SQRT (A**2 + B**2)
WRITE (PRT,20) A, B, C
```
(d)
```
MULTIPLY HOURS-REG BY RATE-REG
     GIVING GROSS.
SUBTRACT DEDUCTIONS FROM GROSS
     GIVING NET.
```

(7) Why would a mathematician prefer FORTRAN to COBOL for programming a statistical report?

(8) What are the advantages of programming in a high level language

(a) from the programmer's point of view?

(b) from the data processing manager's point of view?

(9) Now that high level languages have been introduced, can we do without low level languages and machine languages? Explain your answer.

(10) The following program segment is written in a computer language called BASIC. Would you consider it a high level language? Give reasons.

```
  1 REM TO FIND THE AVERAGE OF A
    SET OF NUMBERS
 10 LET C = 0
 20 LET A = 0
 30 READ N
 40 IF N = 0 THEN 90
 50 PRINT N
 60 LET C = C + 1
 70 LET A = A + N
 80 GO TO 30
 90 LET B = A/C
100 PRINT 'AVERAGE OF',C,
    'NUMBERS =',B
110 END
```

(11) The following program segment is written in a computer language called APL. It is performing the same calculation as the program segment in question 10. What differences do you notice?

```
NUMB ← □
□ ← (+/NUMB) ÷ ρ ×
```

8 Disk and Tape Storage

There are other ways of storing translators and large volumes of information, as we shall see in this chapter by considering disk and tape storage and methods of processing information using them.

For several reasons it is desirable to have the translator stored in a medium other than cards. Besides the facts that cards wear out, and that a stack of cards is easily dropped and disarranged, a card reader is a relatively slow form of input to the computer.

One of the major advantages of a computer is its speed. Internally a computer is capable of performing millions, or even billions, of instructions per second. However, a card reader has not yet been invented that senses the holes in the cards at anything near that speed. An average speed for card readers is 600 cards per minute or 800 columns per second. Therefore, by the slow input of instructions or data we are holding up the fast internal processing. Several units have been designed to cope with this problem and we shall consider two of these now.

Magnetic Tape Units

Magnetic tape drives can 'read' information from magnetic tape and transfer it to main storage at rates up to 1 250 000 characters per second. Magnetic tape is much the same as the tape used on a tape recorder and is usually about 13 mm wide. Information is stored on the tape in the form of magnetized spots called bits. These are arranged in tracks along the length of the tape. The width of the tape allows up to nine tracks. The tracks across the width of the tape provide one column of information, that is, one character or instruction (see diagram 8.2).

Since only nine tracks or positions at most are present, we cannot use Hollerith code to represent our information. One of the tracks is always used to contain a **check bit**. Several coding methods are in existence for representing characters on magnetic tape. One of the most commonly used methods is Binary Coded Decimal (BCD), which is used with 7-track tape. There are two zone positions (B and A) that are combined with numeric positions 8, 4, 2, 1 to represent all numbers, letters and special characters. Study the diagram of a piece of magnetic tape coded in BCD.

Diagram 8.1 Tape drives

Diagram 8.2 Magnetic tape coded in BCD

The check bit is not used in the coding of information. As the information is written on the tape, the number of bits in each character is calculated. An extra bit, if required, is put in the check row. The tape is described as having **even** or **odd parity**. For even-parity tape, the total number of bits per column must be even and the check bit is added if necessary to make it so. Similarly, for odd-parity tape, the total number of bits must be odd and the check bit is used to achieve this. For example, the letter A in BCD uses three bits:

B	A	8	4	2	1
1	1				1

Therefore, if the tape is even parity, the check bit is required; if the tape is odd parity, no check bit is required.

The information is packed very closely on the tape and may contain up to 246 characters per millimetre. Compare that to the amount of information in a punched card.

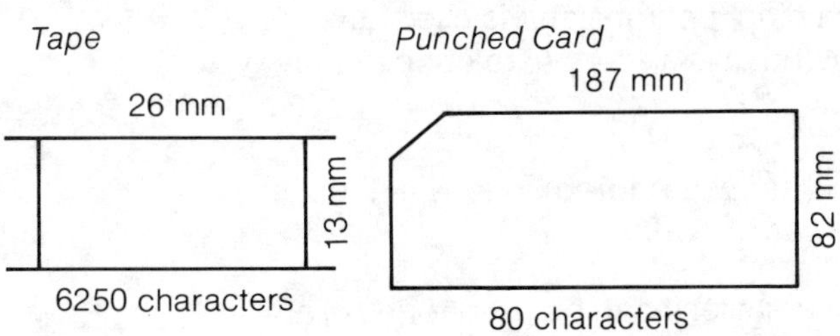

Magnetic tape is usually stored in reels containing about 732 metres of tape. To calculate the amount of information we can store on a reel of tape, we must know the density of the tape, that is, how many characters may be stored per unit length. For example, the number of characters that can be stored on 732 metres of tape at a density of 32 characters per millimetre is $732 \times 32 \times 1000$ or 23 424 000 characters—over 23 million. How many cards does that represent? $23\,424\,000 \div 80$ gives 292 800 cards or about 146 boxes!

How does the information pass to and from the tape? The tape drive has a read/write head over which the tape passes. Instructions from the CPU determine whether the head will read or write. Magnetized spots are 'written' on the tape according to impulses received from the CPU. The tape is taken up on a second reel and can be read repeatedly without destroying the information. The bits are sensed and impulses are sent to the CPU. Writing will destroy information present on the tape and replace it with new information. In other words, reading is nondestructive and writing is destructive.

The speed at which the tape passes over the read/write head and the density of the tape give us the rate at which information is transferred to main storage. For example, tape that has a density of 32 characters per millimetre and a speed over the read/write head of 1905 millimetres per second, has a transfer rate of 32×1905 or 60 960 characters per second.

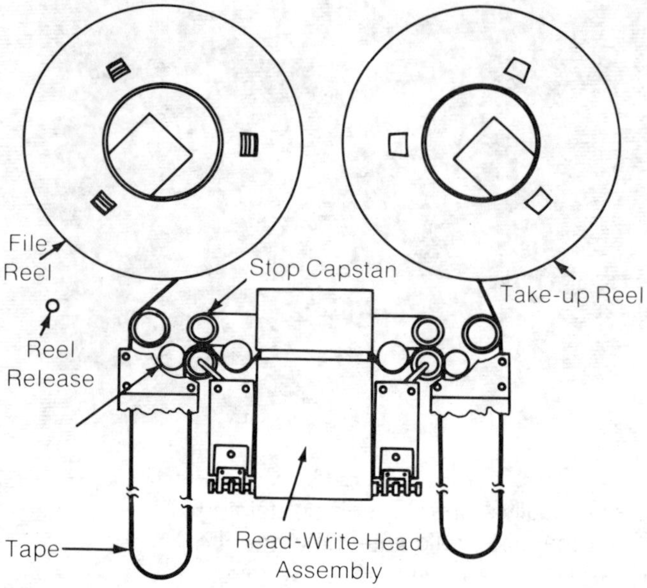

Diagram 8.3 Mechanism of a tape drive

Once certain information on a tape is no longer required, the tape can be re-used. We cannot reuse cards unless we are prepared to fill up the holes! Also, the life of the tape is considerably longer than the life of the cards. The tape has a lead-in piece for the operator to thread through the tape drive. Apart from this piece none of the tape is physically handled by the operator. In the newest tape drives even this handling has disappeared since the tape is self loading. Cards must be handled by the operator. Cards are affected by dampness, which makes them swell, and by dryness, which makes them cling together. Both of these conditions can cause them to jam or get bent in the card reader. The tape, when not in use, is fully protected by a plastic cover.

Suppose we add two tape drives to our computer system and store the translator on tape. Consider the following procedure to process a program:

(1) Mount the correct tapes on the tape drives by threading the beginning of the tape across the read/write head and around the take-up reel.
(2) Place a card, called a *control card*, in the card reader to issue an instruction to read the tape.
(3) Place the source program and data in the card reader.
(4) Start the card reader.
(5) The control card is analyzed.
(6) The tape unit is activated and the translator is transferred to main storage.
(7) The source program is read and translated and the machine language version is stored on the second tape.
(8) If there are no errors, the machine language version is read from tape into storage.
(9) The data is processed.
(10) The tapes are rewound to the beginning.

There are several points to note here:

– this method is much faster than reading the translator from cards.

– the machine language version is on tape and if there are errors the tape can be re-used. If the machine language version is a card deck and it has errors, we normally have to throw it out and get a new correct machine language deck by translating the corrected source program again.

– two tape drives are rarely sufficient as the translator normally requires space for intermediate work areas for tables, for accumulating errors, and so on, before producing the machine language version. Thus, **scratch tapes** are required. Many more instructions can be translated, and therefore larger programs can be written, if these **auxiliary storage** areas are available. Auxiliary storage is storage other than main storage.

– the tape containing the translator is used as auxiliary storage but it is also *input* to our computing system.

– when the translator was stored on tape in the first place, the tape was the *output* unit.

– a tape unit is versatile; it can be used for auxiliary storage, input and output. Is this true of a card reader or printer?

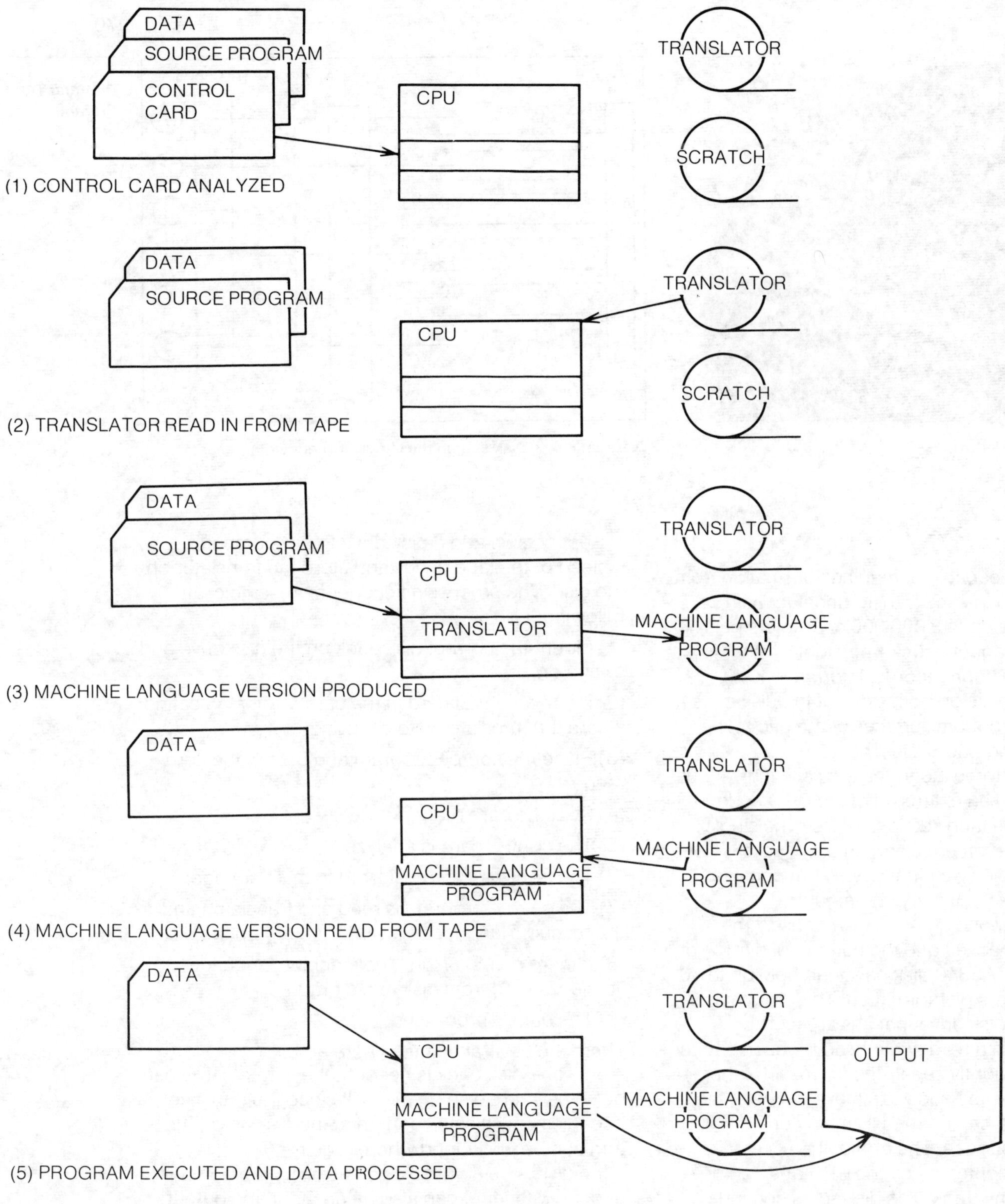

Diagram 8.4 Processing data using a translator stored on tape

Diagram 8.5 Disk drive

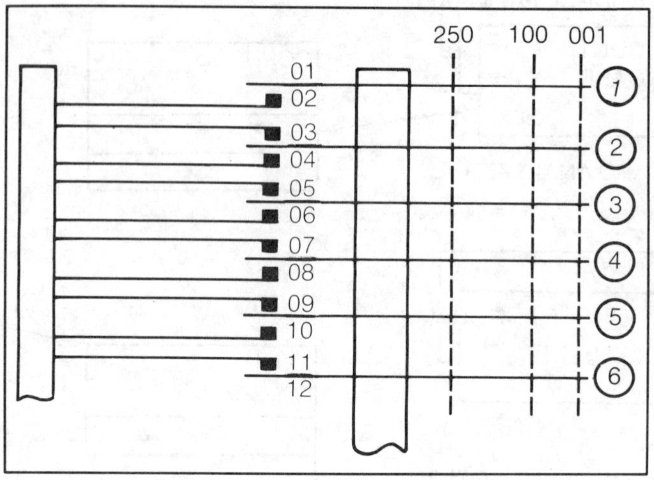

Diagram 8.6 Disk schematic showing read/write heads

Disk Units

A **disk drive** is capable of reading information from a magnetic disk pack and transferring it to main storage at rates up to 3 000 000 characters per second. The magnetic **disk pack** looks rather like a stack of phonograph records. Information is recorded on tracks on both sides of the disk except for the top and bottom surfaces of the pack. The tracks are concentric circles, not a spiral. Information is stored along the tracks using various codes including an extension of the BCD code we discussed in the tape section. There is no single check bit, however; checking on disk packs is done in a more complex way that we will not consider here. Disk packs hold varying amounts of information, depending upon how densely the information is packed and the number of disks. For example, an IBM 3340 disk pack can hold up to 70 million characters of information. The disk pack is inserted into a disk drive that has an access mechanism with a read/write head for each surface. The disks are slightly separated from each other so that the read/write heads can move between them and information can be read from any one of 200 tracks on any surface. The arm of the access mechanism is controlled by the CPU and can be positioned at any track. The disk spins continually when mounted and switched on.

Suppose we add a disk drive to our computer instead of the tape drives and store the translator on the disk. The processing sequence resembles the following:

(1) Mount the correct disk pack on the disk drive and switch on.

(2) Place a control card in the card reader indicating where the translator is to be found.

(3) Place the source program and data in the card reader.

(4) Start the card reader.

(5) The control card is analyzed.

(6) The translator is transferred to main storage.

(7) The source program is read and translated and the machine language version is stored on the disk.

(8) If there are no errors, the machine language version is read from disk into storage.

(9) The data is processed.

There are several points to note here:
– only one disk pack is needed; the scratch area can be somewhere else on the disk since the translator occupies only a small portion of the disk area. The arm can be positioned where required.
– the disk is being used as an auxiliary storage unit and, as with tape, can also be an input and output unit.

Diagram 8.7 Data module or disk pack

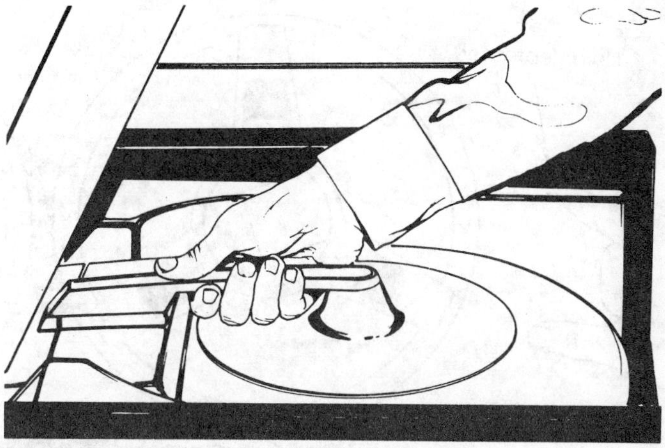

Diagram 8.8 Loading a data module

– because of the ability to access information directly from various places on a disk by repositioning, the arm of the disk is said to be a **direct access storage device**. Direct access is not possible with a reel of tape. If we need information 456 metres from the beginning of the tape, then we must wind 456 metres onto the other reel.

Processing Methods

We have discussed storing the translator on disk or tape, and it is equally possible to store data on disk or tape. For large amounts of frequently used data, disk or tape is a most practical solution to the storage problem.

Let us consider two of the methods of processing information:

(1) *Sequential processing*: Data items are processed one after the other in some sequence. Data read by the card reader is processed sequentially. The cards are read one after the other and the reader cannot read card number 6 and then skip back and read card number 4. Tapes are usually processed sequentially; information is read from the tape as it winds from one reel to another. However, it is possible to back up or back space the tape. This means item number 6 could be read and then the tape back spaced and item number 4 read, but it is a time-consuming operation and not frequently used.

(2) *Random processing*: Data items are processed in any order. Cards cannot be randomly processed. Tape can be randomly processed, since we have the ability to back space, but it is inefficient. Information stored on the disk can be randomly processed very easily since the arm can be placed at any specified place.

The tape and disk can be compared to a tape recorder and a record player. Suppose a tape and a long-playing record have the following selections on them in this order:

PALOMA BLANCA
AQUARIUS
THE STING
JEAN
SNOWBIRD

In order to play *Jean* followed by *Paloma Blanca* on the tape recorder, we must advance the tape to the beginning of *Jean*, play the selection, reverse the tape to the beginning of *Paloma Blanca* and play the selection. The record player arm can be positioned at the beginning of *Jean* and when it has played, the arm can be lifted up and placed at the beginning of *Paloma Blanca*. The record can, of course, be 'processed' sequentially as well!

Information on disk can be processed sequentially or randomly with equal ease. Information on tape can be processed sequentially with ease but random processing is inefficient.

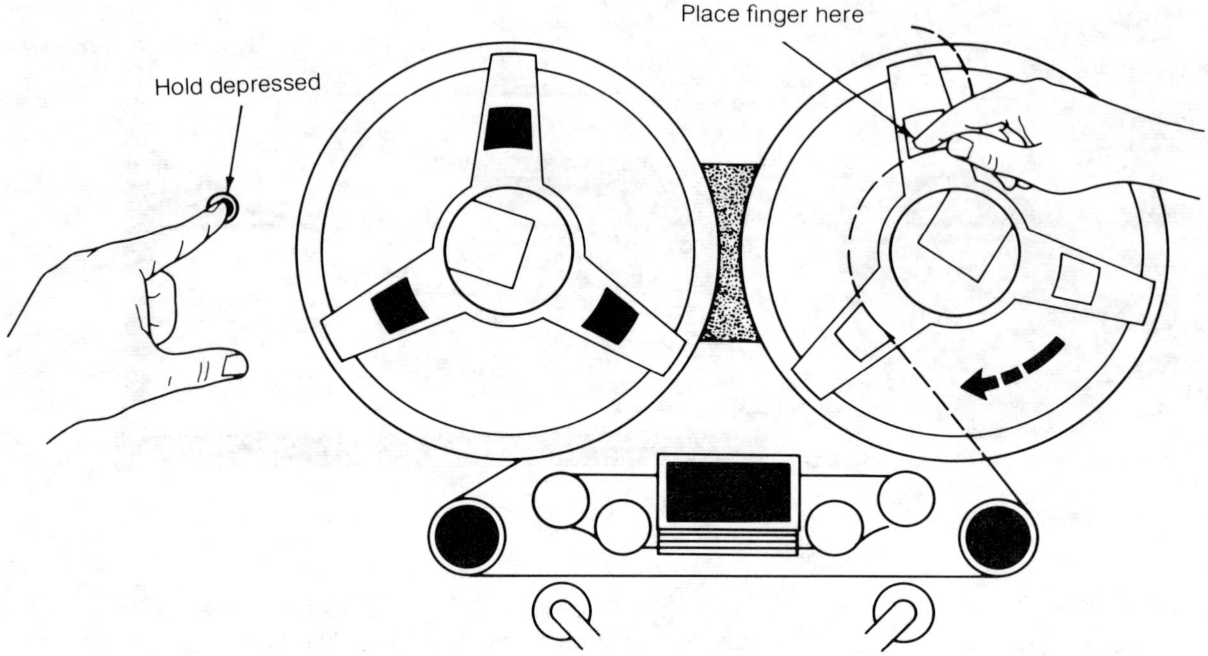

Diagram 8.9 Part of a tape drive showing tape being threaded over the read/write head

Let us review some of the facts we would have to consider in deciding between disk and tape for a system. It is possible, of course, to have both included in one computing system.

Capacity:

1 disk pack: 70 million characters
1 tape reel: 23 million characters

Note: These are sample capacities only; many variations exist. In practice these figures would be less because space is wasted separating items of information so that they can be easily found.

Cost: A disk pack is more expensive than a reel of tape.

Speed of Access: Information can be transferred to main storage faster from disk than from tape.

Durability: The life of a disk pack is greater than that of a reel of tape and the disk pack is less prone to damage. The disk pack is completely covered with a hard plastic cover which is removed only when it has been mounted on the drive. Some disk packs, often referred to as data modules, are completely sealed in a plastic case. There is no contact between the read/write heads and the surface of the disk. The heads ride a fraction of a hair's breadth above the disk surface. A tape reel must be mounted on a tape drive by an operator and could come unwound in the process. Even if it is a self loading tape there is still contact between the tape and the tape drive.

Method of Processing: Disks can be accessed randomly or sequentially while tape can be only sequentially accessed.

Before we make a decision perhaps the most important question is "What are we going to use it for?" If we keep translators on tape, we will probably have to mount a new tape for each translator, whereas we can store several translators on a disk and access them by using a different control card. At least one scratch tape would require mounting, while another area on disk can be used as a work area. The time involved could be critical. While a tape is mounted, all processing may have to be stopped for at least a minute or two. The disk arm transfers to another track in a fraction of a second. On the other hand, suppose we wish to store information about customers, in customer number sequence, on tape or disk. Since we probably read all the information starting at customer one, there is no advantage to storing the information on a disk. For any commercially used computing system three tapes is usually a minimum whereas one disk could cope with the same amount of processing. How does that alter the cost? Tape as a storage medium is cheaper and less space consuming than disk. Disk is better if we want to jump about in processing, as we would, for example, in randomly reading customer information to answer enquiries. Disk or tape, or a mixture of both, is chosen as part of the computing system according to the jobs the computer is required to perform. We shall discuss this in more detail in Chapter 9.

Buzz Words

Tape drive	Disk pack
Disk drive	Direct access storage device
Parity check	Scratch tape
Odd parity	Auxiliary storage
Even parity	Sequential access
Parity bit	Random access
Data module	

Points to Review

(1) The comparatively slow card reader input unit of a computing system can mean that the full speed potential of the computer is wasted.

(2) A magnetic tape drive is a device capable of reading and writing information at great speed, using magnetic tape as the medium.

(3) A magnetic disk drive is a device capable of reading and writing information using magnetic disks, stacked to form disk packs, as a medium.

(4) Information can be densely packed on tapes and disks.

(5) Tapes and disks are continually re-usable.

(6) One disk drive can operate on a system efficiently but three tape drives are usually required for efficient tape operation.

(7) Areas on tape and disk are used as work areas in the translation from source program to object program, thus saving main storage space.

(8) Tape and disk can be classed as input, output or auxiliary storage.

(9) Tapes are usually processed sequentially whereas disks can be processed sequentially or randomly.

(10) Many factors are taken into consideration before choosing tape or disk, or a combination or both, for a computing system.

What Do You Know?

(1) Record which bits are turned on to code the letters LUNCH in BCD. (See page 178.)

(2) What characters are represented (coded in BCD) on the tape in the following diagram? Is the tape shown even or odd parity?

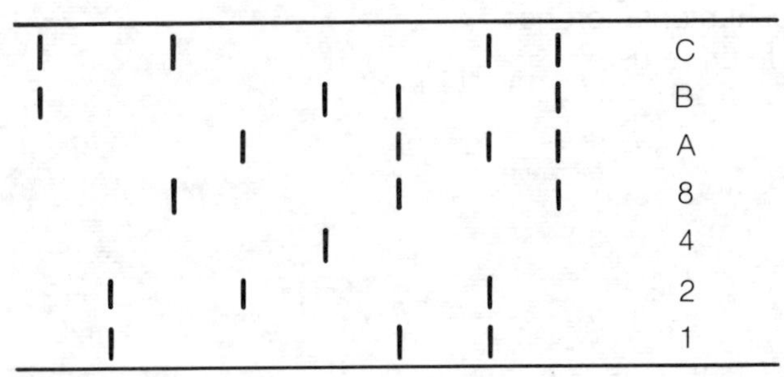

(3) If the letters in question 1 were written on even-parity tape, which extra bits would be turned on? and which turned off?

(4) Information is at present recorded on cards using 315 cards and all 80 columns of the cards. How much tape would this information require assuming no gaps and a tape density of 63 characters per millimetre?

(5) What is the transfer rate for tape that has a density of 63 characters per millimetre and is passing over the read/write head at 2856 millimetres per second?

(6) List some of the advantages of using tape instead of cards to store data.

(7) What are some of the advantages to storing the translator on tape instead of cards?

(8) Research other forms of coding used for recording characters on tape.

(9) A disk is a direct access storage device. Explain.

(10) 7¼ million characters can be stored on one type of disk. How many boxes of cards is this equivalent to? (1 box of cards contains 2000 cards.)

(11) Research one form of coding used for recording characters on disk.

(12) What factors must be taken into consideration before deciding between disk or tape as an auxiliary storage device?

(13) Explain the difference between sequential and random processing and give an example of where each would be applicable.

(14) Compare punched cards, magnetic tape and magnetic disk with respect to the following:

(a) storage capacity
(b) speed of reading by a computer
(c) ease of human reference
(d) ability to be re-used

9 What Is a Data File?

We mentioned in Chapter 8 the possibility of keeping information on tape or disk. Now we will study in more detail the storage media for large volumes of information.

Data Files

Suppose Company A has 1000 customers and certain information is kept about each customer: name, address, balance owing, discount allowed, and so on. Such customer information is called a customer **record** and a collection of records forms a *file*, that is, a **data file** of customer records. Files are kept in many forms and several different storage media, such as cards, tape, disk or file drawer, can be used.

Suppose we set up a data file of records containing information about items stocked at a drug store. Certain criteria must be considered if the file is to be useful.

(1) The file should contain only required information. Initially we might consider the following information sufficient:

item number	re-order quantity
description	minimum stock
cost price	stock room location
selling price	vendor

(2) The file should be efficiently organized. We shall choose to keep the records in ascending sequence by item number. If a disk or tape file is to be established, the information is probably keypunched into cards first.

It is most practical to keep the same information in the same place on each card. It is also desirable to assign a set number of columns to each separate piece of information because it is much easier to write a computer program to process information from the same number of card columns each time. We can write the program so that instructions repeat themselves, doing the same thing each time but using different data. To program instructions to read the same type of data in columns 1-4 on card 1, columns 46-49 on card 2, and so on, is much more difficult. Therefore we establish **fields of data** and the field sizes remain the same for the entire file.

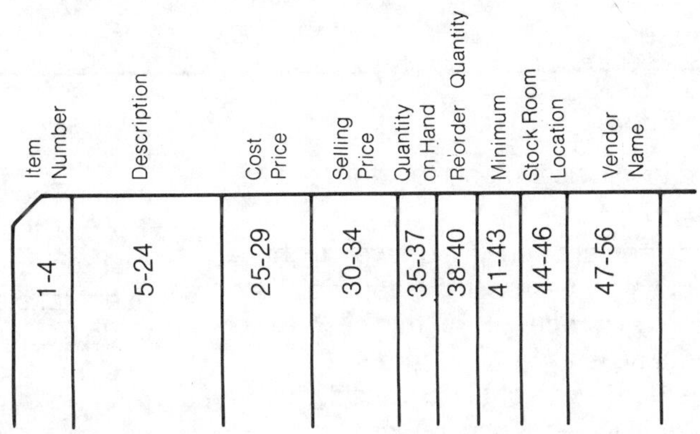

Diagram 9.1

Suppose we assign card columns and establish fields for our item file (see diagram 9.1). Before designing a card we must have some details about the information. For example, we should know the highest priced item, the total number of items, the longest description, the longest vendor name, and so on. In our example we are assuming that the cost price is never more than 999.99 (the decimal point does not need to be punched) and that the quantity on hand is never more than 999. Is any allowance to be made for growth of the file? For example, the total number of items stocked now may be 897 but it is predicted that in two years the stock will be up to 1024. At that time three card columns would not be sufficient to hold the quantity on hand.

Sometimes it is difficult to store all the information on one card and two cards may be necessary. However, if the information requires only four columns on the next card, perhaps the card layout can be revised. For example, we can identify the vendor by a three-digit number instead of by a ten-digit name. The number can reference a second file when the name is required.

The keypunch operator can tab on the keypunch in much the same way as a typist does on a typewriter. She can punch up a drum card that fits on a drum in the top of the keypunch and indicates where the tabs or stops are set. This way it is easy for her to make sure that each field starts in the correct column.

(3) The file should be easily accessible and up-to-date. To achieve this we must consider carefully the storage medium for the file.

Media for Data Files

We will look at four possible media for storing data.

(i) *A File Drawer*
Filing the records on cards in a file drawer might be the method employed if we are implementing a manual operation. All processing in this case is manual and updating is a clerical chore. If we consider this method, we might also consider putting the items in alphabetic sequence, rather than numerical, since human beings find it easier to look up *toothpaste* than to remember that toothpaste is item number 14726. The file information is easily accessible and, with a small number of items, is by far the most economical. Isolated items of information are easily found; that is, random access is comparatively fast. Sequentially dealing with all items in the file could be tedious and prone to error. Order writing, checking stock, and updating take a great deal of time since typing, checking, calculations, and so on, are done manually.

(ii) *Punched Cards*
For a medium-sized file this method of storage is an excellent idea. Presumably there is access to a computer or to electromechanical equipment. The information is keypunched and then listed on the computer or other equipment so that visual checking for errors is relatively easy. The card file can be sorted into any desired sequence using a mechanical device such as a sorter. Updating is done by writing a computer program to produce new updated cards or by hand-filing changes. Any statistical reports can be produced easily and rapidly. Information about individual items can be retrieved randomly by clerical staff.

(iii) *Magnetic Tape*
For large files tape storage is very good. The information can be put on cards and then read by the computer and stored on tape, or it can be keyed straight onto tape by using a device similar to a keypunch. Although the latter method is faster the cards are sometimes valuable for checking or for back-up in the event the tape is inadvertently destroyed. Updating the tape, statistical reports, stock checking, and so on, are done via simple computer programs. Enquiry into the file is not quite so easily accomplished. Suppose we require information about four items from an item file of 8729 items. The items are numbers 2062, 5691, 24 and 7469. Although we need only four records, *all* records up to number 7469 have to be read and this might take as much as ten minutes! It is much faster to do the job manually in a card file. However, if most of our processing requires looking at all records, then the enquiry problem is minimal.

Updating tapes is done by creating a second tape using a sequence of steps such as the following:

(a) Read a card.

(b) Read a tape record from tape 1.

(c) Compare item numbers.

(d) If unequal, write existing record on tape 2 and return to (b).

(e) If equal, write new updated record on tape 2.

(f) Return to (a).

Error checks and last record checks are required as well. Tape 2 becomes the new master item file. Tape 1 can be reused or kept as back-up in case tape 2 is destroyed or is wrong.

(iv) *Disk*
For medium or large files disk storage is also very good. Information is initially created on the disk using either cards or tape. Updating can be done very easily either randomly or sequentially. For randomly updating the file, the following steps may be used:

(a) Read a card.

(b) Read the record with the same item number as the card.

(c) Write the record back on the disk at the same place.

(d) Return to (a).

In disk storage the same disk area can be re-used for the updated file as was used for the original. Also we have the added advantage of being able to find single items very rapidly.

File Size

Some of the terms used above, such as a medium-sized file and a large file, are misleading and need some explanation. A file of 2000 records can perhaps be considered a medium file, and one of 10 000 records can be considered a large file. But if the 2000 records are 1000 characters each and the 10 000 records are 200 characters each, then the total volume of characters is the same in each case! A large file usually means a large number of records. The volume the file occupies depends upon the record length. Both must be considered when setting up files.

A point to note is that some of the tape and disk area is wasted leaving gaps between the records so that we cannot actually store, for example, 23 million characters on tape or 70 million on disk.

Choosing the Correct Storage Medium

The file storage medium chosen depends upon many factors. Before any decisions are taken as to the most practical way of storing a file, many calculations are made and many questions are asked.

Calculations

(1) Record length

(2) Number of records initially required for present file

(3) Growth allowance—extra records to be added each month, each year

(4) Total number of characters involved.

(5) Number of cards, tapes and disks required

Questions

(1) How often is the file updated?

(2) How many times is it used per week? per month?

(3) Is it accessed randomly?

(4) Is all the information required each time?

(5) How much time does the processing take? For example, how long does it take to update the file?
manually (3 days?)
cards (4 hours?)
tape (½ hour?)
disk (¼ hour?)

(6) Which method is least error prone?

The method and storage medium chosen depend upon the applications that use the file, the cost, the computer time available and the equipment available. After all these points have been taken into consideration, the most practical and economical method is chosen.

Typical Files

Following are two typical files, one stored on tape, the other on disk.

Hydro Customer File

Record layout

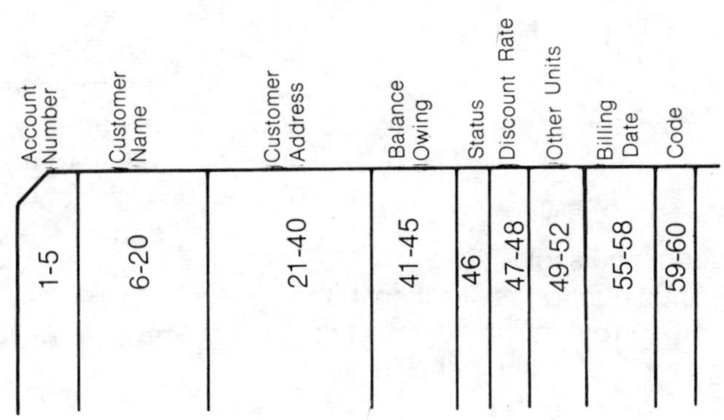

Number of records: 100 000

Each eight records will take about 30 mm of tape (allowing for the gap between records). Therefore, the file fits on one tape with an allowance for growth.

Processing: sequential

The file is required for the following:
(a) Sending out customer bills (every 2 months)
(b) Updating the file with the amount paid (every 2 weeks)
(c) Printing a list of the customers with an excessive unpaid balance (every month)
(d) Deletion and addition of customers (every 2 months)
(e) Statistics (every month)

Olympic Games Record File

Record layout

Type	Country Number	Country	Gold	Silver	Bronze	4th	5th	6th	Total Points	Time of Last Update	Date	Number of Records Held	Number of Records Broken
1	3	15	3	3	3	3	3	3	4	4	4	3	3

Number of records: 400

The file easily fits on one disk pack.

Processing: random and sequential
The file is maintained during the duration of the games for keeping current the standings of the countries taking part and most processing is random.

The file is used in the following way:

(a) Production of daily reports of status in the three areas (track and field, swimming and other events) plus a total status report. Reports are produced in total point sequence and alphabetic sequence by country.

(b) Continual updating as events take place.

(c) Continual enquiry as T.V. and radio stations request information.

(d) Disk copy operation every 30 minutes for back-up.

The two applications are entirely different and the best method was chosen for each. The second example requires some complex programming to make sure the enquiries always receive priority over other uses for the information. This is quite possible.

Sociological Problems

In setting up and maintaining files, not only must we consider the physical problems involved but also the ethical and legal problems. Are we keeping information about people on file to which we legally have no right? What security is there for making sure that the wrong people do not have access to a file? Should school history files be available to employees? Should we in fact keep a kindergarten through grade 13 file? Surely it is valuable to have complete medical files accessible by doctors, specialists and surgeons. A file for checking the validity of credit cards certainly helps safeguard our own money. How do we control file contents and the people having access to them? These problems are receiving a great deal of discussion today and, with an increasing awareness of how the computer operates, you should be able to differentiate between valid arguments and political scare tactics, and to be aware of where complete files are an excellent idea and where they represent an invasion of our privacy.

Buzz Words

Data fields
Data record
Data file

Points to Review

(1) Card columns are grouped to form fields of information.

(2) Fields of information are grouped together to form a record.

(3) A collection of similar records forms a file.

(4) Data files should (a) contain only required information, (b) be well organized, (c) be up-to-date and easily accessed, to be of any value.

(5) There are many storage media for data files, including a file drawer, cards, tape and disk.

(6) Sequential updating of a tape file involves creating a second tape.

(7) Sequential or random updating of a disk file does not require extra disk space or another pack.

(8) The file storage medium is chosen after carefully studying the file characteristics and the processing required.

(9) Ethical and legal problems must be given careful consideration.

What Do You Know?

(1) Assign an appropriate number of card columns for fields for the following information:

student number
name
initials
street address
city

Customer Number	Name	Balance Owing (dollars)	Discount Rate
1-4	5-20	21-24	25

(2) In the above record
(a) what is the largest number of customers possible?
(b) what is the greatest possible balance owing amount?
(c) how many possible discount rates are there?
Explain each answer.

(3) You are required to design the record for a student information file. What questions would you have to ask before assigning field lengths for the following information?

student number	last term marks
name	home room
initials	teacher code number

(4) Draw a flowchart to show how active items for the month would be accessed and listed on the printer, using cards with item numbers punched for the active items and a master item file on tape in item number sequence.

(5) Calculate how many reels of tape would be required for the following file:
100 000 records, each 240 characters long.
Each 10 records require an additional 13 mm of tape.
Characters can be stored on the tape at 32 characters to the millimetre. (Assume tape is 732 metres long.)

(6) It is estimated that the number of records for the file in question 5 will increase by two percent next year. Will the same number of tapes be required?

(7) Records are to be put on disk. They are five hundred characters each and every five records require twenty extra characters for identification purposes on the disk. How many records could be placed on a disk pack with 70 million characters capacity?

(8) Choose the best storage medium for the following files and justify your choice:

(a) 200 records, 500 characters each, accessed randomly for updating frequently, processed sequentially once every two months.

(b) 4000 records, 200 characters each, processed sequentially each week.

(c) 250 000 records, 1000 characters each, randomly accessed frequently, sequentially processed monthly.

(9) Three files now exist with student information. It has been decided that there is much duplication and that one well-organized file would be an improvement. Suggest what the consolidated record should contain giving the field and an estimated number of characters. The most frequently used information should be at the beginning of the record. Who should have access to the file and what should be its life span?

(i) Registration file: student number, name, address, date of birth, last school, last grade, parent or guardian, phone

(ii) Guidance file: name, home room, student number, date of birth, previous school, subjects now taken, last year's grades, repeated grades if any, parents, possible career, last date of interview, summary of interview (1 sentence), out of school activities, home phone, medical status

(iii) Office file: student number, name, home room, date of birth, last school, number of days absent to date, subjects taken, last year's result (average and pass or fail), home phone, parents' names, nurse visits (last date)

(10) The following information is kept on file about items stocked:

item number, description, cost price, selling price, vendor number, vendor address, quantity on hand, re-order quantity, minimum stock, vendor catalog number.

Certain information is used daily as orders are filled, but much of the information is used periodically only. It has been decided that it would be more practical to split the file into two files: an active file referenced daily and another file used less frequently. Suggest a record layout for each file.

10 Data Processing Techniques

This chapter deals with electromechanical and computer methods for sorting, collating, reproducing and interpreting, and introduces the concept of a data base.

We mentioned in Chapter 1 that some of the electromechanical equipment produced in the fifties is still in use. Some companies keep equipment such as sorters, collators, reproducing punches and interpreters to relieve the load on their computer. Electromechanical equipment of this type is often called unit record equipment. It uses units of information recorded on cards, or unit records, as the input medium. These are the punched cards we describe in Chapter 2. While the processes of sorting, collating, reproducing and interpreting are still important in data processing, it is possible today to have the computer perform all these operations. In this chapter we will take a brief look at these processes.

Sorting

Sorting is the process of rearranging records into numeric or alphabetic sequence. If performed manually, this is a very tedious and time-consuming operation.

Electromechanical Sorting Using A Sorter

A mechanical sorter can be used to sort cards into sequence according to certain card columns. Cards are placed in the machine hopper. To the left of the hopper are thirteen compartments or pockets that receive the cards. The thirteen receiving pockets are arranged from left to right: 9, 8, 7, 6, 5, 4, 3, 2, 1, 0, 11, 12, R. Cards pass through the sorter at the rate of up to 2000 cards per minute. The cards must pass through the machine once for each column of numeric information to be sorted. For example, if the cards are being sorted on a 3-digit field, they must pass through the machine three times. The sorting progresses from right to left, column by column, across the field.

When the start key is pressed, the cards are automatically fed from the bottom of the stack and advanced between a sorter brush and a metal roller. As the brush drops through the first punched hole In

Diagram 10.1 Sorter

the column, contact is made with the metal roller to close an electric circuit. A chute blade corresponding to the punched hole is electrically opened and the card is directed by the chute and a number of feed rollers into the proper pocket. Cards with a one-punch drop into pocket one, with a two-punch into pocket two; and so on. If there are no punches in that column, the card falls into the reject pocket. Cards are collected from the pockets and placed in ascending sequence with the zeros first, then the ones, then the twos and so on. If the field being sorted is greater than one column, then the next pass is made. A column selector knob (or knobs) can be moved to indicate the card column required for each pass.

Selection switches or digit suppression keys are used when only cards with certain punches are to be selected. In alphabetic sorting the cards must pass through the sorter twice for each column, one pass to select the zones and the second pass to select the digits. Cards with a single punch in a certain column can also be selected by using the selection switch. For example, customers in a certain geographical area, coded 1 on the cards, could be selected. This would not disturb the sequence of the file. Some sorters can provide a count of cards processed or can be used merely to count the number of cards in a deck.

Computer Sorting

Sorting on an electromechanical sorter is restricted to an eighty-character record (a card), whereas computer sorting does not restrict the number of characters in the record. Most computer manufacturers provide programs to sort records as part of the computer's software. The programs are called general purpose sort programs or sort utilities and each user must specify, using control cards, pertinent information about the data to be sorted.

There are several techniques that can be employed in sorting records. The most efficient technique for a particular sort problem depends upon several factors, some of which are the availability of extra storage (tape or disk), the size of main storage and whether the time taken for the sort is critical. We will look at three sorting methods.

(1) *Selection Method*

One of the simplest methods of sorting is to pick out the smallest of the records (for a sort to ascending sequence) and place it in another file area in position one, pick out the next smallest and place it in position two, and so on. This method requires a work area equal to that of the original file and is a slow method of sorting. The file has to be read completely as many times as there are records.

Read the file once and pick out the smallest
Read the file a second time and pick out the second smallest
Read the file a third time and pick out the third smallest
And so on

(2) *Exchange Method*

Successive records are compared and exchanged when found to be out of sequence. Consider the following list of record numbers that we want to get in ascending sequence.

1) 3
2) 1
3) 7
4) 4
5) 2
6) 9
7) 5

(a) Compare records 1 and 2 and exchange if necessary
(b) Compare records 2 and 3 and exchange if necessary
(c) Compare records 3 and 4 and exchange if necessary
And so on.

	a	b	c	d	e	f	g
1)	3 >	1	1	1	1	1	1
2)	1	3 >	3	3	3	3	3
3)	7	7	7 >	4	4	4	4
4)	4	4	4	7 >	2	2	2
5)	2	2	2	2	7 >	7	7
6)	9	9	9	9	9	9 >	5
7)	5	5	5	5	5	5	5

This successive comparison is repeated, starting with records one and two again, until no more exchanges take place. This method requires no more storage than the file already occupies. There are many refinements to this technique that can improve the speed of sorting.

(3) *Sort/Merge Method*

The group of records is stored in two separate areas. Pairs of records, one from each area, are compared and placed in sequence. Each pair, now in sequence, is thought of as a string. Pairs of strings (consisting of two items each) are merged into sequence. Now there are strings consisting of four items each. Pairs of strings are again merged into sequence. This continues until the records are completely sequenced.

Original File
13
69
56
3
8
22
35
83
61
49
37
75
59
18
70
31

Split Into Two

A	B
13	69
56	3
8	22
35	83
61	49
37	75
59	18
70	31

Paired and Sequenced Successively

Pairs	Groups of 4	Groups of 8	Merged
13	3	3	3
69	13	8	8
3	56	13	13
56	69	22	18
8	8	35	22
22	22	56	31
35	35	69	35
83	83	83	37
49	37	18	49
61	49	31	56
37	61	37	59
75	75	49	61
18	18	59	69
59	31	61	70
31	59	70	75
70	70	75	83

We have taken the simplest example of a sort/merge. It can be made more sophisticated and therefore more efficient.

In some instances only the record number and the field to be sorted, instead of the entire record, are read into main storage. It is often possible to get all the record numbers and sort fields into main storage at the same time whereas it is not possible to get in all the records. These are sorted so that a table of record numbers in the required sequence is obtained. Then the records can be accessed or a new file built in this sequence.

Collating

Collating is the arranging of information in a predetermined pattern. It is really an extension of the sorting function to include the processing of two files to be matched, for example, making sure that every customer is represented in a name file and an address file; or merged, for example, placing new customers in alphabetic sequence in an already existing file.

An electromechanical collator is capable of matching, merging and also sequence checking and selecting. Sequence checking is the process by which the ascending or descending order of a file is verified. Selecting allows certain cards to be withdrawn from the file.

These four functions can be performed on card, tape or disk files by writing the appropriate computer program. A program to select certain records is quite easy to write. Sequence checking and matching programs are a little more difficult to write, since it is not very practical to have the computer stop when, for instance, an out-of-sequence situation occurs. The program has to be written to cope with all the possibilities without stopping. The merging operation as we have seen is used in a computer sort operation.

Reproducing

Reproducing records means the exact copying of the records, usually to produce a duplicate file. Duplicate files are necessary for back-up, for use in another area, and so on.

A reproducing punch enables duplicates to be made of an original card file. The entire card can be duplicated or only certain columns. Also, the information from one card can be punched into a deck of cards. This is called **gang-punching**.

Programs can be written to reproduce cards, tape or disk and also to copy the information to other media. For example, a tape file can be punched out into cards. Manufacturers usually provide utility programs to perform this type of operation. In general utility programs involve certain functions common to all data processing installations, such as converting from one media to another or record comparison. They serve the computer installation much as a reference library serves a school. Selective copying in any media is required and is not difficult to program.

Interpreting

Interpreting

It is often necessary to have the holes in the cards interpreted, or printed, and thus easily readable. For example, hydro bills, time cards and telephone bills must be readable.

It is possible to have a keypunch with a special feature on it that allows for pre-punched cards to be fed through and interpreted. The letters appear above the column interpreted. There is also an electromechanical interpreter that can print one or two lines on the top of the card as it feeds through. Each character printed takes up a little more room than one card column. Sixty printed characters fit along the eighty columns of a card. In order to print two lines the card must be fed through the machine a second time.

The equivalent function on the computer could be the printing out of card, disk or tape files, which is done using utility programs either provided by the manufacturer or easily written. Cards can be interpreted by some card readers equipped with the feature to do so.

Introducing the Database Concept

We have discussed in this chapter and in Chapter 9 some of the basic techniques employed in processing data so that the data can be used to produce useful reports for those requiring them. Let us review some of those ideas:

(1) Data is kept in an organized form in records
(2) A group of records with the same format and type of information forms a file
(3) A series of instructions called a program must be written to process the records in the file. For example, you may wish to write instructions to the computer to sort the records, select those required, update them or gather statistics about the information contained in them.

As the data processing function in any company expands, new files are built and new programs are written to access both the original and new files. A significant amount of time is spent updating files, sorting data and making program changes. Many computer installations find that over the years they have established many files, each with several unique programs to process them. There is a tendency to duplicate information in several files. For example, in a student record system the student number probably occurs in several files and even the student name, a much longer field, may be repeated. When a new student arrives in a school several files may have to be updated. Why not combine all information about the student into one record? You were in fact asked to do this in Chapter 9, question 9. This is certainly done in many cases. Remember that the programs written to process those individual files will in all probability have to be altered to be valid with the new combined file.

Why then can't there be a filing system allowing generalized processing, just as there is a generalized sort/merge program? In fact recent developments in data processing are moving towards just this. Installations are combining their data files and eliminating duplicated items to form a **database**. All programs, and therefore all users, would be able to access the data contained in the database. Instead of files containing specific items of data we can establish a pool of information (the database) from which it is possible to extract sets of data; for example, the set of customers who have exceeded their credit limit, or the set of customers with back orders.

Sophisticated programming has been developed to allow the database to be set up and pre-processed so that the application programs using the data do not have to be altered as the database is changed. In other words 'generalized programming' can take place. Disk storage or direct access storage of some type is necessary for a database.

Database Management System

Let us take a closer look at a system involving a database. A system of this type is often referred to as an information management system, database management system, database/data communication system, or is given a specific name by the company marketing such a system. The important overall functions of such a system are to provide programs for organizing and managing the data and to provide programs for processing the data.

Specifically, some of the functions that have to be taken care of by the database managment system are:

(1) To organize the storage of the data:
The sequence of the fields in the records must be established, the type of data identified (for example alphabetic, numeric), and the field lengths kept.
(2) To organize the retrieval of the data:
The required set of data must be located, in sequence if required, and formatted for the user.
(3) To authorize access to the data:

The person requiring the data must have access to it. If all data is kept in one place then some of it may only be available to certain people. For example, salary information may only be available to authorized managers.
(4) To supervise the status of the data:
It must be ensured that data is not lost during the updating of the database.

Storage of the Data

The initial storing of the data is very important since the data organization or data structure can influence, among other things, the time it takes to find the data and the volume of storage required. The database will be used by many departments in an organization and must therefore be set up to quickly and efficiently accommodate their needs.

Setting Up Records
One of the simplest methods of organizing records is to store the data in each record in the same sequence, as we discussed in Chapter 9. For example, the fifth field may always be the re-order quantity, and will always start at the seventeenth character of the record. Space will be left in each record for any items omitted in that particular record. Fields are then located by their relative position.

	Part	Desc.	Q.O.H.	Pr.	Reord.
Record 1	1234	NAILS	024	.89	200
Record 2	1235	SCREWS	250	.84	240

Another relatively simple method of setting up records is to include the field names as part of the record.

Record 1
1234 DESC NAILS QOH 24 PR .89 REORD 200
Record 2
1235 DESC SCREWS REORD 240 PR .84 QOH 250

The sequence in which the fields are stored does not matter in this case. If the fields are different lengths then **delimiters** are needed to show where each different data item starts. A slash (/) might be used as a delimiter. No space need be left for missing fields but extra space is required for the field names and more complex programming is required to locate the delimiters.

1234/ITEMDESC/NAILS/QOH/24/PR/.89/REORD/200

Other more sophisticated methods of storing data have been devised, one of which employs a technique involving **pointers**. For example, if a customer has certain items on order, pointers at the beginning of a record may indicate the start of fields containing details of those items.

1237 20 35 50 15 SLEEPEZE 10 LAZYBOY 5 BEDCHAIR

↖ ↑ ↗
Pointers

This method does not require much extra space in the record for the pointers, but allows the records to have varying numbers of fields. Updating the records can be complex, since if a new field is added a new pointer must be inserted.

Retrieval of the Data

Retrieval of a particular set of data means that we shall have to find more than one record. Thus the order or sequence in which the records are stored is also important. We shall need a fast way of finding the required set of data without reading the entire database.

Suppose student records are stored in student number sequence but class lists are required in alphabetic sequence. A directory is set up to indicate the first record in the required alphabetic sequence, as in example 1.

Example 1: DIRECTORY

TYPE	*CLASS*	*POINTER*
ALPHA	9A	507
ALPHA	9B	510
ALPHA	9C	515
ALPHA	10A	421

The 'Type' indicates the sequence or set of records. 'Class' further delimits the set of records. 'Pointer' gives the number of the starter record in the set. In Example 1, entry 1 indicates that an alphabetically sequenced set of records for 9A starts with record 507.

Each record contains a pointer to the next record in the required sequence as in Example 2.

Example 2: DATA

Student Number	*Class*	*Name*	*Pointer*
421	10A	Adams	425
-			
-			
-			
425	10A	Black	426
426	10A	Brown	432
-			
-			
-			
507	9A	Cranston	511
-			
-			
-			
510	9B	Brubacher	512
511	9A	Curry	520
512	9B	Dawes	525
-			
-			
-			
515	9C	Archibald	519

If you follow the sequence for 9A, the first record is number 507, which points to 511 as the next one, and 511 in turn points to 520. Therefore the records are **chained** together to create a list of students in name sequence.

Using a directory and a series of pointers, any set of data can be sequenced. For example, in a student database, sets of data may be required for class lists (as above), honour students, graduating students, students on certain buses and male/female students. This is one comparatively straightforward but flexible method of accessing sets of data. Of course, if a student is added then the pointers must be changed, and if a student is removed the chain is broken! The programming required for taking care of all such details is complex.

Requesting and Processing Data from the Database

Suppose we step through the series of events that could take place when a user, via a program, requests information to produce a report and update records in a database.

User (via a program)	*Database Management System*
(1) Submit the program for processing	(1) Check the user's security to access the data.
(2) Program requests the first record	(2) a) Check the field names: —are they valid? —is the user authorized to update them? b) Determine how to access the data on disk (directory? pointers?). c) Return the requested data to the program.
(3) Process the data: —update —gather statistics —start printing the report	
(4) Return the updated record to the database management system	(4) a) Replace the existing disk record with an updated version b) Store the change in a change 'log' for backup.
(5) Loop back until the entire data set is updated	
(6) Finish printing the report.	

This is a simple example and there are many other functions performed by the database management system. The user may have to pay for the service which means statistics have to be kept, such as CPU time, disk storage used, and the number of lines printed. We have not discussed in full data storage methods or the security mechanism that would be required.

Some of the Advantages

There are a number of advantages to using a database approach:

(1) There is no duplication of data and therefore no wasted space.
(2) No sorting is required.
(3) All data is in one place and thus updating is done once only.
(4) All programs can be written to access the data from one source. In some cases multiple databases are established which can interconnect.
(5) The security problem is reduced. There is only one source of restricted data.
(6) Data can be added to the database without program changes being required.

A database system requires a large amount of direct access storage such as disk storage. This is not a problem in a large installation, since such storage is one of the few things in this world that is becoming cheaper! A database can provide the basis for an extremely flexible information system for a large number of users, and many installations are moving towards the implementation of a database management system. However, remember that setting up a database and implementing a database management system is complex, requiring a sophisticated computer system and skilled personnel.

Buzz Words

Sorting	Database
Collating	Delimiter
Interpreting	Pointer
Reproducing	Chained Records
Merging	Collating sequence
Matching	Utility program

Points to Review

(1) Unit record equipment exists to perform certain functions and relieve the work load of the computer.

(2) Computer programs can be written to perform all functions for which electromechanical unit record equipment is designed, except interpreting.

(3) Sorting is the process of organizing records into a particular sequence. There are a variety of techniques for computer sorting.

(4) Collating is the arranging of information in a required pattern.

(5) Reproducing is the process of copying all or part of a record.

(6) Interpreting is the process of printing out the characters represented by the holes on a card.

(7) Multiple files can be combined into a database.

(8) A database management system of some sort is required to organize and manage the database.

(9) A database management system consists of a complex set of programs.

(10) The method employed to initially store the data to form a database is very important.

(11) Sets of data can be retrieved from the database by the user. Sorting is not required.

(12) Chaining is one method of sequencing sets of data in a database.

(13) A database system requires large amounts of direct access storage.

What Do You Know?

What Do You Know?

(1) A file containing a two-digit account number in columns 1 and 2 is to be sorted mechanically. Indicate which cards will fall in which pockets on the two passes through the sorter.

Account numbers:

27, 54, 25, 32, 41, 74, 19, 66,
82, 09, 79, 18, 22, 85, 61, 47

(2) Draw a diagram to show how the account numbers in question 1 can be sorted using the sort/merge method.

(3) Two files are to be matched on the name field. Show which cards will fall into each stacker.

Primary File		*Secondary File*	
Brown	Eccles	Brown	Frank
Bunt	Frank	Bunt	Green
Carew	Green	Carew	Harrow
Chapman	Hunt	Cheam	Hunt
Cheam	Jackal	Crew	Keir
Dunn	Keir	Eccles	Lundy

(4) Discuss the advantages and disadvantages of having an electromechanical sorter as part of a computer installation.

(5) How many passes are required to sort 20 000 cards electromechanically into alphabetic sequence using card columns 1 to 5 inclusive? If operator time is ignored, how long would this take on a 1200-cards-a-minute sorter?

(6) Draw a flowchart for a computer program to perform a selection sort using records in main storage.

(7) Draw a flowchart for a computer program to sequence check a file and print out those records that are out of sequence.

(8) Tell why you think it would be necessary to

(a) sort an alphabetic student file to student number sequence
(b) reproduce a master customer file
(c) interpret a name and address card file

(9) When might it be necessary to

(a) select cards from a card file?
(b) merge records into an existing master file?
(c) select unmatched cards from two card files?
(d) sequence check a deck of cards?
(Give examples not quoted in the chapter.)

(10) Suggest the items that might be contained in a database for:

(a) college students
(b) hospital patients
(c) criminals
(d) bank customers

(11) Suggest sets of data that might be accessed from the above data bases. Give reasons why such sets of data might be extracted.

(12) Why do you think a slash (/) was chosen as a delimiter? Can you suggest other suitable delimiters?

(13) Using the following information, establish a directory and assign pointers in the appropriate records so that the following sets of data can be quickly found:
(a) alphabetic sequence of names
(b) Winnipeg taxpayers
(c) those with assessments in the five to ten thousand category. Remember to keep the pointers in the same sequence in each record!

	Name	*City*	*Assessment*
1	Jones	Toronto	5000
2	Smith	Vancouver	4500
3	Brown	Victoria	7000
4	Dean	Toronto	10000
5	Black	Winnipeg	5000
6	Arnold	Vancouver	15000
7	Grant	Toronto	5500
8	Saunders	Winnipeg	6000
9	Peabody	Victoria	12000
10	Kreiner	Winnipeg	5500
11	Preisner	Vancouver	4000
12	Cranston	Toronto	11000

11 Putting Together An Efficient System

We have discussed in earlier chapters various units of a computing system. We will now look at how the hardware functions with the software to achieve an efficient operation.

Throughput

One of the computer's main advantages is its speed. What speeds are we talking about? Today's computers are capable of executing millions, and in some cases billions, of instructions per second. For example, the CPU could perform one million additions of two numbers in one second. If you can add two single-digit numbers in one second, it will take you approximately three hundred days to finish the same task—assuming that you work nonstop day and night. And your accuracy at the end of that time would certainly be in doubt! Other computer units, like card readers and printers, do not achieve such speeds yet. The cost of renting or buying computer equipment in general is proportional to the speed and capacity of the equipment; that is, the faster the unit, the more you pay; the greater its capacity (CPU, disk pack, for example), the more you pay.

The most important timing consideration connected with a computing system is **throughput time** by which we mean the length of time needed to complete the entire operation. Consider the instruction "Read a card and print a line." What is the total time for the operation? There are three times to consider:

(1) time taken to read a card,
(2) time taken to store and retrieve this information (processing),
(3) time taken to print the information.

Input and output units do not operate at CPU speeds. Card readers can read cards at up to 1200 cards per minute and printers can print at up to 18 000 lines per minute. Obviously, the CPU can do many calculations while one card is being read or one line is being printed. If only one or two processing instructions are involved, then the throughput time is dependent upon how fast the card reader operates or how fast the printer can print lines. The throughput is said to be **input/output bound**. In many cases we can **overlap** input/output with processing; in other words we can use the same time interval for two or more tasks and thus improve our throughput. Study the following examples, assuming reading and writing use one thousand time intervals and the CPU one time interval for each operation: *Throughput*

Example 1: Read and write three cards, no overlapping.

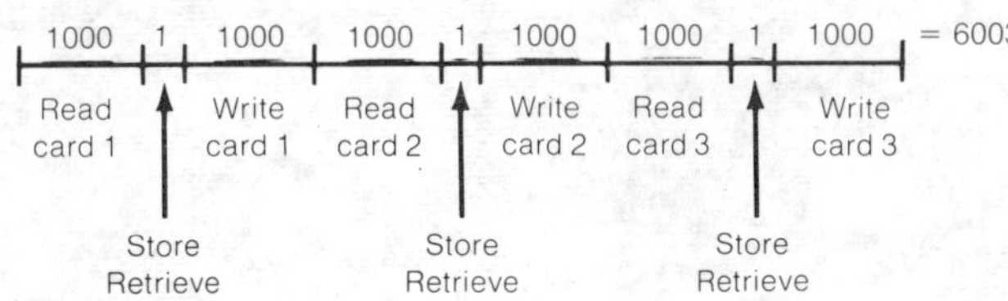

Example 2: Read and write three cards, reading and printing overlapped.

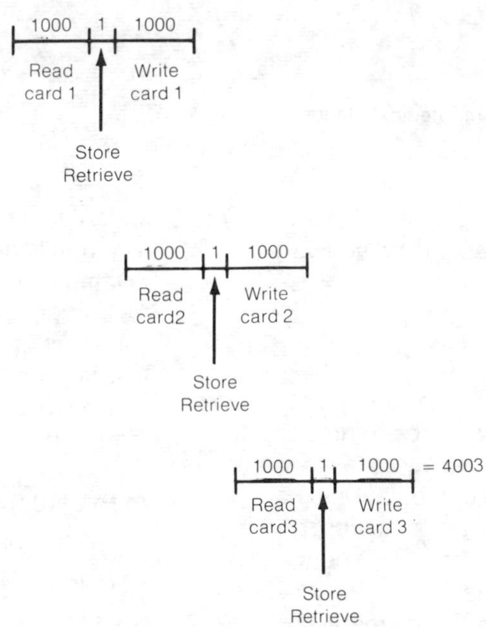

Notice that, in example 2, while card 1 is being written card 2 is being read. In example 1 the total time was 6003 time intervals; in example 2 the total time was 4003 time intervals. Overlapping has improved the throughput by approximately 30%. The

Diagram 11.1 Medium-size computer installation

ability to overlap certain operations is achieved by a combination of hardware design and software programming.

A Balanced System

By carefully selecting units that balance for a computing system we obtain the best throughput rate. Computers today do a variety of tasks. Some of these tasks involve massive computations that require the CPU to do a great deal of work and the throughput is therefore CPU bound. Others are input/output bound. Some tasks require very few cards to be read but produce many many sheets of output. It is practical then to combine a slow reader with a fast printer. The speeds of all the units are known and it is possible to calculate the time involved for a particular job with a fair degree of accuracy. The transfer rates of information from tape and disk do not usually slow down throughput to any extent if the tape and disk are efficiently used. Randomly accessing a tape file is not efficient, for example, and is very time consuming. The operations of tape and disk can also be overlapped with that of other units.

Diagram 11.1 shows an average-size computing system used by a medium-size company for their data processing. The system consists of:

(1) a card reader	800 cards per minute
(2) a card punch	200 cards per minute
(3) CPU	1 million bytes of main storage (with console)
(4) a printer	1100 lines per minute
(5) a disk unit with 5 drives (and 1 spare)	500 million characters (total capacity)
(6) 6 tape drives	
(7) console typewriter	

Diagram 11.2 Console and console typewriter

We have not mentioned the **console** and **console typewriter** before. The console with its buttons and switches, together with the console typewriter, is the operator's means of communicating with the computer. The console has switches to turn on the power for the system or power-up the system. The operator starts and stops the system working by means of console buttons. Before we can understand fully the use of the console, we must take a closer look at the computer software, particularly that part called the **operating system**.

The Operating System

An operating system is a set of processing and control programs that can improve the overall functioning of the computer. Some of the capabilities of the control program are

— supervising all operations,

— causing the correct translators to be loaded into main storage,

— allowing the computer to process a stack of jobs one after the other with no operator intervention,

— keeping a catalog of all information permanently stored on disk.

The processing programs include

(1) language translators

(2) utility programs that perform such tasks as

copying disks,
copying tapes,
punching into cards the contents of a tape,
printing out the information on disk,
listing a deck of cards,
and so on.

There are several levels of operating systems, some more sophisticated than others. Since we have a disk on our chosen system, we probably select a Disk Operating System to help in the smooth operation of the system. The operating system is provided by the computer manufacturer and we can tailor it to our needs. For example, we may never write any program in COBOL in which case we would not include the COBOL compiler on the disk.

Processing a Job Stream

A **job stream** is a series of jobs that we want to process one after the other. What happens when we have the following job stream?

(1) A FORTRAN program to produce a statistical report. The required data is stored on the second disk file (called STAT).

(2) A PL/1 program to update an inventory file on tape

(3) A deck of cards to be listed (80/80 list, that is, merely write on the printer the characters punched in the 80 columns of the card)

First we must be quite clear where everything is (see diagram 11.3). The operator makes sure of the following:

(1) The two tapes are mounted and the units are made 'ready'. The inventory file is on tape drive one and a scratch tape is on drive two.

(2) The required disks are made 'ready'. Disk one contains the operating system including three translators plus many utility programs and control programs. One of the control programs can access the catalog or 'library listing' of all stored information such as translators, files and utility programs. Space is still available on the disk. Disk three contains the file STAT which the FORTRAN program will use.

(3) The card reader has in it the required cards. Each job requires a set of **control cards**. Control cards indicate to the operating system what its next task will be. These cards are analyzed by a control program. Some examples of the information found on control cards are

(i) a job card indicating the beginning of a new program
(ii) the translator required
(iii) the files required
(iv) where the files are stored (disk,tape)
(v) whether the program requires extra disk space (for establishing a file) or a tape (for copying) and so on.

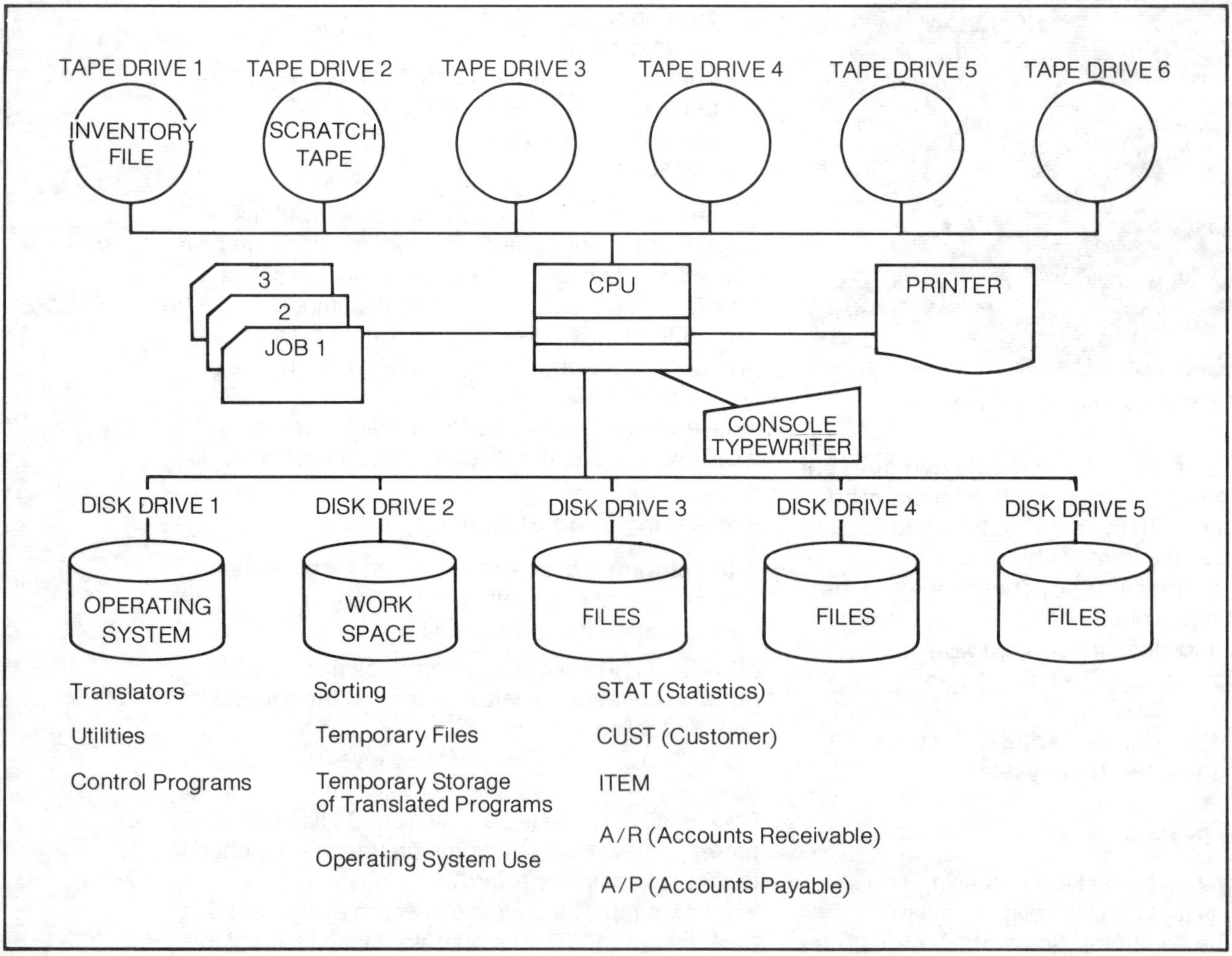

Diagram 11.3

Job 1	/ /JOB REPORT	The next job is called REPORT.
	/ / FORTRAN	FORTRAN translator needed.
	/ / OPTION LIST	Print out the FORTRAN program
	/ / FILE, DISKS, STAT	A file on disk called STAT
	/ / XEQ	
Job 2	/ / JOB UPDATE	The next job is called UPDATE.
	/ / PLI	PL/1 translator needed.
	/ / OPTION NOLIST	Do not print out the PL/1 program
	/ / FILE, TAPE1, INV	A file on tape called INV is required.
	/ / SCRAT, TAPE2	A tape is required for the updated INV file.
	/ /XEQ	
Job 3	/ /JOB LIST	The next job is called LIST.
	/ /UTIL, CARD, PRNT	Utility program is required for copying cards to the printer.
	/ /XEQ	

Diagram 11.4 Control cards

Control cards vary from job to job and for different operating systems. The control cards for our three programs could appear as in diagram 11.4.

We can now push the START button on the console. Immediately some lights on the console flash, indicating that there is some processing going on. The following sequence of events takes place:

(1) A control program called the **supervisor** is moved from disk into part of main storage.

(2) The supervisor causes the first card to be read into main storage.

(3) The first card is analyzed and, since it is a JOB card, the printer moves up to a new page. Certain checking is performed; for example, the supervisor counters are reset, the disk arm may reposition, and so on. Another card is read.

(4) The second card is analyzed and, since a translator is required, the library list is checked to make sure it is present.

(5) The translator is loaded into main storage, probably overlaying all but a small portion of the supervisor. This remaining part of the supervisor is called a **skeleton supervisor** and is always in main storage.

(6) The translator reads the other control cards and stores the pertinent information. The program is then read and translated. The translated version (in machine language) is stored temporarily on the disk as the translation proceeds. The program is listed on the printer since the option LIST is specified.

(7) At the end of the translation the supervisor is returned to main storage and takes appropriate action depending upon an error-free translation or one with errors.

(8) Assuming no errors, the program is loaded into main storage replacing all but the skeleton supervisor. The program is then executed using the file STAT stored on the disk.

(9) At the end of execution, control returns to the skeleton supervisor that has remained in main storage.

(10) The next card, a JOB card, is analyzed.

And so the processing continues with no interference from the operator.

There could be some interesting deviations from this continual efficient operation.

What happens when a program gets into a continuous loop? This is wasting very valuable computer time and requires operator intervention.

The operator can use the console typewriter or one of the buttons on the console to interrupt the program and cause control to be returned to the supervisor. The supervisor then causes cards to be read until a new JOB card is found.

What happens if processing stops for some reason? There are many reasons for this: perhaps the card reader has run out of cards, perhaps the printer is out of paper, and so on. Contrary to popular belief the flashing lights mean very little to a computer operator. He becomes concerned when they stop flashing! He then either receives a typed message on the console typewriter telling him what the problem is or analyses the lights (that is, which ones are 'on', which are 'off') to discover what is wrong.

What happens if the program has errors and cannot execute? Then the supervisor is recalled from the disk and cards are read until the next JOB card is found. No operator intervention is required.

The operating system can cope with most situations but an operator is necessary to keep an eye on things and, of course, to load the required tapes, disks, cards, etc. The console typewriter lists out certain control cards so that the operator can see how the jobs are progressing.

The console typewriter has been replaced by a video display unit on many computers. In chapter 13 you will read more about such units.

If a program has been thoroughly tested and is run on a regular basis then it is usually stored in machine language form. Only a load program is then required to move the machine language program to main storage where it can be executed immediately. The time normally spent in translating the program each time it is used is saved. There are usually different libraries for different types of programs, for example, a source library for untranslated programs and an object library for machine language programs.

We shall see in a later chapter that the operating system can be even more sophisticated than the one we have considered here. This sophistication adds to the complexity and responsibility of an operator's job.

Buzz Words

Throughput time	Operating system	Console	Skeleton supervisor
Input/output bound	Control cards	Console typewriter	Job stream
Overlap	Supervisor		

Points to Review

(1) Throughput time is the time needed to complete a job.

(2) Throughput time can be improved by overlapping the operation of certain units.

(3) An operating system consists of a set of processing and control operations that will improve the efficiency of the system.

(4) The operator communicates with the system via the console and the console typewriter.

(5) Control cards indicate to the operating system what it is required to do.

What Do You Know?

(1) What is throughput time?

(2) What is meant by overlapping card reading with printing on the printer? Why is it advantageous?

(3) Explain the functions of an operating system.

(4) What are utility programs and what functions do they perform?

(5) List some of the tasks a computer operator performs.

(6) What are control cards? What types of information do they contain?

(7) A COBOL program is to be translated but not executed. The translator is on a disk. Suggest control cards that might be used and list the series of events that will take place.

(8) What are the functions of the computer console and console typewriter?

(9) What is in main storage when
  (a) a program is being translated?
  (b) a program is being executed?
  (c) control cards are being read?

(10) If the operating system were stored on tape instead of disk, suggest any differences there might be in the steps involved in processing the three jobs in diagram 11.4.

12 The People Who Work in a Computer Installation

We now have some idea of the hardware and software that make up the computer installation. What about the people-ware?

How is a computer installation run? How many people work there? What do they do? In answering questions such as these about the people and their jobs in a data processing installation, suppose we consider a medium-sized installation using a computer like the one we discussed in Chapter 11, operating in the administrative area of a department store. Assume the the following applications are implemented and running: payroll, accounts receivable, inventory control and charge account billing. Vendor billing and accounts payable are to be implemented within two years eventually leading to a complete budget control system and a warehouse control system aimed at reducing the stock kept at the warehouse. Notice that as well as applications implemented at present we have listed the applications to be implemented in the future. These are already scheduled because no computer installation is ever at a standstill. There is always work being done to improve present applications and implement more.

The **data processing manager** is responsible ultimately for the successful operation of the installation and probably reports directly to the president or vice president of the company. He has had experience in the data processing field for several years as a project leader, systems analyst or supervisor. He is responsible for hiring the data processing staff and supervising their training, recommending new equipment, for expanding the applications and for submitting a budget. His department, and the computer, should provide a service facility to all areas of the company, to ease their routine tasks and to improve their efficiency, thus contributing to the growth and prosperity of the company. He must be very familiar with the entire company's operation. As well as reporting to top management he meets frequently with managers of all departments using the computer. His staff organization varies greatly but for a department store the following set-up is appropriate.

Diagram 12.1

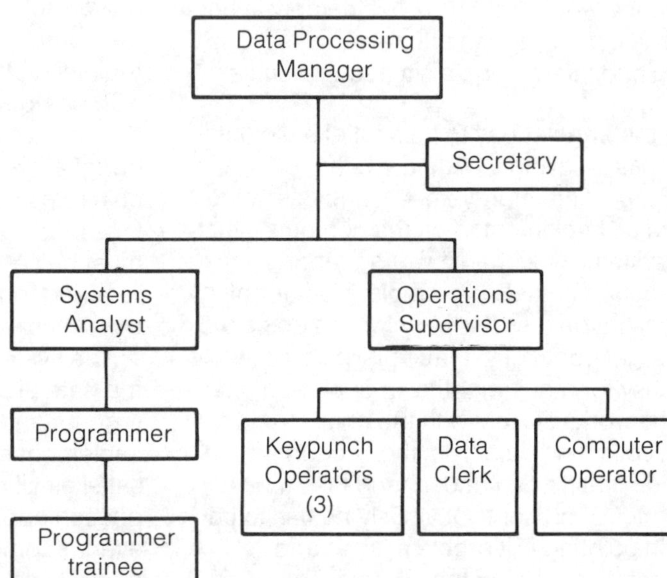

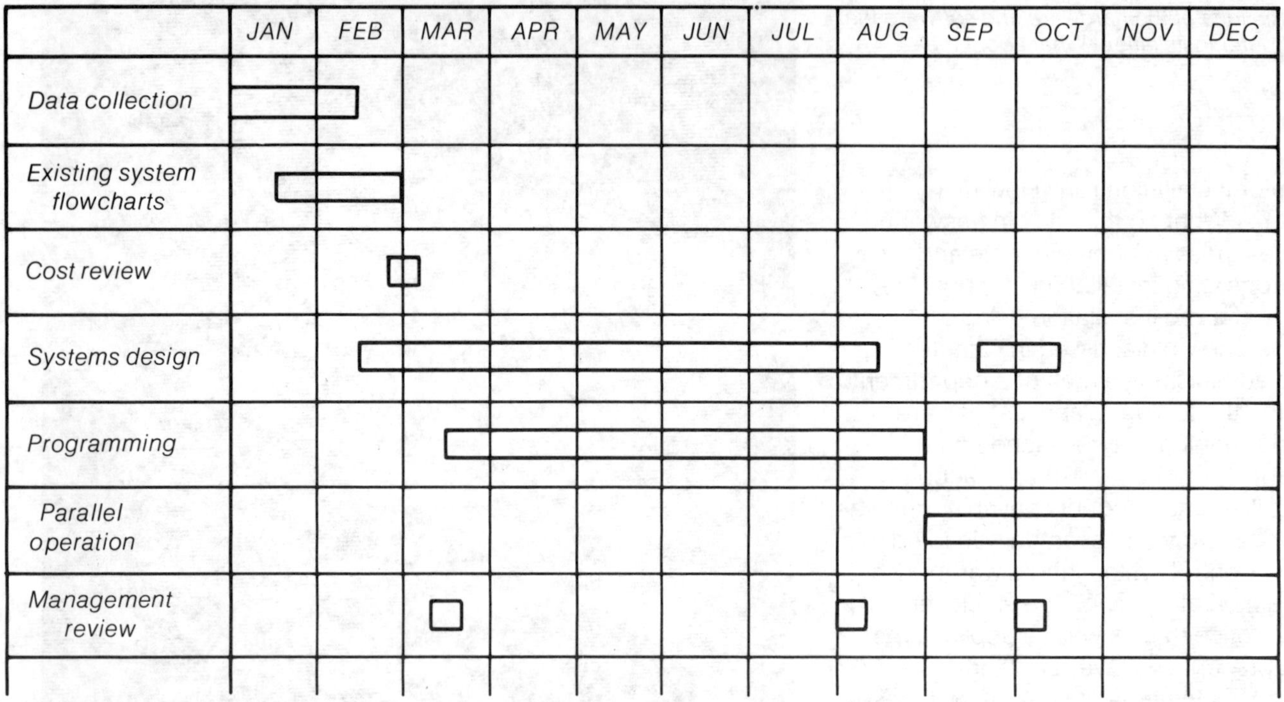

Diagram 12.2 Schedule for implementing a new system

The **manager's secretary** performs the usual secretarial duties but probably is familiar with computer terminology and basic computer concepts. Such knowledge would help her considerably in her job so that she can cope with phone conversations, report typing and interpreting a situation when her boss is out.

The **systems analyst** has to be a bit of a diplomat. Part of his job is studying a manual system in operation, suggesting improvements and designing the system to be implemented on the computer, that is, drawing systems flowcharts, writing reports and collecting required data. For example, his current assignment might be responsibility for designing a complete budget control system. This job probably keeps him busy for many months. In approaching this design he works closely with the chief accountant, collecting data from the accounting department so that he can understand how the system operates at present. Obviously he has to be very tactful in pointing out problem areas and inefficient operations. Using the information he has gathered and having discussed his ideas with the accountant and other personnel concerned with the system, he designs the new system. He must follow closely the recommendations made and make sure the output of the system is acceptable to the recipients. In the technical area he has to be familiar with computer languages and with file and record design, he has to understand fully the computer hardware and software available, and he has to be able to estimate the computer time and personnel time involved in implementing the system. Also, he must be sensitive to problem areas: controls required, growth allowance on files, implementation deadlines, and so on.

The systems analyst makes recommendations to the data processing manager. For example, he might recommend that an extra disk drive be rented to implement successfully a budget control system that satisfies all departments. He might recommend a phased approach to the implementation. He may even recommend that the idea of a total budget control system be dropped because the computer is too small, because there is insufficient staff in the installation, because he has received no cooperation from the departments concerned, because the present system is eminently satisfactory and there is nothing to be gained from changing it, and so on. It is then the manager's decision whether to follow the recommendations. The systems analyst's job is a responsible one and he must be familiar with the aims, organization and running of the company. A systems analyst usually begins as a programmer and, as he gains experience and maturity, he is promoted to systems analyst. A good systems analyst has a wide choice of excellent and challenging jobs available and can move on to be a project leader or manager.

The **programmer** does the writing of programs to perform the tasks outlined by the systems analyst. A programmer receives systems flowcharts and input and output formats from the analyst and then codes, debugs and tests the programs required, usually to meet a given deadline. A programmer must be skilled in the computer language he is to use and a good programmer is probably proficient in at least two computer languages. The learning of additional languages takes two or three weeks full-time study. The programmer is familiar with all aspects of the computer he is using: the operating system used, the utilities available, the particular language features implemented on that computer, and so on. He is sensitive to the most economical size of program possible with the available CPU and work areas, and he knows how to make up test data to test all parts of the program; particularly the error routines.

The programmer confers with the analyst frequently and discusses codes to be used, tables to be built, data file layouts, and so on. He makes recommendations to the analyst about computer time required, programmer time required and the number of programs required, perhaps saying that a deadline cannot be met unless he has more computer testing time. In most installations certain times are set aside for the programmers to test their programs, probably once a day, and the programmer must estimate how long it will take to debug his programs given this schedule. A good programmer requires only one or two runs to remove all keypunch errors. Then he has to find logic errors using the program test data and his original flowchart. He must prepare full documentation for the programs when they are operational, including detailed flowcharts, program listings with ample comment statements and operator instructions with error messages and the action to be taken. As he becomes experienced he probably helps with systems design and systems studies in order to progress to systems analysis.

Programmer

Diagram 12.3

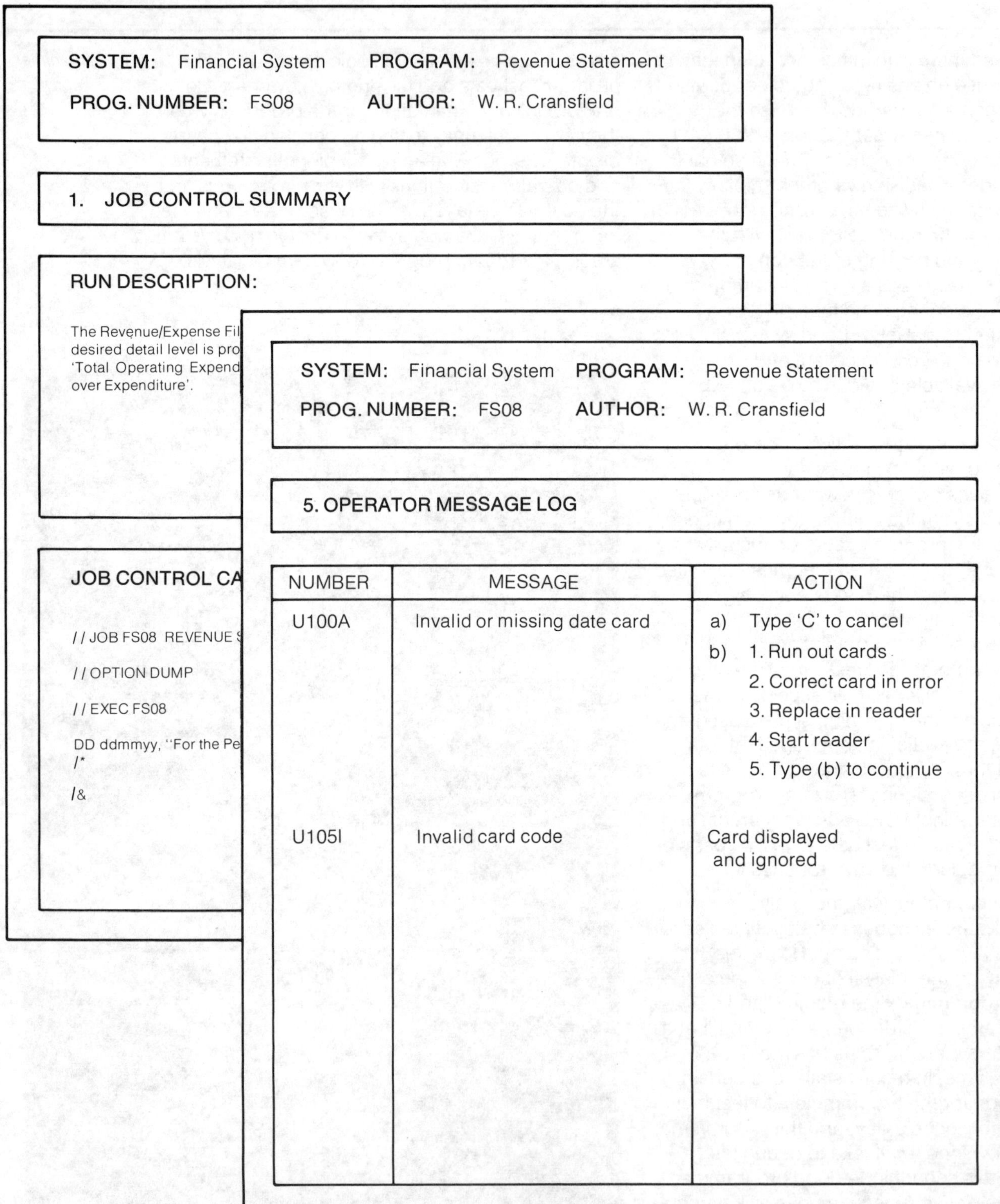

SYSTEM: Financial System PROGRAM: Revenue Statement
PROG. NUMBER: FS08 AUTHOR: W. R. Cransfield

1. JOB CONTROL SUMMARY

RUN DESCRIPTION:

The Revenue/Expense Fil
desired detail level is pro
'Total Operating Expend
over Expenditure'.

JOB CONTROL CA

// JOB FS08 REVENUE S
// OPTION DUMP
// EXEC FS08
DD ddmmyy, "For the Pe
/*
/&

SYSTEM: Financial System PROGRAM: Revenue Statement
PROG. NUMBER: FS08 AUTHOR: W. R. Cransfield

5. OPERATOR MESSAGE LOG

NUMBER	MESSAGE	ACTION
U100A	Invalid or missing date card	a) Type 'C' to cancel b) 1. Run out cards 2. Correct card in error 3. Replace in reader 4. Start reader 5. Type (b) to continue
U105I	Invalid card code	Card displayed and ignored

Diagram 12.4 Sample computer centre documentation

A **programmer trainee** is likely working in his first job and has less than one or two years experience. He writes some of the programs closely supervised by the other programmer or the analyst. He may be given short unrelated programming tasks such as the alteration of existing programs, the programming of extra reports using existing files, and so on. As he gains experience he is given more responsible work. Writing the programs for a system is a job requiring skill, a great deal of care, attention to detail and exhaustive testing. Writing payroll programs, for example, is not a task delegated to a junior programmer. A small oversight on the part of the programmer could cause chaos.

The **operations supervisor** is responsible for the efficient running of the computer system. This includes the scheduling of the computer time and the supervision of related personnel (keypunch operators, data clerk and computer operator). He is also responsible for making sure that the hardware is always functioning efficiently and for scheduling preventative maintenance by the manufacturer. He sees that the library of magnetic tapes and disks is correctly labelled and maintained and that the operating system is functioning with sufficient back-up. He checks the quality of the output before it leaves the computer room. He makes recommendations about physical layout and resources, such as air conditioning, storage space, false flooring. He keeps statistics on the time used by specific departments, schedules reruns if required, supervises keypunch personnel and sees that their schedules are maintained. He reports to the data processing manager if the system is overloaded and might recommend that another shift be run. He submits requirements for keypunches and other unit record equipment and for installation supplies such as cards, paper, printer ribbons, tape reels and disks. The operations supervisor could move to a larger installation where he would have more responsibility or he could move into other areas of the installation.

The **keypunch operator** keypunches programs and data required for the applications. A keypunch operator is fast, careful and accurate in operating a keypunch. She does not necessarily understand programming languages but keypunches what is printed on the coding sheets. (It is the programmer's responsibility to see that his program is readable.) If data is being keypunched and it is critical, that is, it is necessary that errors be nonexistent or minimal, then the data may be key verified. A verifier is operated in the same way as a keypunch and looks just like a keypunch but, instead of punching holes into the cards, it senses holes already in the cards. The same information is keyed using the punched cards instead of blanks. If the operator keys ABCD from the original document and ABCD is punched in the card, then the keypunching is accurate. If she keys ABED and ABCD is punched in the card, a red light appears. She then checks to see whether she is wrong or the keypunching is wrong and takes appropriate action. Programs that are keypunched are not usually key verified since the programmer can determine any keypunch errors made. Keypunch operators can progress to be supervisors of several operators or they can move into other areas of the data processing installation if they have the ambition to learn more about the computer.

Data Control Clerk

The **data control clerk** is responsible for controlling and checking all input and output connected with the installation. Incoming data is checked for completeness. For example, an adding machine tape should arrive with a bundle of cheques, and three boxes of cards should be present when three are specified. She keeps a log of data accepted, its completeness and the time of acceptance and maintains a schedule of input and output. After being checked for completeness, all output is distributed by the data control clerk according to the schedule. For example, one copy of two reports goes to the president, three copies of the statistical report go to the accounting department and other copies go to be filed. The data control clerk makes sure the computer operator has all the required data for running a program or series of programs at the scheduled time.

A data control clerk must be familiar with the company organization and know whom to contact when input is missing or when output will be late. She may move eventually into supervisory work, programming or other areas connected with the installation. It is desirable that the control clerk understand basic computer concepts and computer operation.

SYSTEM: Financial System	PROGRAM: Revenue Statement
PROG. NUMBER: FS08	AUTHOR: W. R. Cransfield

2. SETUP INSTRUCTIONS

CARD IDENT.		CARD INPUT DESCRIPTION	SOURCE
CODE	COLUMNS		
DD	1 – 2	Date Card	Standard Date Card

DASD DRIVE	PACK I.D.	I/O	SOURCE	DISPOSITION
091	111111	Input	Library	Library

TAPE DRIVE	TAPE I.D.	RING	SOURCE	DISPOSITION
None				

PRINTER SETUP		PUNCH SETUP
Revenue Report FORM — 8½ ⋆ 13	PRINT POSITIONS — 1 – 120	DESCRIPTION — None
TAPE — Formaliner	LINES/INCH — 6	ELECTRO NO —

SPECIAL COMPUTER SETUP INSTRUCTIONS

REVENUE STATEMENT

For the Period	Page No.
Apr. 1 – Jan. 31, 1969	1

Account No.
40-0000-000 41-0000-000 42-0000-000

Current Month			Year to Date		
Budget	Actual	Variance	Budget	Actual	Variance

Diagram 12.5 **Sample computer operator instructions**

Computer Operator

The **computer operator** actually runs the computer. He checks the schedule and, using the operator instructions provided, makes sure that the correct disk and tapes are mounted, the forms are correct and the control cards and data are ready. He watches for error indications and takes appropriate action, reports equipment malfunctions and generally makes sure the computer is kept running with as few halts as possible. He constantly checks the computer console typewriter for messages and checks the console lights to make sure the computing is proceeding as it should. A computer operator must understand the functioning of the equipment with which he is working and usually studies programming as well. A computer operator in a small or medium-sized installation can move on to a larger installation where he would have responsibility for more complex equipment or he can train as a programmer or become an operations supervisor.

Although the only jobs that have really been indicated as female occupations are those of the keypunch operator and the data control clerk, there is no restriction in the data processing industry to jobs available to men only. There are many female programmers and analysts. Computer operators tend to be men, probably because there is often shift work involved.

We have looked at the personnel working in one installation. There is a great deal of variation in the number of people and their job definition in different installations. In a small installation jobs may be combined so that the keypunch operator is also the computer operator and there is a programmer analyst instead of a programmer and an analyst.

Diagram 12.6 Using this mini computer, one person may perform the function of a programmer, keypunch operator, computer operator and data control clerk.

In a large installation there could be more than one computer operator: a senior operator might have another operator or a trainee under him. Also there could be specialization among programmers: a software programmer responsible for maintaining the operating system, writing specialized routines to be incorporated in language translators and so on; scientific programmers responsible for scientific applications and a senior programmer in charge. A librarian may be employed to organize and control a tape library if hundreds of tapes are involved. There are many other jobs we have not discussed. The data processing industry has a tremendous number and variety of challenging jobs available and there is great potential for job advancement. In working with computers, however, you must be prepared to work odd hours, to study continually, to be resourceful and to have a sense of responsibility.

Running An Installation

What are some of the important considerations in running a successful installation?

(1) *Sufficient controls*
Data coming in is checked and reports going out are checked. Programs should have built-in controls for checking the accuracy of the data, for sequence checking, for checking for blanks in a certain field that should not be blank, for checking a customer number and name in an update card against a file record before updating the file and for producing a hash total of incoming data. For example, it might be that customer numbers are added. The total really has no meaning and so is called a hash total, its only value being that it provides a check. A hash total of customer numbers on incoming cards can be made on an adding machine. This is compared with the hash total accumulated on the computer as the data is processed. Any difference indicates an error. In any systems design adequate checks are incorporated by manual, mechanical and programmed controls.

(2) *Accurate scheduling*
This means that each application must be timed. Adequate time must be allowed for the operator to load tapes and disks. Programmers must be allowed test time. Time must be scheduled for maintenance and for back-up procedures (copying master files, for example). Priorities must be worked out; for example, the payroll would take priority over updating a customer file. Forecasts of the overloading of one shift must be made so that personnel can be employed and trained.

(3) *Management reporting*
The data processing manager must make regular reports to management. He must make sure that his problems, progress, implementation schedules, proposed development and budget requirements are known by the top management of the company.

(4) *Personnel training*
The manager must have a training program for his staff. The installation personnel will be dissatisfied if they do not see their careers progressing and in order to do this the personnel must be kept up to date on the latest developments in the industry. Large installations often run their own courses and training sessions and most computer manufacturers provide courses for their customers. As well, the data processing manager would be very wise to organize seminars for people indirectly connected with the computer so that they understand its capabilities and limitations.

(5) *Control of restricted information*
Any information that is to be available only to specific people must be adequately protected and locked up. Today, many people are unhappy about the keeping of comprehensive records on disk or tape. They feel that unscrupulous use of this information is an invasion of their privacy. And it certainly is! On the other hand, for years personnel files have been kept in locked cabinets, available to unscrupulous people by various dishonest means. The same is still true, except that it is probably harder to get at the information as disk packs and tapes cannot be read by the human eye. The problem is not with the computer but still with the people involved.

(6) *Maximum utilization of the computer installation*
The computer installation personnel must be continually working towards the most efficient use of the equipment. Can time be saved by using off-line

equipment? Can a program be made more efficient by using improved logic or different programming language features? Can other applications be implemented? Can other departments be served? Until the computing system is being used efficiently twenty to twenty-four hours a day, it is not being used economically. Many installations run three eight-hour shifts. Others run only one shift but rent time to other users for second or third shifts.

(7) *Planning*
Planning for future applications is essential. Time schedules must be drawn up for systems to be implemented within the next few years. Such a schedule might include
(i) study of the present method used and gathering of related information,
(ii) design of a computerized system: systems flowcharts, file design, form layouts, card design, and so on,
(iii) program writing,
(iv) testing,
(v) parallel runs,
The accountant cannot ask for a total budget control system and expect to have it by next week. When the system is ready to be implemented, it should be done in parallel with the existing method. For example, dummy cheques are produced on the computer and compared with the real cheques.

The economical use of the computer is a combination of the maximum number of hours of usage and the efficient use of that time. Scheduling, future planning, control and a responsible data processing manager with an interested and capable staff results in a well run and profitable computer installation.

What Do You Know?

(1) You are applying for a job as a data processing manager in a medium-sized computer installation. Write a letter addressed to the vice president of the company, giving a resume of your previous employment, education and qualifications.

(2) List the various tasks that an experienced programmer might be expected to do. What background knowledge would he require?

(3) For a month collect information from your town's newspaper about job advertisements connected with the computer under the following headings: job, salary, experience required, education. In what areas are the greatest number of jobs available? Summarize the educational requirements for each job type.

What Do You Know?

(4) Explain what is meant by a hash total. When is it used?

(5) Student marks are to be submitted to the computer centre on cards by the staff. The cards contain a student number, name, subject number and a mark. These cards are used to update a student file on disk. The student report cards are produced by the computer. Suggest manual, mechanical and programming controls that should be incorporated.

(6) Payroll cheques are to be printed on the computer for eight hundred employees. Suggest controls that are necessary in the operation.

(7) As a system analyst you are given the following job assignment: The village of Little Blandings is to be surveyed by questionnaire to assist the council in choosing a solution for the following problems. Construct a set of questions so that decisions can be made to the satisfaction of the majority. Only yes/no answers can be processed. Those filling out the questionnaire should be aware of the implications in their answers (for example, increased taxes).

(i) A highway has to be built through or near the village and there are several alternatives:
(a) The highway can incorporate the main street.
(b) The highway can be one mile from the centre. There is no feeder road at present (increased taxes).

(ii) The local school is not big enough.
(a) Supply portables (minimum cost, limited life, buses needed).
(b) Build a new addition to the school (increased taxes and buses).
(c) Build a new school to serve the new subdivision (increased taxes and buses).

(iii) The village square is in bad shape. The suggestions for dealing with it are:

(a) Pave it (no upkeep).
(b) Returf it (upkeep).
(c) Mixture of both.
(d) Provide benches with (a), (b) or (c).
(e) Provide a fountain with (a), (b), (c) and (d).

(8) The following tasks are to be performed on the computer and unit record equipment by the operator during an eight-hour shift that starts at 4 p.m.

(i) Payroll: 3-hour run–3 tapes–cards–normal paper for first two hours—cheques for one hour—1 scratch disk, 1 disk with operating system.
(ii) Reproduce cards: 1 hour
(iii) Sort cards: ½ hour
(iv) Testing job for programmer: 1½ hours—1 scratch disk, 1 disk with operating system—cards—normal paper
(v) Billing: 2½ hours—1 scratch disk, 1 disk with operating system—master file tape and 2 scratch tapes—special paper.

Draw up a suitable schedule. Tapes take two minutes to load and unload, disks, three minutes. There are four tapes and two disks on the system as well as a card reader and a printer. The installation has a sorter and a card reproducer. It takes three minutes to change the paper in the printer and one minute to initially load the card reader. The times given are actual run times and do not include tape changing, disk loading, and so on. Another operator takes over at the end of eight hours.

Use the following headings for the schedule: Job, Approximate start time, Operation, Anticipated run time, Loading time, Elapsed time. Indicate whether you anticipate a job to be running when the new operator takes over.

(9) The following letter has been received by the computer centre manager from the chief accountant who understands little about computers. Reply to the letter explaining tactfully what is involved to supply the information requested.

Dear Mr. Jones,
I understand that you keep on file in your department, information about our personnel from which you produce the pay cheques. I would very much appreciate a statistical breakdown by section of the salaries of our employees (see enclosed document) and also a name and address listing in alphabetic sequence. I would appreciate having this information by the morning.
Yours truly
James Anstey

(10) What talents and experience would you think necessary for the person running a one-man computer installation consisting of a small computer, with several applications running and two or three to be developed?

13 Another Look at Input/Output Units

Now we will study some of the other input/output units that are in use.

We have discussed in detail the most commonly used input/output units of a computing system: the card reader, the card punch, the printer, the console typewriter, disk and tape. There are many more units available, some of which are mentioned below.

Visual Display Unit

Several visual display units are available and they can be used either as input or as output units. One such visual display unit consists of a cathode ray tube (like a TV screen), a program function keyboard, a light pen and a keyboard. The complete unit is connected to the computer and is under the control of the CPU.

The display area is 28 by 21 cm and is divided into a grid of addressable points. Colours for display terminals vary but are always chosen to be easy on the eye and minimize glare, and the brightness can be adjusted.

The information to be displayed is stored in a **buffer**, a temporary storage which is part of the circuitry of the terminal. The information in the buffer can be transferred back to the CPU for storing permanently, or used in calculations etc.

A visual display appears on the screen when an electron beam in the CRT (cathode ray tube) strikes the CRT screen which is phosphor coated, and therefore glows briefly. The screen display must be continually regenerated since it fades in a fraction of a second. It is regenerated approximately fifty times per second. If the display is not regenerated fast enough the image on the screen flickers and becomes difficult to read.

It is possible to display 1920 characters at one time in 24 rows of 80 characters each. All characters displayed on the CRT are formed from a pattern of small dots of light on a 7 X 9 dot matrix. A small dot of light called a **cursor** is displayed beneath a character or character position on the screen to indicate where the next character entered from the keyboard will be displayed and stored in the buffer. A character which has the cursor under it can be altered or deleted.

Diagram 13.1 Visual display unit

Continuous displaying of information can be achieved by spacing forwards and backwards using special keys. For example, you may browse through a file looking for information, showing screen after screen, until the information is found.

The addressable points in many terminals are sufficiently close together that very smooth curves can be drawn. These terminals are often referred to as **graphic terminals**.

The information to be displayed is provided by the user's program. The visual display unit is just another input or output unit. If the programmer asks for the letter A to be displayed, he specifies:

(1) the display unit as the output unit,
(2) the letter (A),
(3) the size of the letter,
(4) the position of the letter.

The programmer gives instructions in the appropriate language for A to be 'drawn', much the same as you give instructions to somebody plotting an A on a piece of graph paper. A translator program and the operating system take care of the actual transmission of the correct impulses.

We can communicate with the display unit manually in three different ways:

(1) *Using the keyboard*
The program indicates, by displaying a message on the screen, that keyboard input is expected. For example,

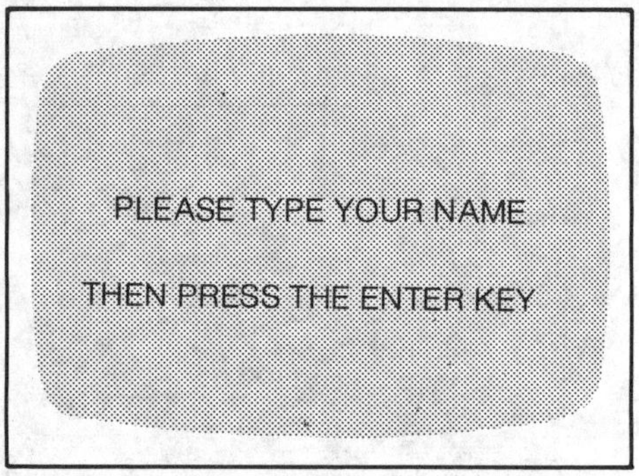

When the name has been typed and the ENTER key depressed, the program accepts the name as input in the same way as it would receive input from the card reader—the typed name is merely a series of impulses from a different input unit. The name also appears on the screen and can be visually checked and altered before transmission to the CPU.

(2) *Using the light pen*
The light pen contains a photo cell that is sensitive to the light spots on the screen. The pen is attached by a cord to the terminal and, when pressed against the screen, sends impulses to the CPU. The light pen, of course, reacts only if the program is asking for a response in that way. For example,

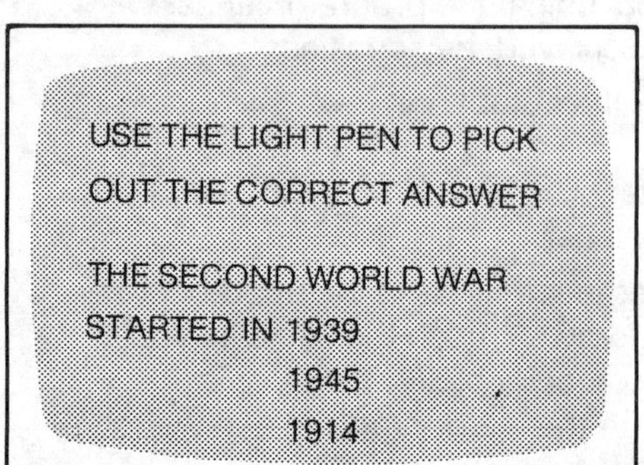

The position from which the impulse is received causes the program to continue accordingly.

(3) *Using the program function keyboard*
There are push-button keys that can cause certain programs, already stored on disk, to be used. These buttons can be used with several switches to give a wide range of combinations. For example, a combination of key 1 and switch 2 might display a routine to teach you how to use the light pen, while a combination of key 12 and switch 3 might increase the size of an image by a certain factor.

Visual display terminals are becoming increasingly popular since they provide instant viewing of information. While the price of paper has been steadily increasing the price of visual display units has been steadily decreasing, contributing to their popularity for many applications. For example, the guidance teacher in a school can review a student's record prior to an interview. A phone call to City Hall about your tax assessment can result in an immediate answer as the clerk causes your tax record to be shown on the screen. Bridges can be designed and altered on the screen until the best design is obtained, at which point a hard copy of the statistics can be printed or the design plotted. The position of space rockets can be displayed and the picture continually altered as the statistics change, thereby giving us a simulation of what is taking place thousands of miles away.

Mass Storage

A **mass storage** system is a unit capable of storing very large amounts of data, and can be used as an input and output unit. It can store up to 470 billion characters of information. The data is stored on small cylindrical data cartridges. Each cartridge is approximately 5 cm in diameter by 10 cm in length. The cartridge contains a spool of tape about 18 m long. Just over 16 m of this is useable, and can store up to 50 million characters. The rest is lead in tape at either end. Depending upon the volume of storage available in a particular mass storage system, there are up to 4000 data cartridges incorporated into the unit in a honeycomb arrangement of storage cells.

Diagram 13.2 Mass storage system

The data is stored on the data cartridge in an image of the way it would be stored on a disk. How is this enormous volume of data controlled and made available to the user? The mass storage system is attached to the central processing unit of the computer, which controls the processing of data. Let us follow through what happens if a certain file or data set is required that is stored on the mass storage system.

First, the location of the file is determined by searching a set of tables containing information about location, size, type etc. of the data files. A device called an accessor then moves to the physical location of the data cartridge. The cartridge is removed from its cell and placed in a data recording device. The requested data is then transferred at high speed to a disk pack. Since the data is stored on the cartridge in the image of a disk it can then be accessed in the same manner as a regular disk pack. Getting the information to the disk from the cartridge is called **staging**. When updated or new data is transferred back to a data cartridge, it is termed **destaging**. Overall control of the mass storage system is provided by a special control unit.

Data can be transferred to more than one disk pack. Thus the whole process of accessing information can be thought of as a massive electronic library, with a 'librarian' (mass storage control unit) placing 'books of information' (data cartridges) in 'carrolls' (on disk packs) where they are 'read' (accessed) by the various 'users' (programs).

Isn't this series of steps time consuming? Yes, it does take longer than accessing records directly from a disk file, but the time should be compared to that required to find information from a tape since mass storage is intended to be a replacement for the massive tape libraries kept by some organizations.

When information is required from a tape in the library, the following process takes place:

(1) The tape librarian locates the tape.
(2) The tape is transported to the computer room and loaded on the tape drive.
(3) The tape is searched sequentially for the required information. If the information requirement is known ahead of time, then the tape can be mounted ready for access.

This process involves manual assistance, which is not as fast or accurate as electronic means.

There should be a saving of "people" time in using mass storage—time spent by tape librarians and operational personnel. Other advantages include no physical handling of storage media and a saving in space, since mass storage eliminates tape libraries and tape drives required to provide access to large volumes of data.

Mass storage units have come into existence because of the masses of information today being stored. This information is relatively useless unless it can be accessed *as required*. Since modern computers can run many jobs at the same time (multiprogramming—see Chapter 15) a media was needed to keep up with the constant demand for data required for those jobs. Mass storage provides a media that is less expensive than disk and faster than tape. Many businesses have initially used a mass storage system to replace tape but are finding that it provides them with the volume of storage and access flexibility to tackle data processing problems previously impossible or impractical with tape.

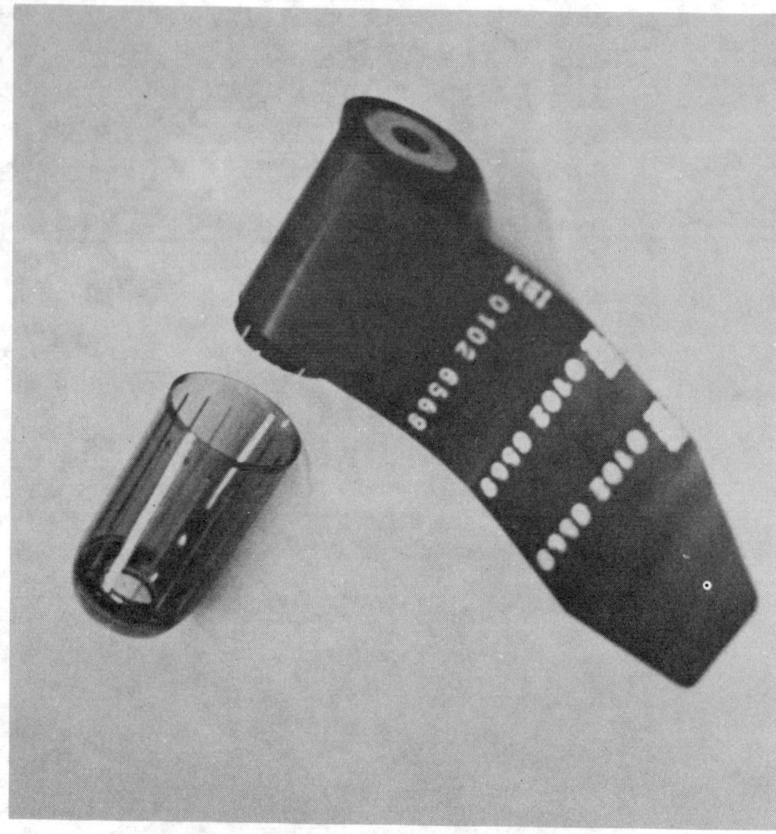

Diagram 13.3 Data cartridge

Diagram 13.4 The two data cartridges in this diagram may store the same amount of information as one disk pack.

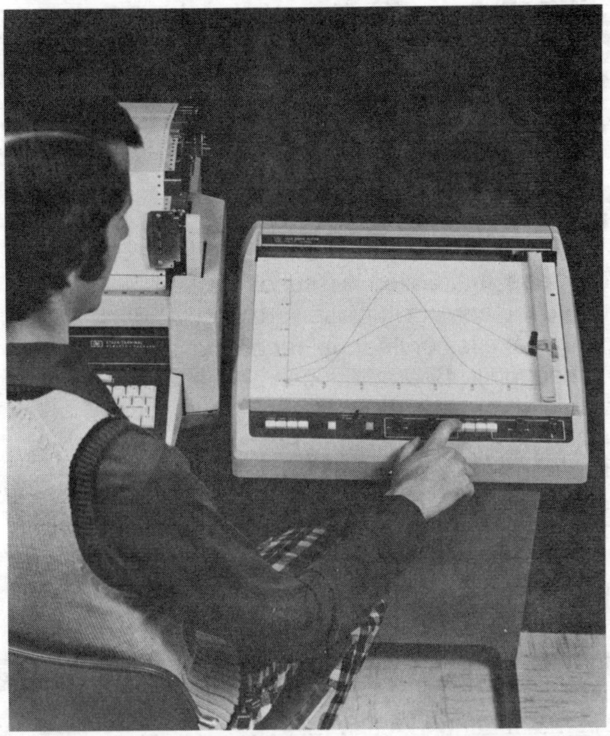

Diagram 13.5 Graphic plotter

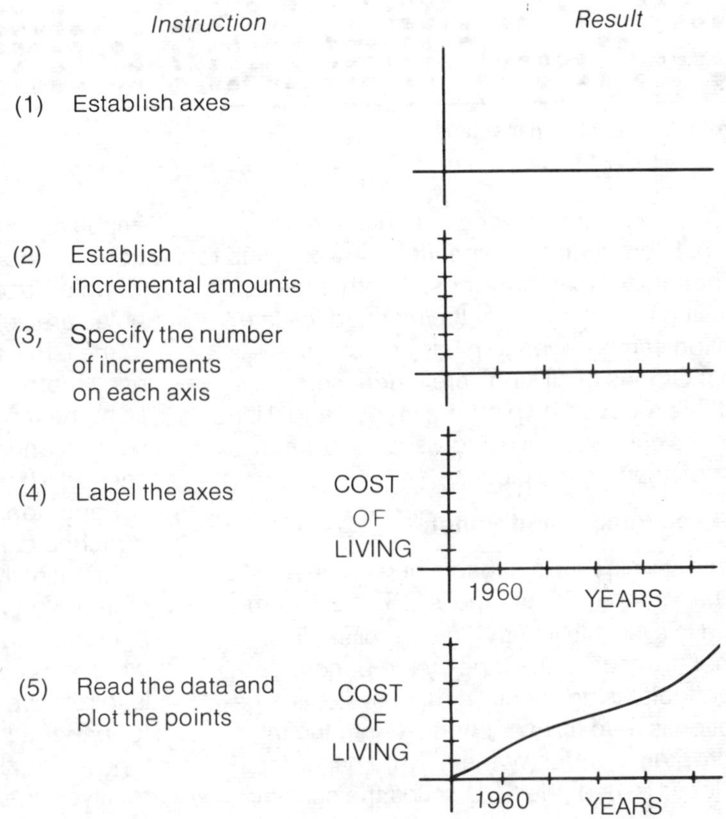

Diagram 13.6 Graphing the increase in cost of living.

Plotter

The plotter is an output unit only and is capable of producing bar charts, engineering drawings, graphs, and so on. A ballpoint pen is mounted on a horizontal bar, along which it can move in both directions. This carriage (pen and bar) is fixed above a moveable roll of paper. The paper can move vertically, that is, up and down, and the pen can be raised or lowered onto the paper. By the combined movement of the two moveable parts, the paper vertically and the pen horizontally, any type of curve, line or character can be drawn.

All instructions to the plotter are under program control and the programmer refers to the plotter in much the same way as he does to the printer. The pen can be instructed to be raised or lowered; that is, to be off or on the paper, and to move backwards and forwards across the paper, and the paper can be advanced or retracted. Plotter instructions are the same type of instruction as is required for drawing a graph or a scale drawing on a piece of graph paper. Suppose we wish to plot the rise in the cost of living over a period of years. Our program should include a series of instructions like those in diagram 13.6.

When you give instructions to the plotter it is important to remember the *raise pen* and *lower pen* instructions. The entire set of instructions given without the correct use of these could result in a hopeless mess. For example, were the pen not raised after one operation, as it moved to execute the next operation, it would draw a line getting there.

The plotter produces lines or curves by joining tiny lines that are a few millimetres long. These tiny lines can be in any one of four directions, giving an excellent approximation of a perfectly smooth curve. The paper in the plotter is either 30 cm or 79 cm wide, depending upon the model, and is a continuous roll. The pen can be changed easily to produce drawings of different colours.

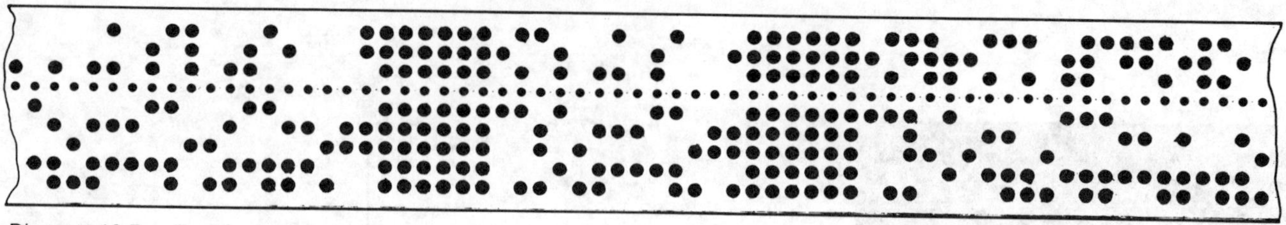

Diagram 13.7 Punched paper tape

The plotter is a useful piece of equipment to engineers in producing engineering drawings and to cartographers for map drawings. Weather maps are drawn using a plotter so that the most up-to-date information can be given to pilots and ships' captains. Graphs of all kinds are much more accurately produced by plotter than by hand. Hard copy of designs outlined using visual display units can be obtained on the plotter.

Paper Tape Reader and Punch

Equipment exists that is capable of reading and writing paper tape. Paper tape is l.27 to 2.54 cm wide and is available in varying size rolls. Small round holes, made in the tape by the punch, represent data using special coding systems. The information is read from or punched into the tape under program control. When a 'write paper tape' instruction is issued, the CPU sends the correct impulses to the paper tape punch and causes the correctly coded information to be punched. Similarly, when a 'read paper tape' instruction is issued, the holes are sensed and the correct impulses are sent to the CPU. Since the tape is continuous, records of any length can be kept on it. Characters can be read from the tape at rates of 150 to 1000 characters per second and punched at 15 to 150 characters per second, depending upon the equipment used.

Paper tape has many of the same uses as punched cards. Although it cannot be interpreted automatically, as punched cards can, it is easier to store than punched cards and is not prone to bending and warping. Paper tape is continuous and it is not as easy to remove or alter one part of it as it is to remove or alter a punched card. One of the uses for paper tape is in the printing industry for typesetting. Paper tape readers and punches provide relatively inexpensive input and output units.

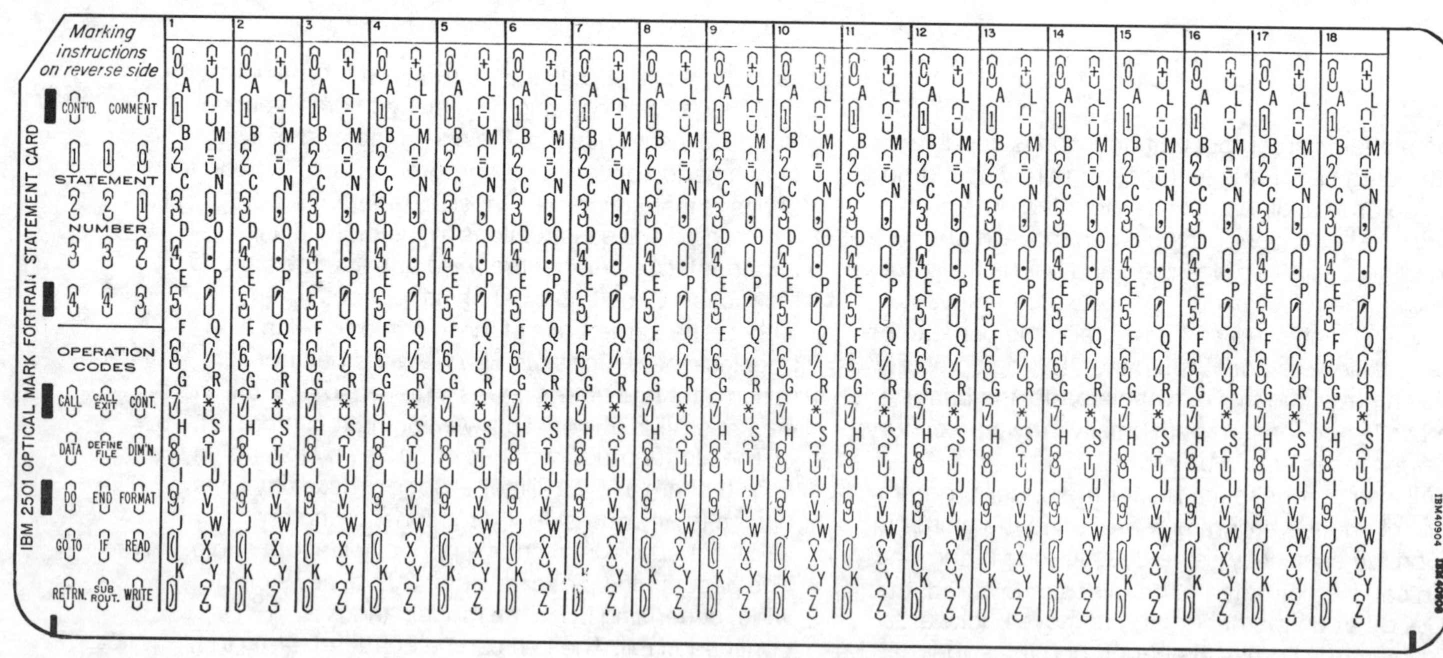

Diagram 13.8 Optical mark reader card

Character Recognition Input Units

Optical Readers

There are several units in existence capable of 'reading' marks on cards or documents. This means that one step in getting data into the computer, namely keypunching data from source documents to cards, is eliminated, and we can use the original document as input. There are several types of optical readers.

(1) *Optical Mark Card Reader*
An ordinary card reader can be changed to allow it to accept marks made with a lead pencil on a specially designed card. Instead of sensing holes, the reader senses pencil marks. Any mistakes in data or in a program can be altered by erasing the mark and recoding the same card. This unit has particular application in schools and colleges where the keypunching bottleneck is a real problem.

(2) *Optical Mark Page Reader*
This unit can read an entire page of pencil marks and transmit the information to the CPU. This type of equipment has application in many areas: test scoring, survey projects, sales reporting, water, gas and electric meter readings.

(3) *Optical Page Reader*
It is possible to have typewritten documents or handwritten characters 'read' by a special reader. The characters must be in predesignated areas and handwritten characters must be carefully formed (see diagram 13.9). The document is read by a small, precisely controlled light spot, which finds and scans each individual character. As the light spot passes over a character, reflected light is converted to a unique combination of electronic signals. When errors do occur the operator has the opportunity to make corrections. If the error is too extensive the document is rejected. Errors that can be corrected are displayed in a 127 mm display tube and corrections made via a keyboard. For example, in diagram 13.9.1 the 5 is composed of two separate lines, which is not allowed. In 13.9.2 the 4 and 5 are run together, which makes them unrecognizable. The equipment must not be set up to be too tolerant or incorrect information will be accepted by the CPU.

Diagram 13.9.1

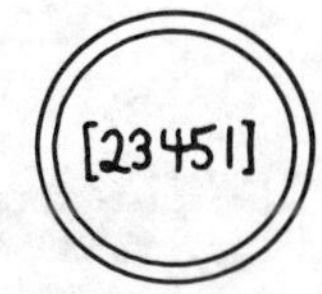

Diagram 13.9.2

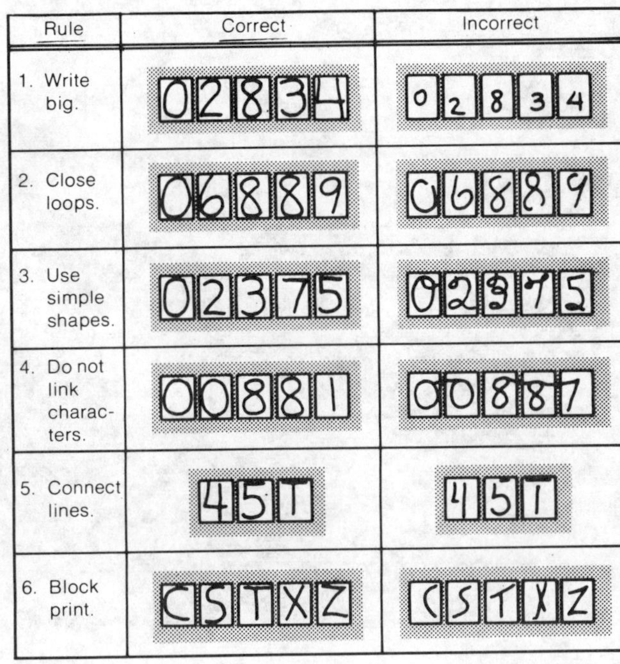

Diagram 13.9.3

The ability to enter our own characters allows a great deal of flexibility using a much smaller area. For example, to enter an age we write in any two numbers. To do this using a mark page reader we have to provide twenty positions for the possible answer, as shown below.

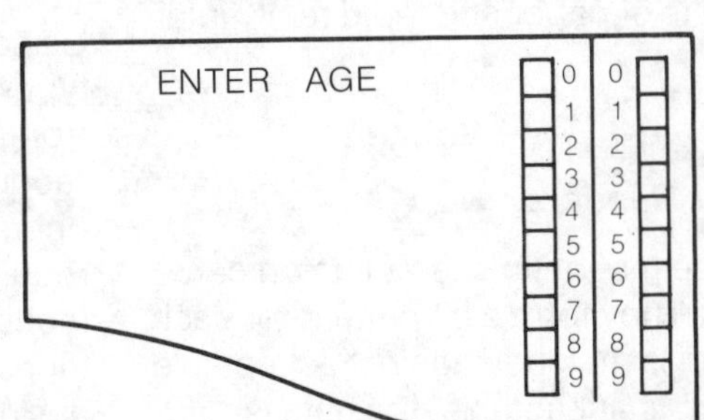

13.10 Sample document read by an optical mark page reader

Diagram 13.11 Optical page reader

The optical page reader also is capable of reading pages produced by a typewriter. Many industries employ the units for updating accounts, order entry, motor vehicle application, insurance policy changes, and so on. It is feasible that in the future programs will be typed on sheets of paper and fed directly into the computer.

Magnetic Character Readers

These units can sense magnetic characters on cards or paper documents. They form a bit pattern for each character, which then is matched against acceptable patterns. If the pattern is acceptable, the data is processed. If not, an error signal is given. These units are used particularly in banks for processing cheques. They have the added capability of being able to sort the cheques according to the magnetic characters on them.

Keytape Unit

Using a keyboard resembling a keypunch or typewriter keyboard, it is possible to type information from original documents and have it immediately recorded on magnetic tape. The unit allows the operator to verify the data and make corrections if required. It is feasible to have several of these units feeding information to the same reel of magnetic tape or in some cases to a magnetic disk. This idea is designed to improve the data entry situation and cut out the keypunch step in data-processing departments.

Diagram 13.12 Keytape unit

Specialized Terminals

Most of the input and output units so far mentioned are used for many applications. They could be classed as general purpose units. There are many input/output units which have been designed for specific industries. For example, there are special terminals for banks, supermarkets, off-track betting, security control and department store sales. There are special terminals for monitoring various production processes in, for example, the chemical, oil and nuclear power industries.

We will take a closer look at the supermarket scanning system, which consists of two terminals. You have probably noticed that most of the items you purchase in the supermarket now have a series of uneven width bars showing clearly on the outside of the package or can. This is called the **universal product code**, and can be read by a scanner which transmits the information contained in the code to a computer.

The scanner is a specialized terminal providing another means of data entry to a computer. The operator moves items across a window in the scanner with the code facing downwards onto the window. A beam of light crosses the code and light is reflected off it. Since spaces and bars reflect different amounts of light, the scanner can differentiate between them, and the bar code is transmitted as electronic impulses which can be translated to identify a unique item. The code can

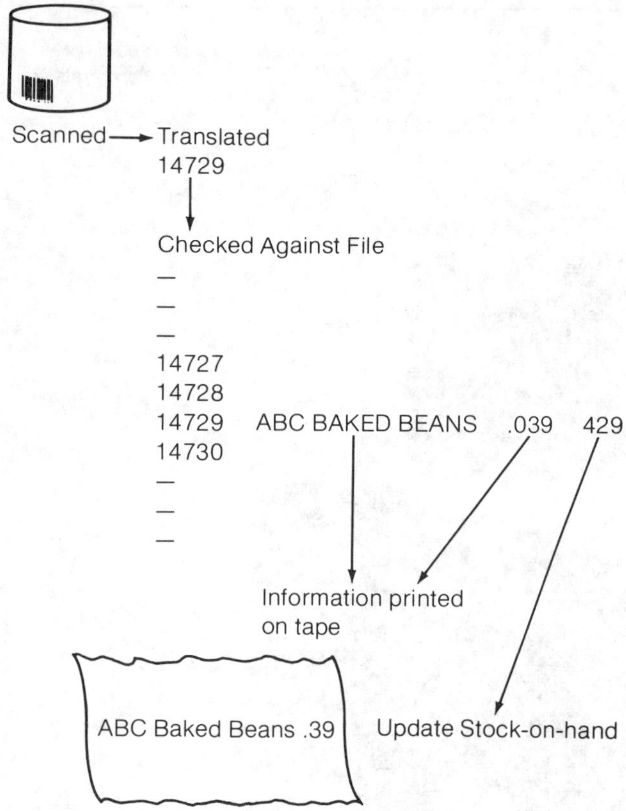

Diagram 13.13

Diagram 13.14 Universal product code

pass across the scanner at any angle, although there is a best scanning position which allows the operator to move items across the scanner at maximum speed.

Not all items in a supermarket will have a universal code on them. For example, a lettuce or a pot roast might be hand priced. There is another terminal provided as part of the system to enable the checkout person to enter information about such items. This terminal would replace the traditional cash register, allowing the operator to key in item numbers or prices. There is a printing unit incorporated into the terminal which prints out an itemized bill for the customer.

When a customer checks out at a supermarket equipped with the supermarket scanning system the cashier either passes the items over the scanner or enters the code or price via the keyboard. The central computer identifies the code and causes the name and price of the item to be printed on the customer receipt tape. Prices are supplied by the computer so there is never any chance of being wrongly charged by a tired or careless operator. The tax, where applicable, is automatically calculated by the computer and the bill is totalled ready for the customer. Meanwhile the computer updates the inventory for that store.

Not only can the checkout be speeded up with this system, but stores can be managed more efficiently. There should be no out-of-stock situations. The number of people stamping prices on items can be drastically reduced, since the majority of items will have the universal product code, and only the shelf need be labelled with the price. Any price changes can be entered into the central computer and the shelf relabelled.

One of the most recent controversies related to the acceptance of the computer has centred around the use of scanning equipment in supermarkets. The main complaint is that the price of the item is not stamped on the item. If a price change is made there is no stock sold off at the old price since the computer is given the new price immediately, which is stored with the item number. The shelf price is changed by altering one card. When the universal code is read by the scanner the updated price is accessed and charged to the customer. Also the lack of price on the item means the housewife cannot compare with last week's purchases. However, an itemized detailed bill is produced for the customer, giving description and price for each item. There is a mistrust by the public of the supermarket who, they feel, can change prices rapidly at will. The supermarkets on the other hand feel they can control inventory more efficiently, reduce out of stock conditions and speed up check out. Will the financial savings be passed on to the consumer? That is another controversial topic!

Buzz Words

Visual display units	Mass storage
Light pen	Magnetic character reader
Plotter	Keytape
Paper tape reader	Paper tape punch
Optical reader	Universal product code
Buffer	Cursor
Data cartridge	Graphic terminal

Projects

(1) Research information about the magnetic drum and the use to which it is put in industry.

(2) Research information about an application using either a plotter or a visual display unit.

(3) Design, flowchart and present a system to allow a company's manager to obtain immediate information about employees for purposes of promotion, review of progress, and so on. Anticipate questions such as

(i) How can the manager find information about a particular employee?
(ii) Where is the information stored?
(iii) How much data is available about the employee?
(iv) What security is there so that nobody else can access the information?

(4) Discuss how a visual display unit can cut down on 'paper pollution'.

(5) Design a card that could be marked by a meter reader and processed immediately by the computer. You are required to provide the meter reader with the following information (prepunched):

(i) meter number
(ii) account code
(iii) address (street and number)
(iv) name
(v) old reading

You must prepare a document to explain clearly to the meter reader how he is to

(a) code the new meter reading,
(b) show that he was unable to read the meter and did not leave the card,
(c) show that he was unable to read the meter and left the card,
(d) indicate the date of marking and his code number or letter.

(6) Research the following statistics to indicate how much space would be required on a data cartridge or data cartridges to keep the following files (record length as indicated):

(i) federal voting population in your province or state (record of 40 characters)
(ii) school student population for the province or state in which you live (record of 1000 characters)
(iii) telephone subscribers for the province or state in which you live and for the largest province or state in your country (record of 50 characters).
In each case comment as to whether you feel mass storage is necessary.

(7) Prepare the dialogue to be displayed on a visual display unit that is to be used to obtain information from students about their proposed careers. A light pen is not available but students can respond by typing single letters or yes/no answers to the questions.

(8) Prepare a 15 minute presentation

(a) protesting the use of scanning terminals and the universal product code in your local supermarket.
(b) defending the use of scanning terminals and the universal product code in your local supermarket.

14 More About Programming Languages

This chapter discusses two high level programming languages in sufficient detail to permit the writing of some simple programs.

FORTRAN

Although FORTRAN[1] was originally written to enable mathematicians and engineers to communicate easily with the computer, it is quite possible to use it for commercial programs.

To Read and Write Out One Card

How do we read and write the 80 columns of a card using FORTRAN? The flowchart indicates that four steps are involved.

(1) Set aside a storage area for the information on the incoming card. The programmer chooses a name for the area and specifies the number of storage positions needed, one for each character. No special characters can be included in the chosen name and it must begin with an alphabetic character. A DIMENSION statement performs this function. The complete statement could be

```
      DIMENSION CARD (80)
```

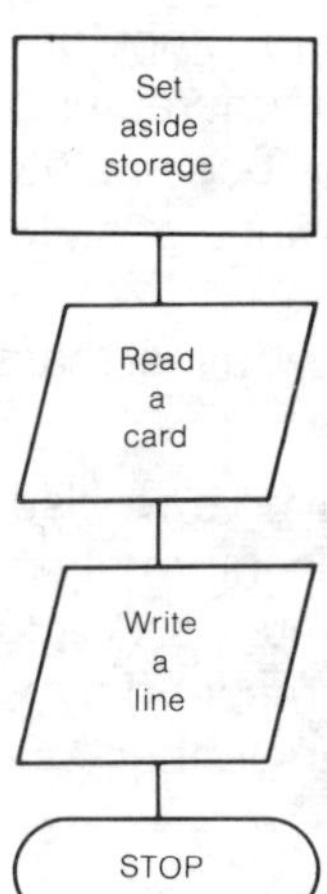

Diagram 14.1 **Flowchart: to read and write out one card**

[1] *The FORTRAN language features used in this chapter, with the exception of the use of quotes in a format statement, are implemented on most computers.*

Here the area is called CARD and 80 storage positions are to be set aside. We can call the area whatever we choose providing we do not use more than five letters or numbers (no special characters) and always start the name with a letter. The following examples are also valid:

```
      DIMENSION C1 (80)
      DIMENSION INFOR (80)
```

The translator takes care of the actual address of the area. We need refer to it only by name.

(2) Read the card from the card reader.

```
      READ (N, 10) CARD
10    FORMAT (80 A1)
```

N refers to the actual unit number of the input unit and depends upon the equipment to be used. For example, using an IBM 1130 computing system, N is replaced by 2 if the 1442 card reader is used or by 8 if the 2501 card reader is used. The statement then reads:

```
      READ (2, 10) CARD
      or
      READ (8, 10) CARD
```

10 refers to statement number 10, which follows; CARD references the area set aside for the information.

Statement 10 is called a FORMAT statement and describes the data using **A** for **A**lphabetic (or character), **I** for **I**nteger, or **F** for **F**ractions (or decimals). By describing our data as 80 A1 we are saying that there are 80 pieces of alphabetic information, each one character in length.

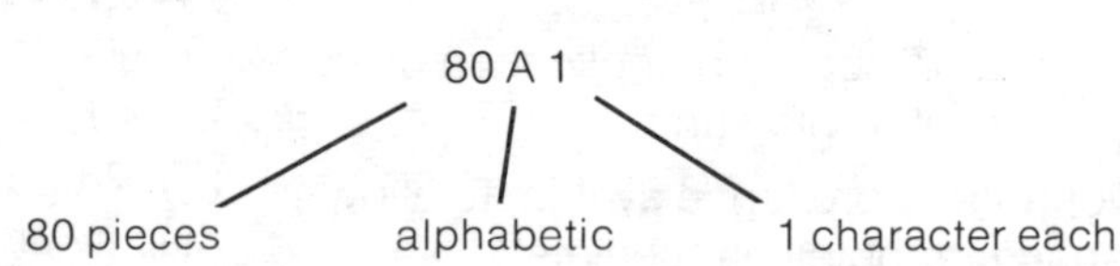

(3) Write the information on the printer.

```
      WRITE (M, 20) CARD
20    FORMAT ('1', 80A1)
```

These two statements are very similar to those for reading the card, M referring now to the output unit. Using the IBM 1130 as an example, 3 refers to the 1132 printer and 5 refers to the 1403 printer. The statement then reads:

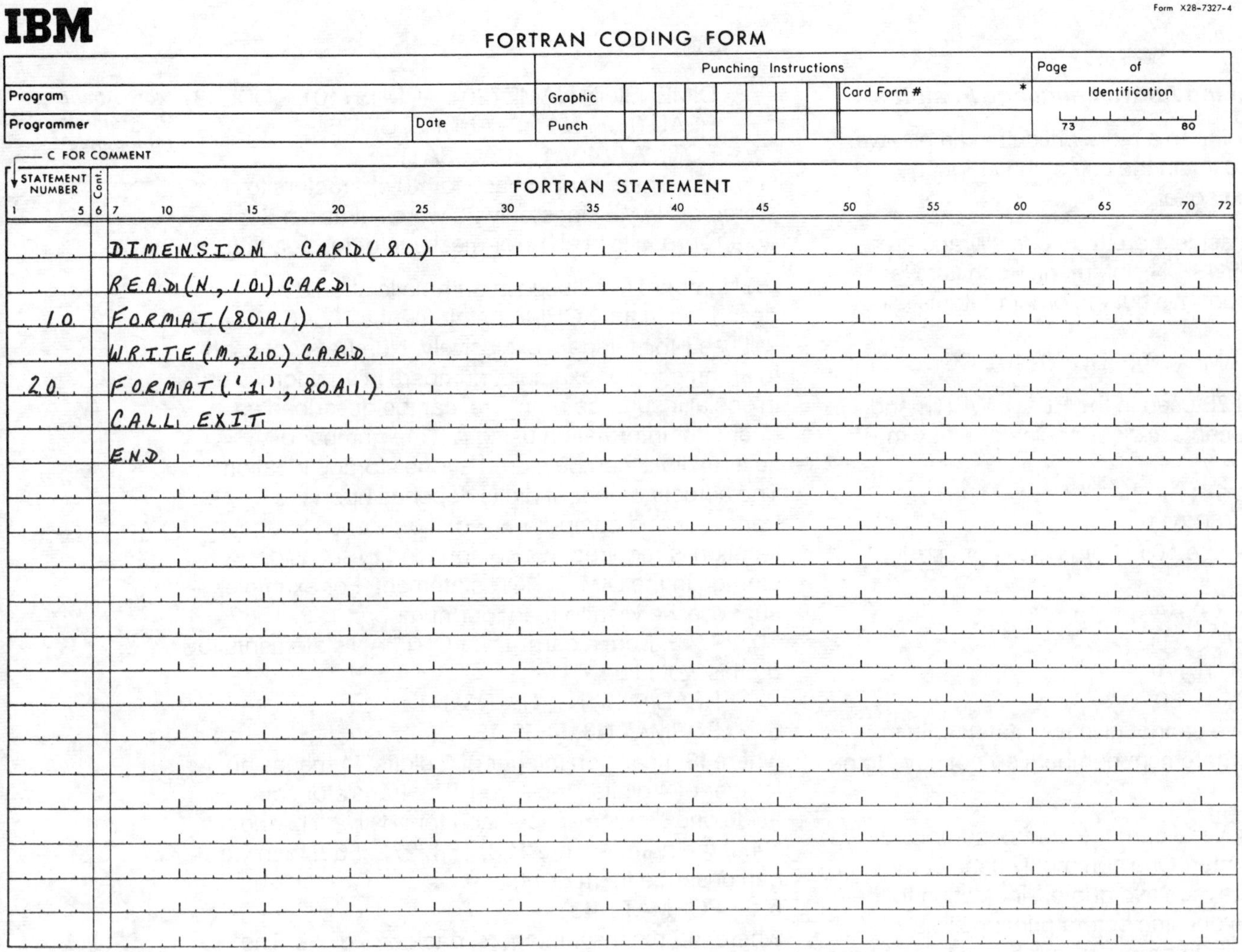
IBM FORTRAN CODING FORM Form X28-7327-4

Program | Programmer | Date | Punching Instructions: Graphic, Punch | Card Form # | Page of | Identification 73–80

C FOR COMMENT | STATEMENT NUMBER 1–5 | Cont. 6 | FORTRAN STATEMENT 7–72

```
      DIMENSION CARD(80)
      READ(N,10) CARD
   10 FORMAT(80A1)
      WRITE(M,20) CARD
   20 FORMAT('1',80A1)
      CALL EXIT
      END
```

Diagram 14.2 FORTRAN coding form

WRITE (3,20) CARD
or
WRITE (5,20) CARD

20 refers to the FORMAT statement describing the output. This time, however, we have preceded the description of data with an instruction telling the printer to skip to a new page before starting to print. The number one in quotes, the first item in the FORMAT statement, indicates this.

(4) To indicate the end of the program we use two statements. CALL EXIT allows control to return to the operating system when the job is completed. END indicates the end of the program. We use the word STOP on the flowchart to indicate we want the program to stop. This does not necessarily mean we wish the computer to stop.

Diagram 14.2 shows a FORTRAN coding sheet and indicates how the statements are to be punched onto cards, that is, where the translator expects to find the various parts. The statement number must be somewhere in columns 1 to 5. Column 6 is left blank. The remainder of the statement goes anywhere between columns 7 and 72. Brackets and commas are required where shown but spacing is not critical. Words cannot be split—a space, however small, indicates the end of a word to the translator. One statement is punched per card.

Further Use of the Above Language Features

Before proceeding to a more difficult example, we should further explain the use of the language features studied so far.

(1) We can set aside more than one storage area using one DIMENSION statement. Each item is separated by commas but the order of items is not important.

```
      DIMENSION NAME (20), ADDRS (40), CODE (3)
```

(2) The 10 and 20 used in the READ, WRITE and FORMAT statements are our choice but they must match.

```
      READ (N, 10) AA
15    FORMAT (80 A1)
```

is wrong: either use 10 in both places or use 15 in both places.

```
      READ (N, 10) AA
10    FORMAT (80 A1)
      WRITE (M, 10) AA
10    FORMAT ('1', 80 A1)
```

is also wrong: we cannot give two statements the same number. Statement numbers do not have to be sequential.

(3) There are several carriage control commands we can give the printer. One commonly used command is ' ', a blank between two quotes, indicating to the printer to space one line before printing. This instruction results in normal printing—one line under another.

(4) One statement can read in more than one piece of information.

```
      READ (N,7) NAME, ADDRS, CODE
```

Each item must be separated by a comma and must be described correctly in the FORMAT statement in agreement with the field sizes on the card and in the same order as the card fields.

```
      DIMENSION NAME (20), ADDRS (40), CODE (3)
      READ (N,7) NAME,ADDRS,CODE
7     FORMAT (20A1, 40A1, 3A1)
```

The order of the format items must agree with the order of the chosen names in the READ statement and the order of information in the READ statement must be the same as on the card.

```
      DIMENSION NAME (20), ADDRS (40), CODE (3)
      READ (N,7) NAME, ADDRS, CODE
7     FORMAT (40A1, 20A1, 3A1)
```

is wrong. There is not space for 40 characters to be stored at NAME since only 20 were set aside. Such an error results in an error message or loss of data.

(5) Numbers to be used in arithmetic should be described in the FORMAT statement as **I** or **F**. We will use **I** for integers exclusively. Numbers not used in arithmetic, for example, numbers in an address or in social insurance numbers, can be described as character information using **A**. One number of several digits can be stored at one storage location. The actual number of digits depends upon the translator and computer used. If only one storage location is required, we do not need to set aside storage in the DIMENSION statement. For example, suppose we wish to read four numbers, 123, 1562, 10, 29743, from a card. The FORTRAN statements to do this would be

```
      READ (N,5) N1, N2, N3, N4
5     FORMAT (I3, I4, I2, I5)
```

where **I**3 means an integer of 3 digits, **I**4 means an integer of 4 digits, and so on. The translator sets aside one storage space each for N1, N2, N3 and N4. If the numbers are 123, 164, 272, 569, then we can describe them using

```
5     FORMAT (4I3)
```

where 4**I**3 means 4 integers, each of 3 digits. The names we assign to integer numbers must begin with the letters **I** through **N**. Since **I** and **N** are the first two letters of the word **IN**teger, this rule is not too difficult to remember.

Correct	*Incorrect*
IA	CODE
JX2	X
KAGE	AGE

When describing integers in the FORMAT statement associated with the WRITE statement, we may need more space allocated on the printer than the number occupied on the card. When the number is printed it may have a sign attached to it, particularly if it is the result of some calculation. Also, if we are dealing with decimals there is a decimal point and possibly a leading zero. A good rule to follow for the format of

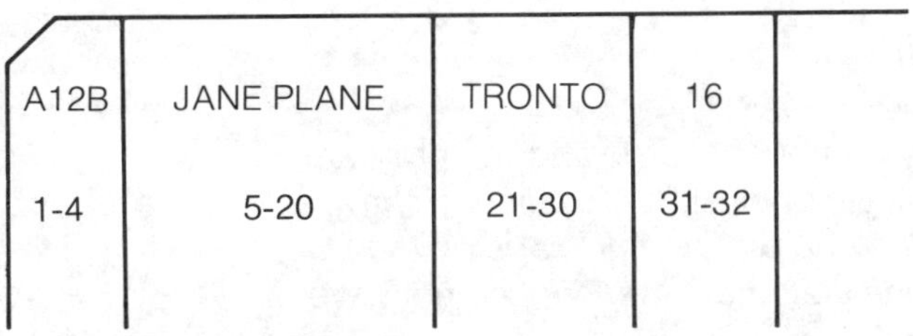

Diagram 14.3 Format of cards to be read and written out

all output numbers, whether integer or decimal, is to add 3 to the number of input digits to allow for any or all of these possibilities.

```
      READ (N, 10) I,J,K,L
10    FORMAT (I3, I4, I5, I2)
      WRITE (M,20) I,J,K,L
20    FORMAT (I6, I7, I8, I5)
```

Suppose we read four fields from the card shown in diagram 14.3 and write out the information on the printer, spacing it suitably to be more readable.

```
      DIMENSION CODE (4), NAME (16), CITY (10)
      READ (N,1) CODE, NAME, CITY, IAGE
1     FORMAT (4A1, 16A1, 10A1, I2)
      WRITE (M,2) CODE, NAME, CITY, IAGE
2     FORMAT (' ', 5X, 4A1, 5X, 16A1, 10X, 10A1,
            4X, I5)
```

Some X's have been added between the output format items. 5X causes 5 spaces between the printed items on the horizontal line, 10X causes ten spaces, and so on. The printed line looks like the following:

```
___A12B ___JANE PLANE_____TRONTO ___16
5        5                10          4
spaces   spaces           spaces      spaces
```

Our program would run successfully on a computer, with the correct control cards, providing we add CALL EXIT and END **statements**.

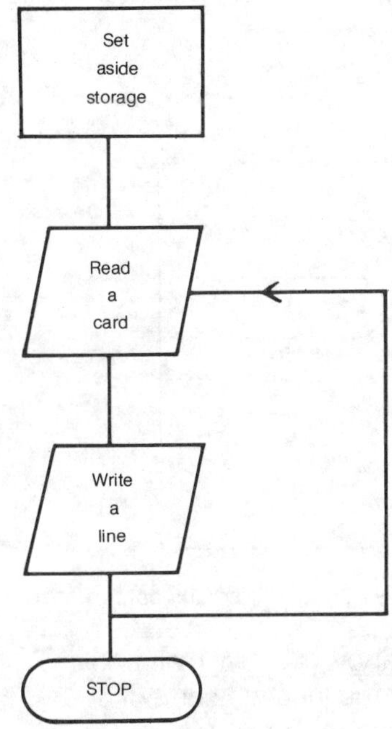

Diagram 14.4 Flowchart: an endless loop

To Read and Write Out Many Cards

Reading and writing one card is a bit of a waste of time. We can add a statement to make the program read and write many cards with the same field lengths and type of information. Each card has a 4-character code, a 16-character name, a 10-character city and a 2-digit age.

```
      DIMENSION CODE (4), NAME (16), CITY (10)
3     READ (N,1) CODE, NAME, CITY, IAGE
1     FORMAT (4A1, 16A1, 10A1, I2)
      WRITE (M,2) CODE, NAME, CITY, IAGE
2     FORMAT (' ', 5X, 4A1, 5X, 16A1, 10X,
            10A1, 4X, I5)
      GO TO 3
      CALL EXIT
      END
```

As the flowchart indicates, the sequence of reading and writing instructions is to be repeated. The statement to which we want to return must have the same statement number as is given in the GO TO statement. Each time the statements are repeated, another card is read and another line is written.

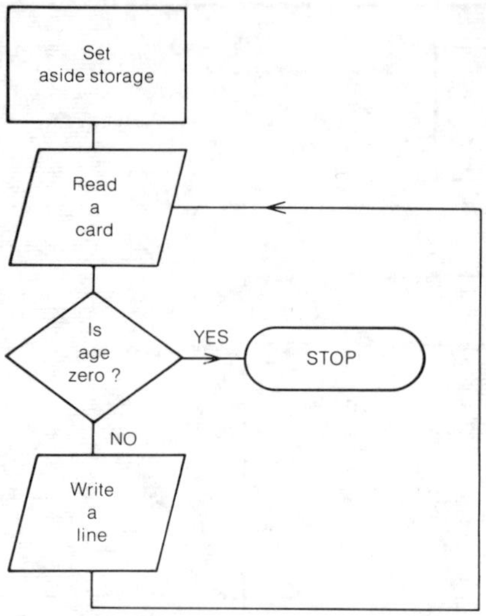

Diagram 14.5 **Flowchart: to read and write many cards**

However, in the program above we are in an endless loop. In order to get out of the loop we can put a blank card at the end of the data and a test in our program to see if the age is zero, as in diagram 14.5. (Blank is usually treated as a zero integer in FORTRAN. If A format is used then they are different.)

The testing statement is an IF statement and looks like this:

```
      IF (IAGE) 5, 5, 4
```

Here, IAGE is tested to see if it is negative, zero or positive. 5, 5 and 4 are the numbers of the statements to be executed next in each case.

```
         5,           5,          4
          \           |          /
        negative     zero     positive
```

If we are interested only in picking out the zero value of IAGE,

```
      IF (IAGE) 4, 5, 4
```

does equally well. Using 5, 5, 4 we also exit from the loop if IAGE is negative. All three numbers must be present in the IF statement. Under some circumstances, they could all be different. Our program now reads:

```
      DIMENSION CODE (4), NAME (16), CITY (10)
3     READ (N,1) CODE, NAME, CITY, IAGE
1     FORMAT (4A1, 16A1, 10A1, I2)
      IF (IAGE) 5, 5, 4
4     WRITE (M,2) CODE, NAME, CITY, IAGE
2     FORMAT (' ', 5X, 4A1, 5X, 16A1, 10X,
              10A1, 4X, I5)
      GO TO 3
5     CALL EXIT
      END
```

We can list any number of cards and our program comes to a logical conclusion *providing we have a blank card at the end or a negative age on the last data card.* Notice statement numbers do not have to be in sequence.

To run the program on the computer it is necessary

(1) to make sure there is a FORTRAN compiler for that computing system,
(2) to use the correct control cards for the computing system,
(3) to code and keypunch the program,
(4) to keypunch the data.

Headings

A well-organized report requires a title or headings on the report or listings. To print headings requires a WRITE statement to be executed once only, before any cards are read. (See diagram 14.6.)

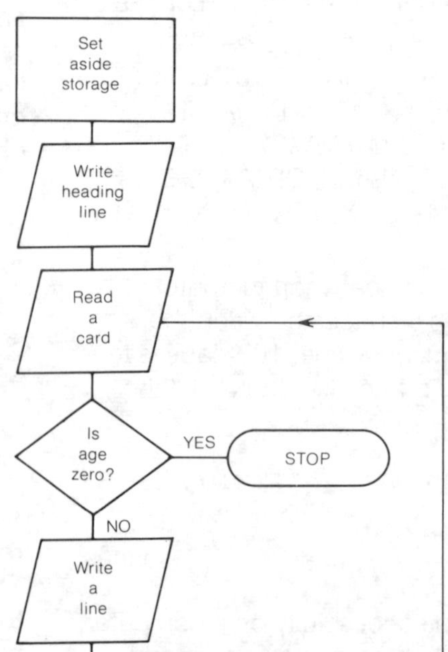

Diagram 14.6

```
     WRITE (M,9)
9    FORMAT ('1', 20X, 'GRADE 11 STUDENT LIST')
```

Since the translator is not looking for information stored under a chosen name in storage, the WRITE statement does not need a list of items. What is to be printed is included in quotes as part of the FORMAT statement. The 20X provides spacing at the beginning of the line and the quotes do not print. Some variations that can be used are:

```
(1) 9  FORMAT ('1', 40X, 'GRADE 11', 20X,
                'APRIL 1977')
```

After skipping to a new page a line is printed as follows:

```
                      GRADE 11          APRIL 1977
______________________        __________
     40 spaces                 20 spaces
```

```
(2) 9  FORMAT ('1', 20X, 'GRADE 11', 10X,
                'STUDENT LIST'//)
```

The two slashes (//) at the end of the line cause the printer to space two lines. (One slash spaces one line, three slashes space three lines, and so on.)

We now have the facility for horizontal and vertical spacing as well as the ability to skip to a new page. Using more than one WRITE statement we can print as many suitably spaced headings as required on our report.

PL/1

A program written in PL/1[1] can be segmented very easily into 'paragraphs' or procedures for such routines as gathering statistics, updating a file record, and so on. There must be at least one procedure in each program. Since we are concerned with writing simple programs, we shall use just one procedure in each program.

The first statement of any PL/1 program is a PROCEDURE statement.

CLIST .. PROCEDURE OPTIONS (MAIN),.[2]

CLIST is the name we have chosen for this particular procedure. The length of the name for a procedure is restricted to a maximum of six characters. All chosen names in PL/1 must begin with a letter and no special characters (*, %, etc.) are allowed. The name is separated from the rest of the statement by a colon : or .., the version used in a particular program depending upon the compiler present to do the translation. The words PROCEDURE OPTIONS (MAIN) complete the statement. Every statement in PL/1 ends with a semi-colon ; or ,..[3] There are few restrictions as to where the statements are punched on cards. Statements may be punched anywhere on the card between columns 2 and 72 inclusive. Punching more than one statement to a card is permissible but not advisable since it can be a problem when debugging.

To Read and Write Out One Card

Suppose we read and write the 80 columns of a card. The flowchart indicates that four steps are involved. The PROCEDURE statement is not indicated in the flowchart.

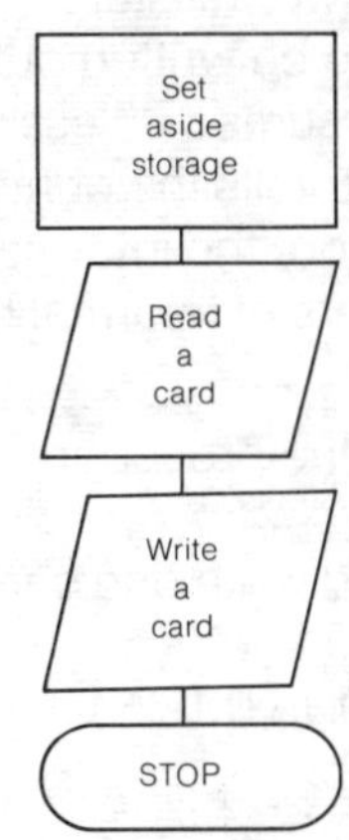

Diagram 14.7 Flowchart: to read and write out one card

(1) Set aside a storage area for the information on the incoming card. The programmer chooses a name for this area and specifies how much storage is needed, one storage position for each character. The name chosen can be any number of characters. A DECLARE statement indicates this step in the program. The complete statement could be

```
        DECLARE CARD CHARACTER (80),.
```

[1]The PL/1 language features used in this chapter are implemented in OS and DOS versions of PL/1 using a 48 character set.

[2]For the Student Language subset of PL/1, use CLIST..PROCEDURE,.

[3]Student Language will accept,.or.,not; and..not:

We have called the area CARD and asked for 80 storage positions to be set aside for character information. The following examples are also valid.

```
DECLARE INFORMATION CHARACTER (80),.
        DECLARE C1 CHAR (80),.
```

The translator takes care of the actual address of the area and we need refer to it only by name. CHAR can be used as an abbreviation of CHARACTER.

(2) Read the card from the card reader.

```
        GET EDIT (CARD) (A(80)),.
```

GET EDIT is the read instruction. GET implies "Obtain from the card reader"; EDIT signifies we are interested in exact details of the information. The card reader is always assumed to be the input unless we specify otherwise. CARD is the area we have set aside for the information. A(80) tells the translator to expect 80 columns of **A**lphabetic (or character) information.

(3) Write the information on the printer.

```
        PUT EDIT (CARD) (PAGE, A(80)),.
```

PUT EDIT is the write instruction. PUT implies "Put out on the printer"; EDIT signifies we will state specifically what the information to be written out looks like. The printer is always assumed unless we specify otherwise. The word PAGE tells the printer to skip to a new page before writing out the information, which is described as 80 characters of information.

(4) Stop.

END CLIST,. indicates the end of the procedure CLIST.

The complete program to read and write one card would be

```
        CLIST..PROCEDURE OPTIONS (MAIN),.
        DECLARE CARD CHAR (80),.
           GET EDIT (CARD) (A(80)),.
           PUT EDIT (CARD) (PAGE, A(80)),.
        END CLIST,.
```

Brackets and commas are required as shown. Spacing is not critical but words cannot be split as a space indicates the end of a word to the translator. Care must be taken to spell the procedure name exactly the same in both places; otherwise, the translator cannot match them. Our program will run on a computer if we have the translator present and if we supply the correct control cards for that computing system.

Further Uses of the Above Language Features

Before proceeding to a more difficult example, we should further explain the use of the language features studied so far.

(1) We can set aside many storage areas using one DECLARE statement and separating the items by commas.

```
DECLARE NAME CHAR (15), ADDRS CHAR (20),
          CODE CHAR (3),.
```

(2) One GET EDIT statement can be used to read in several fields of information rather than one whole card.

```
GET EDIT (NAME, ADDRS, CODE) (A(15), A(20), A(3)),.
```

Each item name in the data list is separated by a comma and must be matched in the item list by the correct description (called format). The two lists must be in corresponding order.

```
                Data List                   Format List
GET EDIT (NAME, ADDRS, CODE)    (A(15), A(20), A(3)),.
             1       2      3        1      2      3
```

is correct.

```
GET EDIT (NAME, ADDRS, CODE)    (A(15), A(3), A(20)),.
             1       2      3        1      2      3
```

is incorrect. In this example the translator is asked to read 3 characters of information and store them at ADDRS, and then read 20 characters and store them at CODE. The instruction causes insufficient data to be stored at ADDRS and tries to store 20 columns of incorrect information at CODE, which is set up to take only 3.

(3) There are other instructions we can give the printer.

```
      PUT EDIT (INFO) (SKIP (2), A(80)),.
```

SKIP (2) tells the printer to move to the next line and then skip 1 more before printing INFO; SKIP (4) would tell the printer to move to the next line and then skip 3 more before printing; SKIP (5), move, then skip 4 lines, and so on.

(4) Numbers not used in arithmetic can be described as character information. Numbers to be used in arithmetic should be declared as FIXED DECIMAL and described using F in the format list of GET and PUT EDIT.

```
    DECLARE NUMB DECIMAL FIXED (4),.
    GET EDIT NUMB (F(4)),.
```

We are using only integers, which are thought of as decimals with no decimal places. For the print out, increase the number in the format description by 3. This allows for the possibility of printing a sign, a decimal point and a leading zero with a decimal number less than one.

```
    PUT EDIT (NUMB) F(7)),.
```

An increase of three is not always required but it is a good rule to follow since it is *always* sufficient.

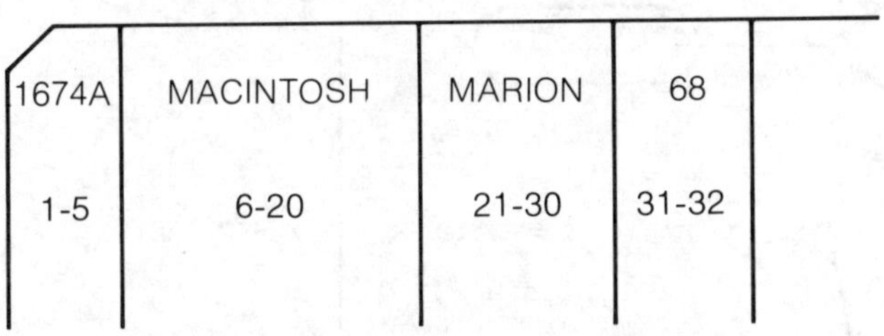

Diagram 14.8

Suppose we read four fields of information from a card (see diagram 14.8) and space it suitably on the printer to make it more readable.

```
CLASS..PROCEDURE OPTIONS (MAIN),.
    DECLARE STUDNO CHAR (5),
            NAME CHAR(15),
            CHRNM CHAR (10),
            AVER DECIMAL FIXED (2),.
GET EDIT (STUDNO, NAME, CHRNM, AVER)
         (A(5), A(15), A(10), F(2)),.
PUT EDIT (STUDNO, NAME, CHRNM, AVER)
(PAGE, X(5), A(5), X(10), A(15), X(2), A(10),
         X(10), F(5)),.
    END CLASS,.
```

We have spread out the program, taking separate lines for each declared item and for the format lists. Each line is punched into a separate card, making the program easy to debug and more readable. We have added a number of X's in the PUT EDIT format list, thus allowing for horizontal spacing. The printed line looks like

```
___1674A_____MACINTOSH _MARION____68
5       10                2        10
spaces  spaces            spaces   spaces
```

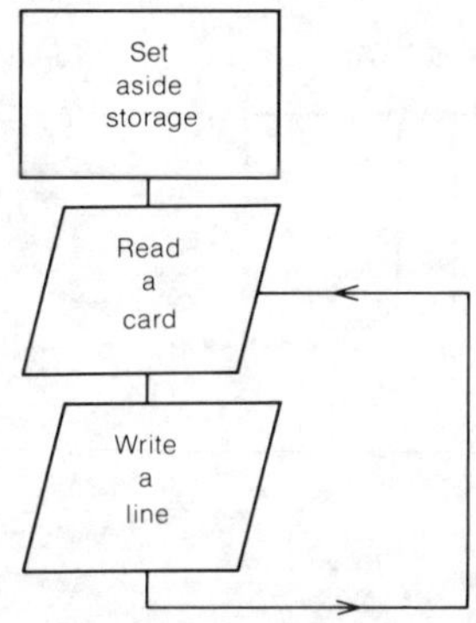

Diagram 14.9 Flowchart: an endless loop

To Read and Write Out More Than One Card

We can add instructions to our program to read and write many cards with the same field lengths and type of information. Each card has a 4-character code, a 16-character name, a 10-character city and a 2-digit age.

```
CLIST..PROCEDURE OPTIONS (MAIN),.
    DECLARE CODE CHARACTER (4),
            NAME CHARACTER (16),
            CITY CHARACTER (10),
            AGE DECIMAL FIXED (2),.
START..GET EDIT (CODE, NAME, CITY, AGE, DUMMY)
    (A(4), A(16), A(10), F(2), A(48)),.
    PUT EDIT (CODE, NAME, CITY, AGE) (SKIP (2),
    X(10), A(4), X(5), A (16), X(3), A(10), X(4), F(4)),.
    GO TO START,.
    END CLIST,.
```

We have labelled the GET EDIT statement START and have given an instruction, GO TO START,., which causes several instructions to be repeated. The label must be spelled the same as the reference to it in the GO TO statement. Since we are now reading more than one card, we must make sure the first card has been completely used up. PL/1 reads data as though it were a continuous stream. The rest of the card has been called DUMMY. We do not have to set aside storage for it; the computer will assign some. It is merely a means of making sure all 80 columns of the card are read with one read statement. However, now we are in an endless loop. (See diagram 14.9).

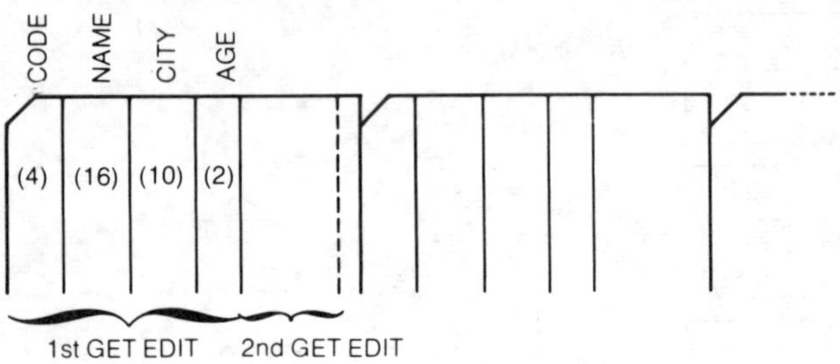

Diagram 14.10

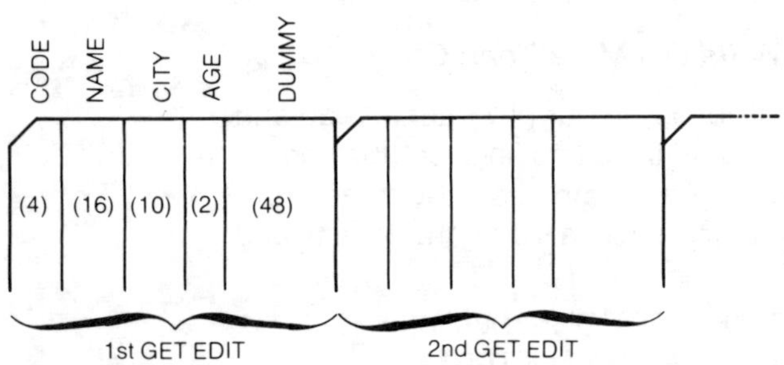

Diagram 14.11

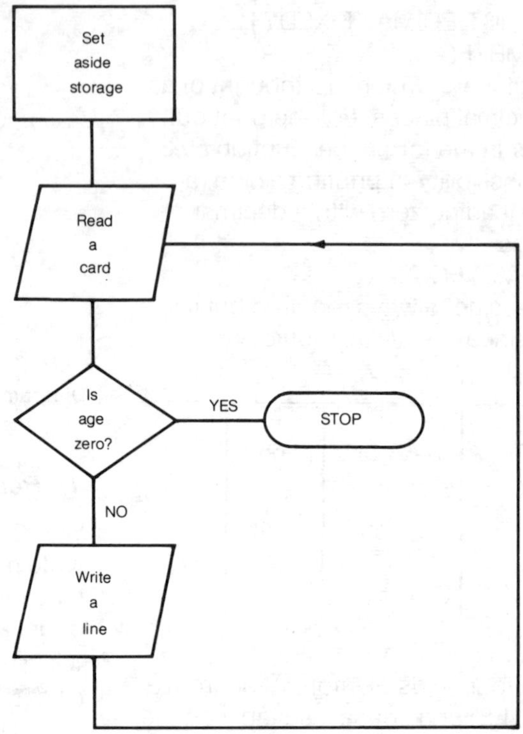

Diagram 14.12 Flowchart: to read and write many cards

To get out of the loop we can put a blank card at the end of the data and a test in our program to see if the age is zero. (Blank is treated as a zero fixed decimal in PL/1. If read as characters, blank and zero are not the same.)

The statement to test the age is

```
IF AGE EQ 0 THEN STOP,.
```

This statement is executed only if the age is zero. It causes the program to stop, not the computer. In other words the operating system will take over. Otherwise the next sequential instruction is executed. Without DUMMY the program would read only one card (see diagram 14.10). The second time the GET EDIT instruction is executed, information is read from the next 32 columns, which are blank. Thus AGE will be zero and the statement

```
IF AGE EQ 0 THEN STOP,.
```

is true. With DUMMY included, the second time the GET EDIT instruction is executed, the information is read from the second card (diagram 14.11).[1] It is also possible to test other relationships using GT (greater than) and LT (less than). There are three others that we will not discuss now.

Our program now reads:

```
CLIST..PROCEDURE OPTIONS (MAIN),.
DECLARE CODE CHAR (4),
        NAME CHAR (16),
        CITY CHAR (10),
        AGE DECIMAL FIXED (2),.
START..GET EDIT (CODE, NAME, CITY, AGE, DUMMY)
        (A(4), A(16), A(10), F(2), A(48)),.
     IF AGE EQ 0 THEN STOP,.
     PUT EDIT (CODE, NAME, CITY, AGE)
(SKIP (2), X(10), A(4), X(5), A(16), X(3),
        A(10), X(4), F(5)),.
        GO TO START,.
        END CLIST,.
```

We can list any number of cards (see diagram 14.12) and our program comes to a logical conclusion providing we have a blank card as the last data card.

[1] *Student language will go to the next card when the GET EDIT is executed again. Thus DUMMY is not required.*

Headings

A well-organized report requires a title or headings on the report or listing. To print headings requires a PUT EDIT statement to be executed once only, before any cards are read. (See diagram 14.13.)

```
PUT EDIT ('STUDENT LIST—GRADE 12')
        (PAGE, X(20), A(23)),.
```

We do not need a list of data items to be located in storage. The information included in quotes, but not the quotes, is printed. There are 23 characters altogether including blanks and the correct number must be shown in the format list. After skipping to a new page the following line is printed.

____________STUDENT LIST — GRADE 12

20 spaces

We can use as many headings as required on our report but they must not appear within the repeating set of instructions. The PROCEDURE and DECLARE statements are always the first two statements of a PL/1 program.

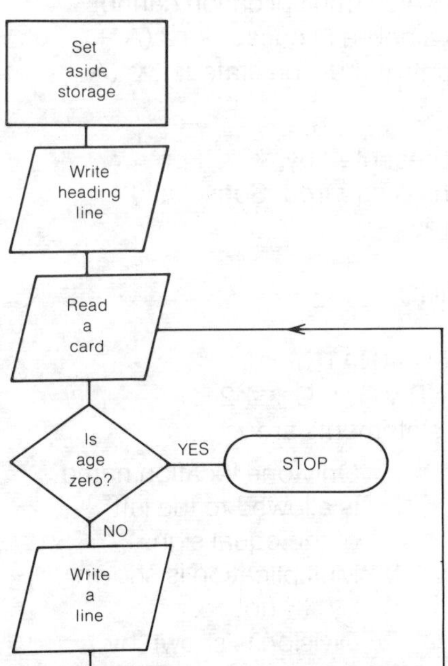

Diagram 14.13 Flowchart: to show where report headings would fit

Use of GET and PUT LIST in PL/1

Use of GET and PUT LIST

To Read and Write Out One Card

It is possible, in PL/1, to use very simple input and output statements that require no precise data descriptions. It is sometimes possible to use this method for input and output in FORTRAN, but it is not always implemented, so we will not discuss it here.

First a storage area is set aside for the data as before.

```
DECLARE CARD CHARACTER (70),.
```

To read the information from the card reader we use

```
GET LIST (CARD),.
```

The first chunk of data on the card is read and stored at CARD. Data is separated into chunks by one or more blanks (see below).

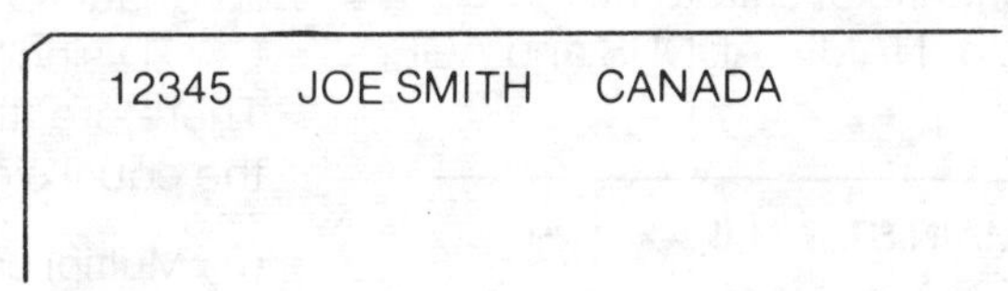

This card contains four chunks of data. All eighty columns of a card cannot be read since the first column at least must be blank.

Referring to the above diagram, suppose we want *Joe Smith* to be one chunk of data. Then it would have to be enclosed in quotes:

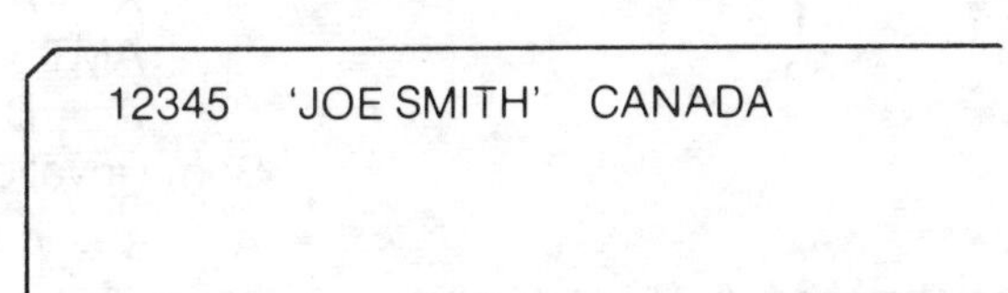

Data is considered to be a continuous stream

In order to write out the data stored at CARD, we use

PUT LIST (CARD) PAGE,.

The information is printed on the printer on the left of the paper, at the top of a new page.

Since we are not using EDIT we have no control over exactly which card columns are read in or where on the page the information is printed. In many instances this is not important. In mathematical calculations, for example, it is not important that the answers appear with precisely ten spaces between them. In programs dealing with commercial data processing however, it is often very important. For example, pre-printed forms may be used and the data must be positioned exactly on the printout.

Further Use of GET and PUT LIST

GET LIST (NAME, ADDRS, AGE),.

causes the first three chunks of data to be stored at the locations set aside for NAME, ADDRS and AGE.

```
'JANE PLANE'   '330 MAIN ST, HALIFAX'   29
```

The order is important since the translator stores the information from the card in the same sequence as specified in the GET LIST statement.

```
123    456    789    102
 ↑      ↑      ↑      ↑
 A      B      C      D
```

Thus in order that D may be read, A, B and C must first be read, even if they are not required in this particular program. The sequence for output must agree with what is required on the printout. For example,

PUT LIST (A,C,D,B),.

would cause 123 789 102 456 to be printed. Vertical spacing can be achieved using SKIP as in the PUT EDIT statement.

Arithmetic

Arithmetic statements in FORTRAN and PL/1 are essentially the same, the main difference being that each PL/1 statement has ; or ,. to indicate the end of the statement. Arithmetic statements in these languages closely resemble algebraic statements. There are, however, some important differences.

(1) Consider the computer language statement

A = B + 4

The symbol = does not always have the algebraic meaning. In computer language, A = B + 4 means *Add 4 to the number stored at B and store the result at A or Replace A by the answer to B + 4.* Thus A = A + 1 is valid in computer language, though it is not valid in algebra.

(2) As a result of this definition of =, statements such as A + B = C + D are not valid in computer languages. The translator cannot interpret A + B = C + D since there is no single location A + B. Therefore, there can be only one name to the left of the equal sign in a computer statement.

(3) Multiplication and division are represented by * and / , *not* by × and ÷. Also, multiplication cannot be assumed as it can in algebra in cases like 2 (A + B). In computer statements it must be stated: 2 * (A + B).

(4) Exponentiation is represented by * *. For example, A * * 2 means A squared. Some valid arithmetic statements are:

```
A = A−1
INT = RATE*PRINC
X = A*2 + B/3
AMT = PRINC* (1 + RATE)
A = B* *2 + 2*B*C + C* *2
```

Some invalid arithmetic statements are:

A + B = A−1	Only one location name is allowed to the left of the equal sign.
INT = RATE × PRINC	Multiplication is shown by *, not ×.
X = A*2 + B ÷ 3	Division is shown by / not ÷.
AMT = PRINC (1 + RATE)	Multiplication cannot be assumed; * must be shown.

Points to Review

The two solutions to the following problem incorporate the language features studied in FORTRAN and PL/1.

Problem: Produce the report as shown given the following input data card layout.

Data Card

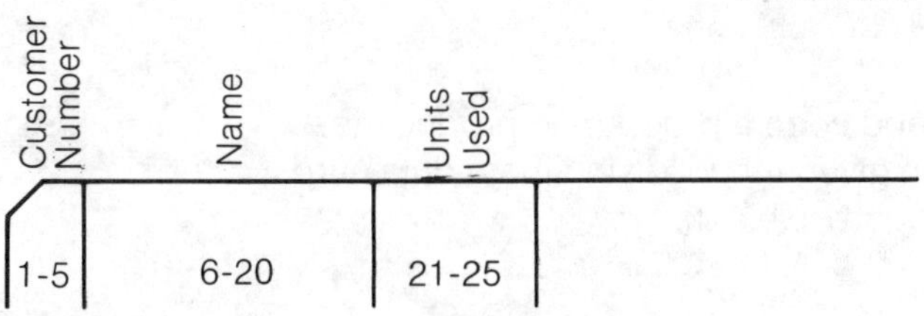

NOTE: Last data card is blank.

Report

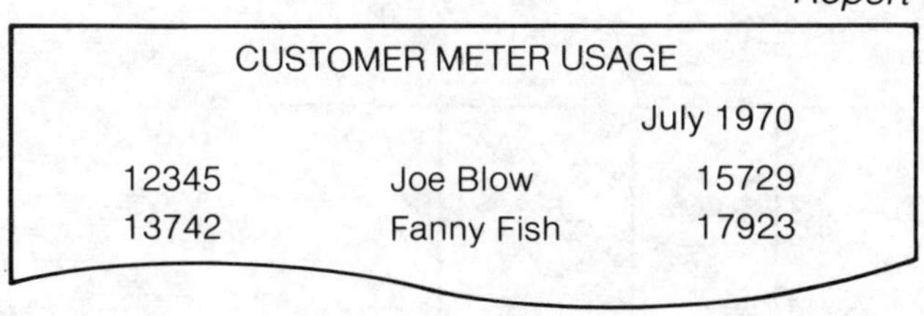

Flowchart

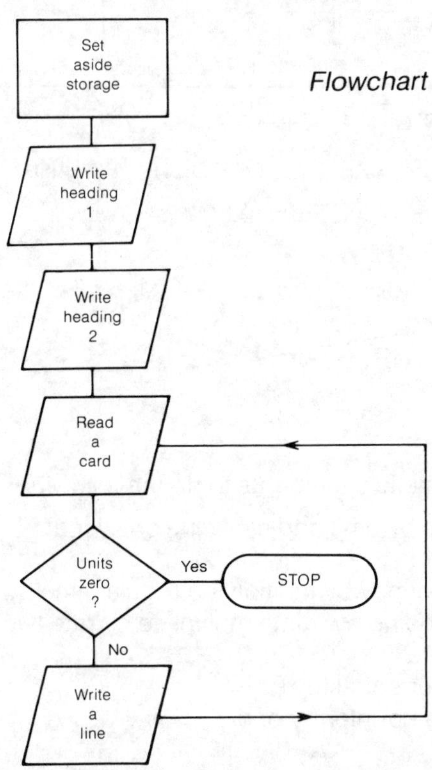

Fortran Coding

```
      DIMENSION CUST (5), NAME (15)
      WRITE (M,10)
10    FORMAT ('1', 20X, 'CUSTOMER METER
               USAGE'/)
      WRITE (M,20)
20    FORMAT (' ', 37X, 'JULY 1970'//)
3     READ (N,30) CUST, NAME, IQTY
30    FORMAT (5A1, 15A1, I5)
      IF (IQTY) 1, 2, 1
1     WRITE (M,40) CUST, NAME, IQTY
40    FORMAT (' ', 5X, 5A1, 4X, 15A1, 10X, I8)
      GO TO 3
2     CALL EXIT
      END
```

PL/1 Coding

```
METER..PROCEDURE OPTIONS (MAIN),.
    DECLARE CUSTNO CHAR (5),
            NAME CHAR (15),
            UNITS DECIMAL FIXED (5),.
    PUT EDIT ('CUSTOMER METER USAGE')
        (PAGE, X(20), A(20)),.
    PUT EDIT ('JULY 1970')
        (SKIP (2), X(37), A(9)),.
START..GET EDIT (CUSTNO, NAME, UNITS,
DUMMY)
        (A(5), A(15), F(5), A(55)),.
        IF UNITS EQ 0 THEN STOP,.
        PUT EDIT (CUSTNO, NAME, UNITS)
(SKIP (1), X(5), A(5), X(4), A(15), X(10), F(8)),.
    GO TO START,.
END METER,.
```

What Do You Know?

FORTRAN or PL/1

(1) Write statements to set aside storage

(a) for all the information on an 80-column card,
(b) for an area called ADRS to contain 35 characters of information.

(2) Write statements to read in the information in question (1).

(3) Write statements to write out the information in question (1) on a new page on the printer.

(4) Write a program to read the card and produce a printed line as illustrated.

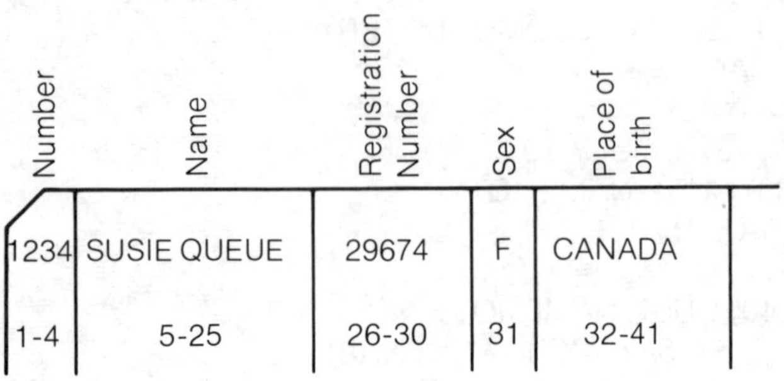

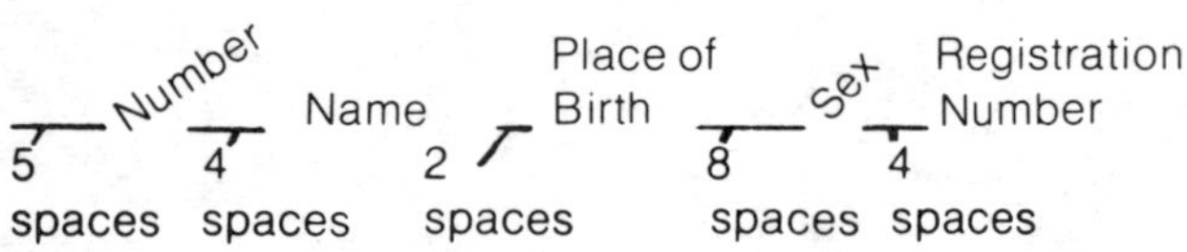

(5) Draw a flowchart and, using the information in question (4), write a program to read and write a set of cards with the same fields. The last card is blank.

(6) Draw a flowchart and write a program to print out only the customers with positive balances. Print the customer name and balance, suitably spaced in each case.

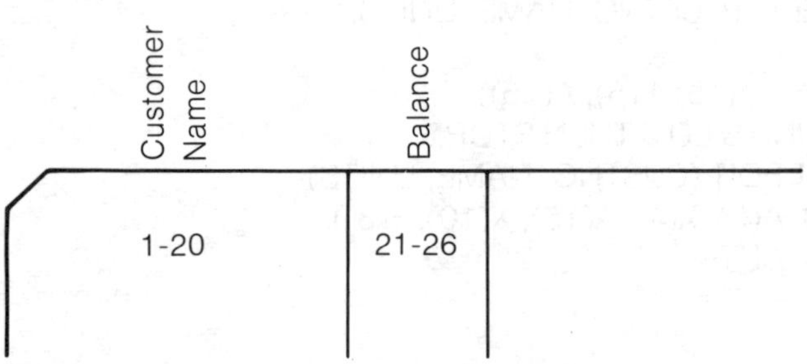

(7) Write statements to print the following page headings:

(a)

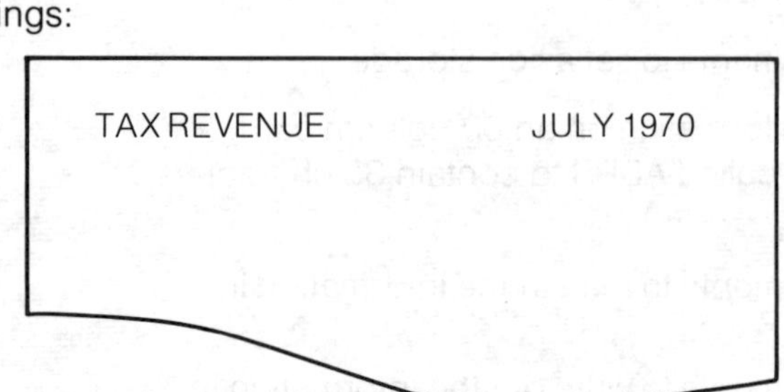

(b)

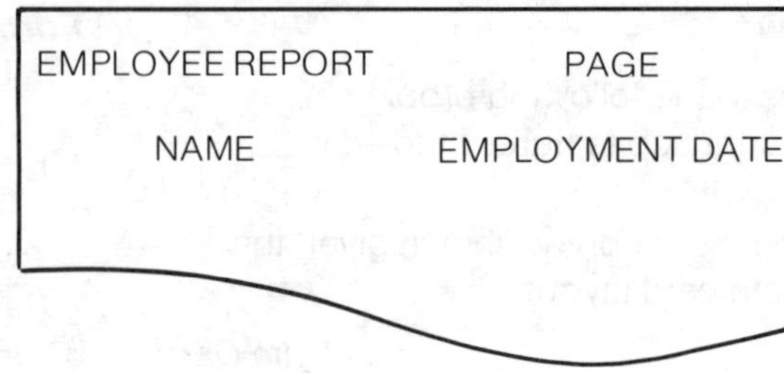

(8) Flowchart and code a program to produce the report as shown given the following input data card layout. The last card is blank.

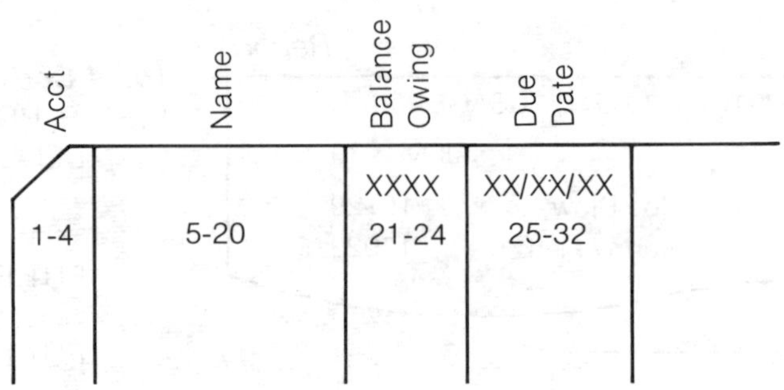

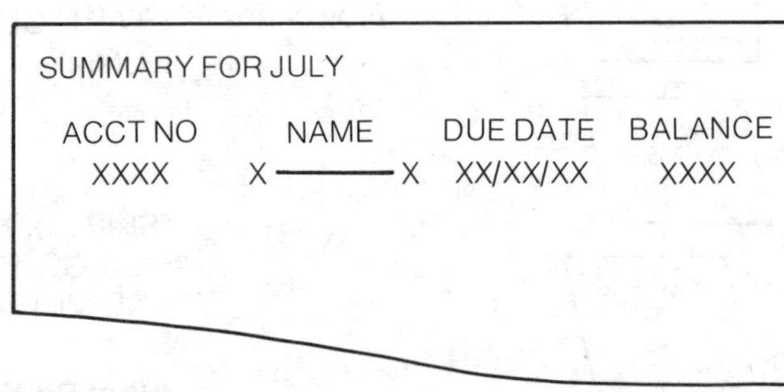

(9) Write arithmetic statements to do the following:

(a) Multiply rate by time and store the answer at gross pay.

(b) Calculate net pay by multiplying regular time by rate one and adding overtime multiplied by rate two and deducting tax.

(c) Set a counter equal to zero.

(d) Increment a counter by one.

What Do You Know?

(10) Flowchart and code a program to list and count the cards in a deck. The last card is blank.

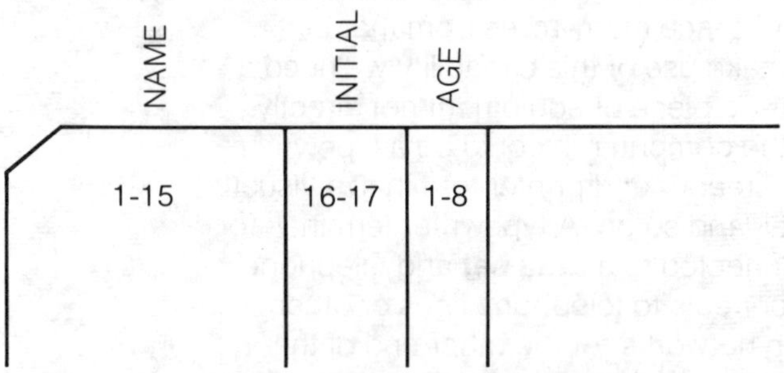

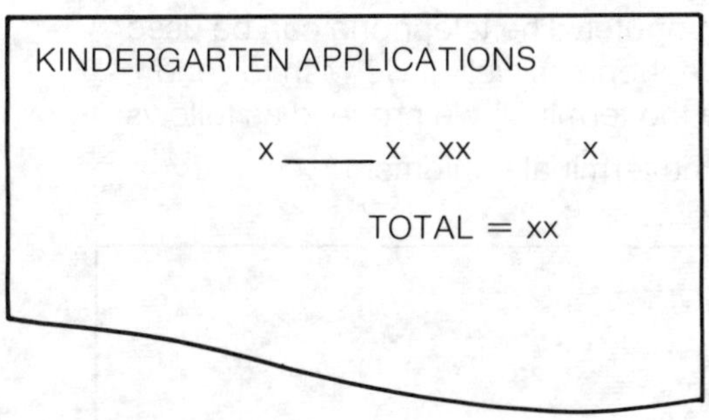

(11) Flowchart and code a program to calculate extensions for the following bill and produce the reports as shown.

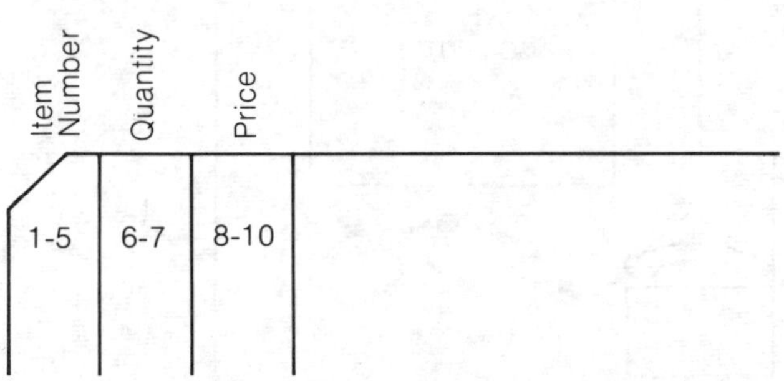

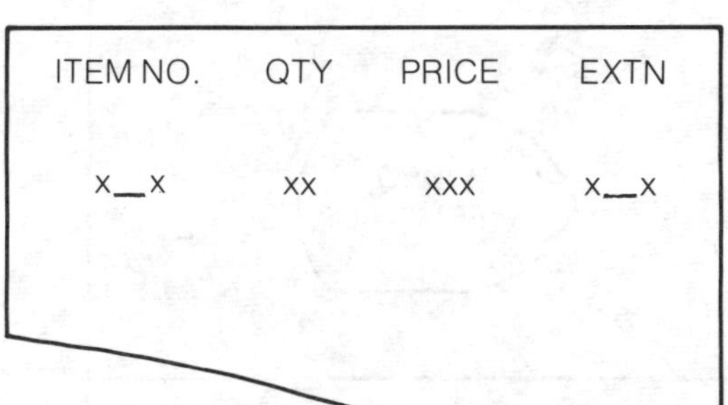

(12) Amend the flowchart and add instructions to question (11) to find the total of the extended prices.

FORTRAN Only

(13) Explain the meaning of the following statements:

```
      READ (N,15) NAME, ADDRS
15    FORMAT (20A1, 25A1)
```

(14) The following program segment to read and write information from a card has errors in it. Correct the errors explaining why they are errors.

```
      DIMNSION CARD (30)
      READ (N,10) CARD
20    FORMAT (35A1
      WRITE (M,15) CARDS
15    FORMAT (1, 30A1)
```

(15) Correct the following statements explaining the errors:

(a) I + J = L + M
(b) KAMT = L(INT + MPP)
(c) M = J ÷ 4

PL/1 Only

(16) Explain the meaning of the following statements:

(a) GET EDIT (NAME, CODE) (A(20) ,A(1)),.
(b) DECLARE CITY CHARACTER (10),.

(17) The following program segment to read and write information from a card has errors in it. Correct the errors and explain them.

```
DECLRE INF CHARACTER (30),.
      GET EDIT (INFO) (A(35),.
      PUT (INF) (A(30)).
```

(18) Correct the following statements explaining the errors:

(a) I + J = L + M,.
(b) KAMT = L(INT + MPR),.
(c) M = J ÷ 4,.

15 More Complex Computing Systems

The more advanced computers now in operation employ some interesting techniques and provide scope for many different and sophisticated applications.

Up till now we have considered a relatively simple computing system, contained entirely in one room and performing only one job at a time. Several units may be used to complete the job but the CPU, at any one time, contains part of the operating system and one set of instructions—possibly a translator or the machine language version of a program written by a user. In this chapter we shall consider briefly some interesting advances in computing: The concepts are quite easy to understand, but the implementation of such systems is very complex. The writing of an operating system to cope with these techniques is a highly skilled job taking many people several years.

Teleprocessing

Teleprocessing enables us to use the facilities of a computer from a place many miles from the computer. To make use of this capability we need a **terminal**, that is, a piece of equipment not directly connected to the computer. It could be a typewriter terminal, a card reader and printer terminal, a visual display terminal, and so on. A typewriter terminal, for example, is connected to a **data set** and telephone that, in turn, connects to telephone lines or other communication networks. At the other end of the network line is another data set, telephone, a control unit and the computer. The telephone can be used as a regular telephone as well. If we wish to send information via the terminal, we proceed as follows:

(1) Switch on the terminal equipment.

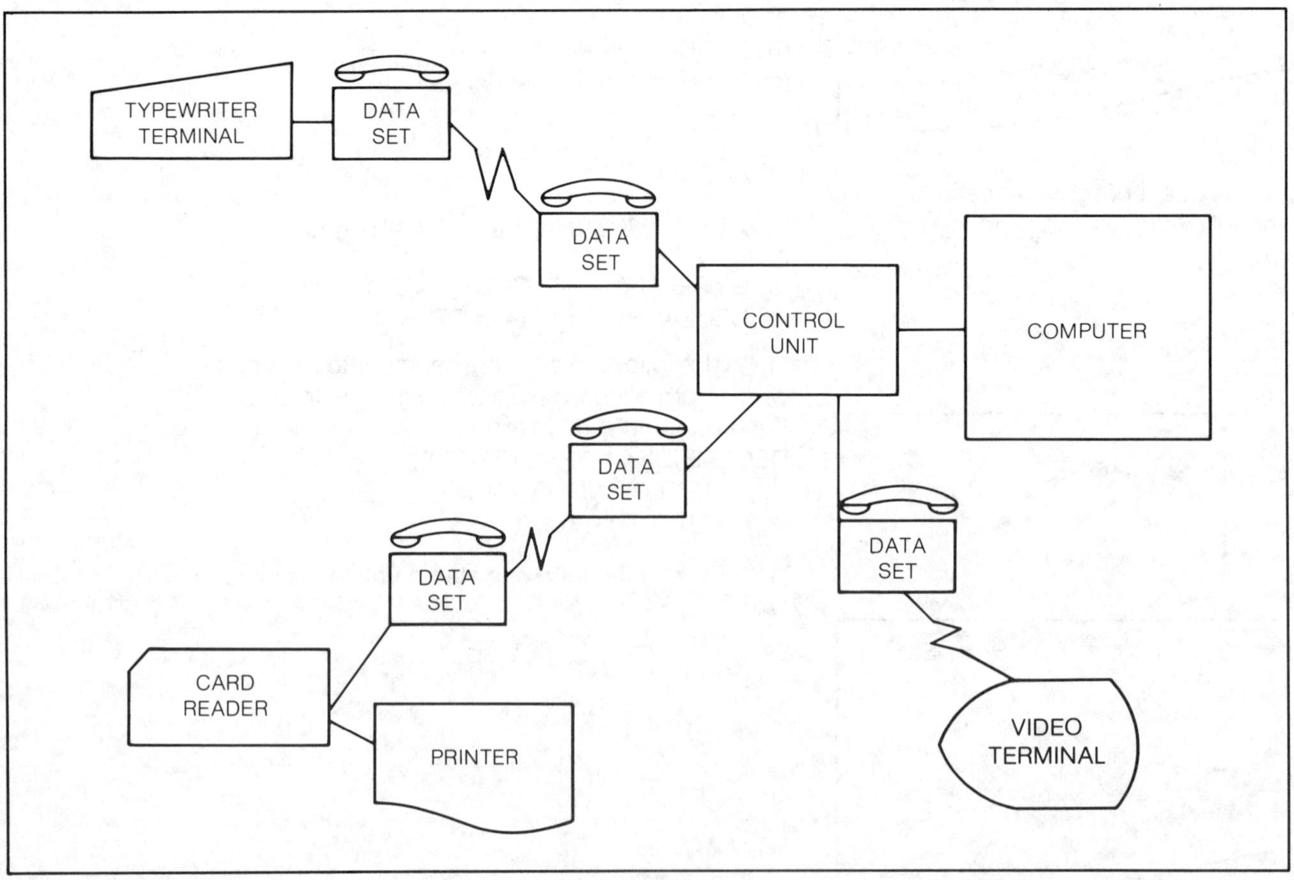

Diagram 15.1 Terminal network

(2) Dial the computer phone number using the terminal phone.

(3) Push the data button, thus indicating that data, rather than conversation, is to be transmitted and replace the receiver.

(4) Type in the information or feed cards from the terminal.

The information is converted by the data set to a series of signals that can be transmitted over communication lines. At the other end the signals are converted back to bits, usually in the control unit, forming bytes or words acceptable to the computer's CPU. The reverse process takes place to return information to the terminal. The data can be checked for validity and either the terminal user or the computer may have to resend the information—just as somebody may not hear clearly what you are saying on the phone and may ask you to repeat it. In some teleprocessing networks the data sets are replaced by control units performing essentially the same functions.

Today there are many teleprocessing networks, which means that many terminal users have access to the same computer. Suppose we have twenty terminals with access to the same central computer. Such a network might be used by hospital staff to enquire from a central file of patient information. How does the computer cope if all twenty enquire at once? The information or **message** as it arrives at the computer is stored in a buffer, a temporary area for the reception of messages. The program must check each buffer continually, and within a certain time period, otherwise information could get lost. The computer does not have complete control over messages being transmitted and cannot indicate to the terminal that the buffer is full. It is much the same idea as a conveyor belt going from one department to another with the beginning of the belt not visible at the end. If the conveyor belt is filled at one end and not emptied at the other, a large pile heaps up. As the program checks the buffer, it empties it of the information it contains. The message is stored,

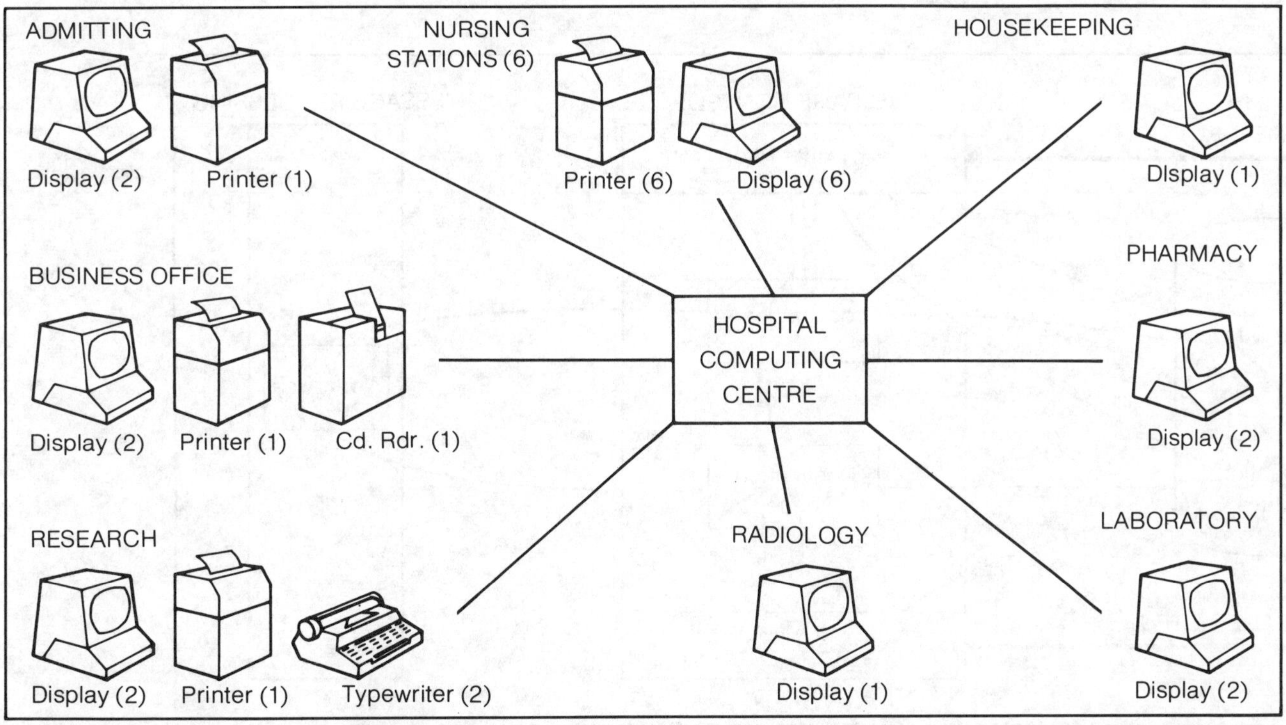

Diagram 15.2 **Use of a terminal network in a hospital**

together with information about the terminal from which it was received, in an area of main storage set aside for this purpose or on disk or tape. The various enquiries form a queue (or line-up) and are processed in sequence. The CPU can operate much faster than the information can be transmitted over communication lines and has no problem checking the buffers. The size and speed of the computer, together with the sophistication of the operating system, will determine how many terminals it can deal with.

Diagram 15.3 shows a schematic of how messages are dealt with after they arrive in the storage buffer. As you can see, several possibilities exist:

(1) The message can be sent immediately to the output queue (destination queue) on a disk if no processing is required.

(2) The message may be sent immediately for processing.

(3) The message may be temporarily stored on the disk to await processing.

Eventually the output messages are collected on disk in a destination queue and transmitted via the buffer area to the correct terminal. The messages could be file records, program statements, and so on.

Some networks are set up for instant turnaround, that is, an answer to an enquiry in one or two seconds, whereas others accept information continually, store it on disk or tape and process it later. It is also possible to do both at once, for example, by using control cards to indicate whether we need an immediate answer or a later answer. The operating system has established priorities and scans the queue for those requiring immediate answers and writes all the others on a tape for processing later. No queue develops if the program keeps up with the enquiries. Normally on a teleprocessing network the queue length varies at different times. For example, enquiry into the hospital patient file might cause a queue to develop at 9 a.m. and 2 p.m. (doctors' visiting times) but not at any other time. Teleprocessing networks employ a technique called **time sharing**: the total computer

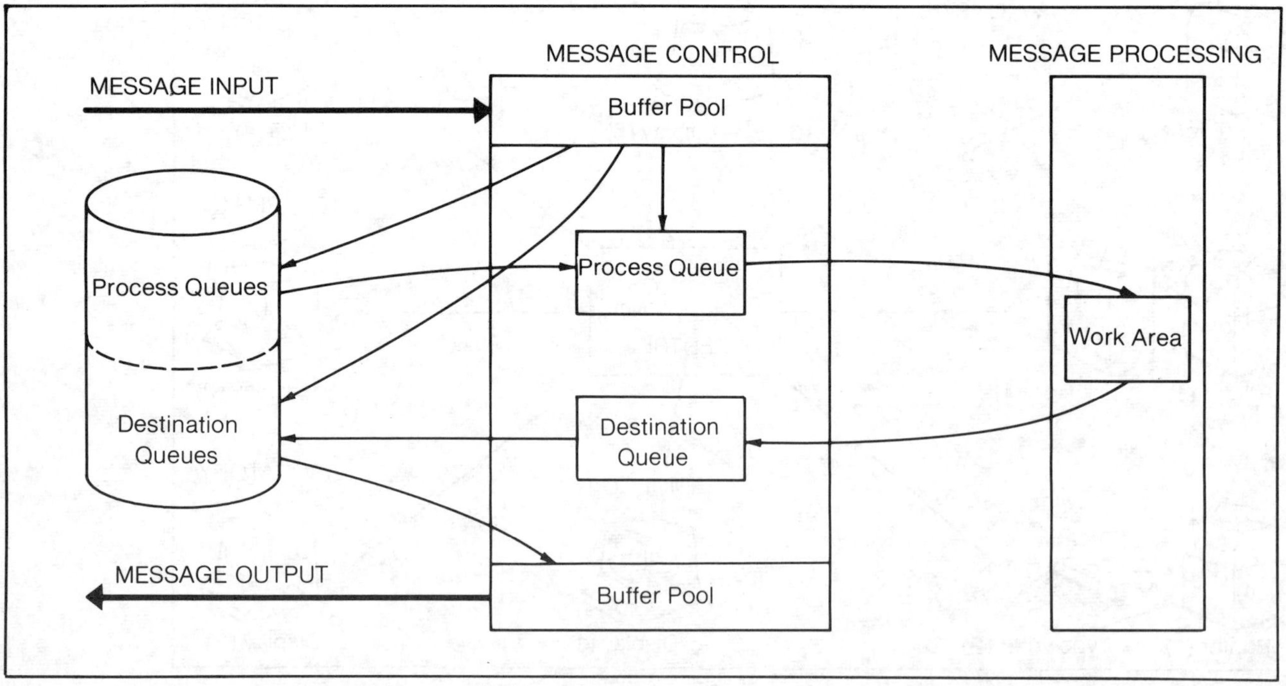

Diagram 15.3 Schematic of message processing

time available is shared among various users and, since the time intervals are so small, each user imagines he is the only one using the computer.

Teleprocessing networks are maintained by many airlines to allow reservations to be made from anywhere in the country. The central computer has files with available seats on all its planes for a certain period of time. The clerk at the reservation desk enquires via the terminal for a specific seat on a specific flight, receives a message as to its availability and then confirms the reservation by entering the customer details. Typewriter terminals or visual display units can be used for such a system. Also in existence are terminal networks for banking. A central file can be updated, immediately reflecting customer deposits and withdrawals. The customer's balance can be checked by enquiry into the file.

Problem solving networks are also in operation. For example, at a terminal you type in your PL/1 or FORTRAN program and have it translated and executed in the length of time it takes you to type it. Your program statements are translated and accumulated as you type. You receive error messages and have the opportunity of making corrections until a correct program is obtained. Then execution of the program takes place. This facility is greatly valued by engineers, research personnel, and so on, who have intermittent problems to be solved and do not require a computer of their own.

Multiprogramming

Using multiprogramming it is possible within one computing system to perform several jobs at once. By using a sophisticated operating system we can effectively divide the main storage of the computer into sections or **partitions**. For example, it is possible to have three jobs going on concurrently in three different partitions:

Partition 1—compiling a COBOL program
Partition 2—copying a tape
Partition 3—updating a payroll file

There may be queuing problems in multiprogramming similar to those in teleprocessing. For example, the programs in two partitions may both require the use of the printer. Usually a computing system that employs multiprogramming techniques has sufficient input and output equipment to make sure there is a minimum of queuing. The sizes of the partitions can be altered for different applications. Careful scheduling is required in multiprogramming since many of the facilities available—registers, arithmetic and logic circuitry, disk working areas, operating system control programs, and so on—are shared by two or more programs. This organization is taken care of by the operating system.

It is possible to combine multiprogramming and teleprocessing. For example, we may establish a partition that is always going to service the terminals. The other part of main storage may contain various programs being processed from a stack of jobs. In other words we have a computer performing routine installation jobs —file updating, accounts receivable, payroll, statistical reports—as well as supporting a teleprocessing network.

Multiprocessing

Multiprocessing

Many large computer installations reach the point where they need more computing power. They must then decide whether to move to a larger computer, if that is possible, get two separate computers instead of one, or go to a **multiprocessing** system.

The use of a technique called multiprocessing permits two computers to essentially function as one computer. The two computers are linked together using a special multisystem unit. One operating system has control of both main storage units and all input, output and storage units.

Moving to a larger computer may require a different operating system, different input and output units and different storage units. If there is a problem with a single large computer back-up computing power must be found.

It is usually cheaper to go to a multiprocessor than to rent or purchase two separate computers. There are no decisions to be made about how to divide the work load between two machines since the single operating system will effectively organize all the work between the two CPU's.

A multiprocessing system may be the best solution to a growth problem. The computing power is almost doubled, main storage is doubled but there is only one operating system to look after. Input and output units, and disk and tape units do not have to be provided for two computers. Should there be a problem with one CPU, processing can continue since each CPU can function separately. It therefore has its own built-in back-up.

Virtual Storage

We have seen that multiprogramming allows more efficient use of the computers' hardware. For example, one program may be making use of the printer while another uses the card reader and yet a third uses arithmetic circuitry to do millions of calculations. Even with many partitions and a sophisticated operating system, full use is still not being made of the central processing unit, which operates at the fastest speed of any of the computer system's units.

Normally, for a program to be executed, all the machine language version of it must be in main storage. There are some exceptions to this rule, but we will ignore them at present. However, at any one point in time not all of the program is required. Consider a commercial program that has several exception routines, for example, listing out-of-sequence customer numbers or punching out cards for customers with zero balances. Most of these sections of the program are run very infrequently, some never, but they occupy space in main storage the entire time the program is being run. At any one time very few instructions from the program are being executed. Extend this to a multiprogrammed system where several programs are being run, and, although the central processing unit is being used a little more, vast areas of main storage are occupied by instructions and possibly data that are used only a small percentage of the total time. Calculations and logic operations are taking place a very small percentage of the time.

A method of improving this usage is to employ a technique known as **virtual storage**. This concept has been implemented on some computers for several years, but recently several manufacturers have announced new and improved implementations of virtual storage. What is virtual storage and how does it work? Suppose we have a very large program to run on our computer and it does not fit into main storage. There are several ways around this problem using conventional programming methods. For example, the program might be split into two or more smaller programs. However, suppose we set aside a special area large enough to contain our program on a device, such as a disk, to which the computer has very fast access. The disk storage that is set aside is called **address space** and is divided into large chunks called **segments,** each segment being divided into smaller pieces called **pages**. For example, we might have segments capable of holding 20 000 characters of information and pages that contain 1 000 characters each. Main storage is now called **real storage** and is divided up into areas called **page frames,** each of which can contain a page of instructions or data (in our example, 1000 characters of information).

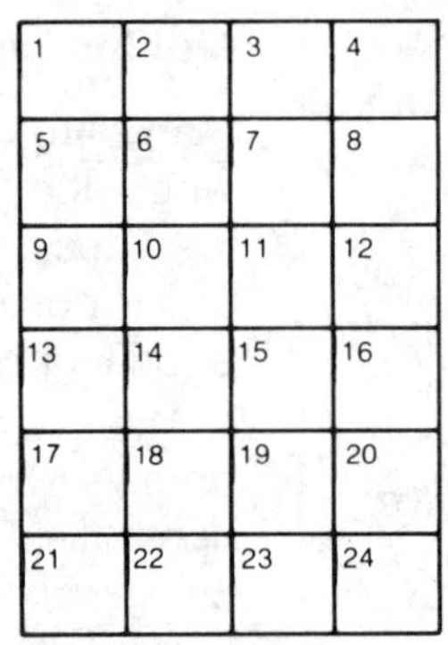

Real storage divided into 24 page frames

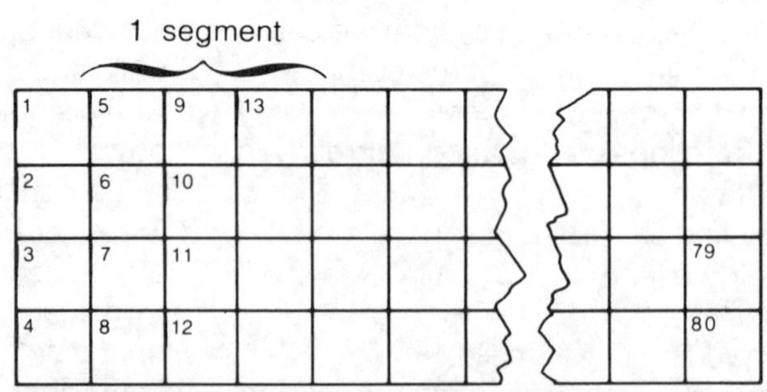

Virtual storage divided into 80 pages or 4 segments

Diagram 15.4

Let us consider how a very large program can be executed using virtual storage. First, the program is translated and the machine language version stored on disk in the normal way. All of the machine language program cannot be read back into real storage since it does not fit. Real storage is filled with as much of the program as it can contain. Suppose in our case we have a real storage of 24 page frames (not realistic, but easy to follow on a diagram). The overflow is put into virtual storage. Thus all the program is automatically divided into equal size pages, some occupying page frames in real storage, others residing in virtual storage. Virtual storage has an area set aside in it that can contain *all* of the program, but, since the majority of the program can be in real storage, only part of it is occupied at present.

As you realized when using the machine language in Chapter 5, the addresses where instructions are stored and where data is to be found are consecutive, and instructions are executed consecutively unless there is intentional branching. When high level languages are used, the translator takes care of assigning actual machine addresses to the instructions. In our program, the 24 pages in real storage are executed and pages 25 and 26, and so on, are required so that program execution can continue. Obviously, one of the pages presently in real storage and no longer required must be overlayed. What sort of havoc will this create with our addresses? There is a very complex mechanism, which is partly hardware and partly software, for completely identifying where in a program a page belongs and for keeping track of which page frames can be re-used immediately by other pages of the program. The pages do not have to be in consecutive page frames in real storage. Each time a

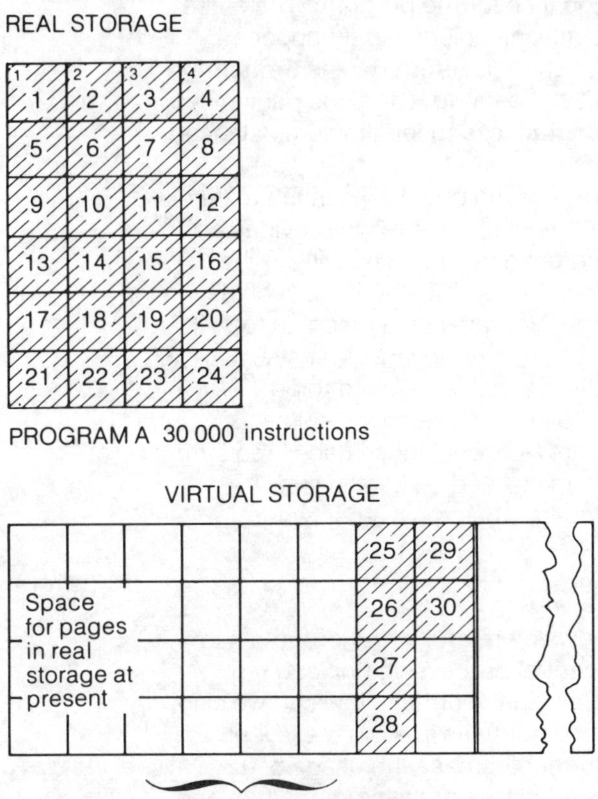

Diagram 15.5

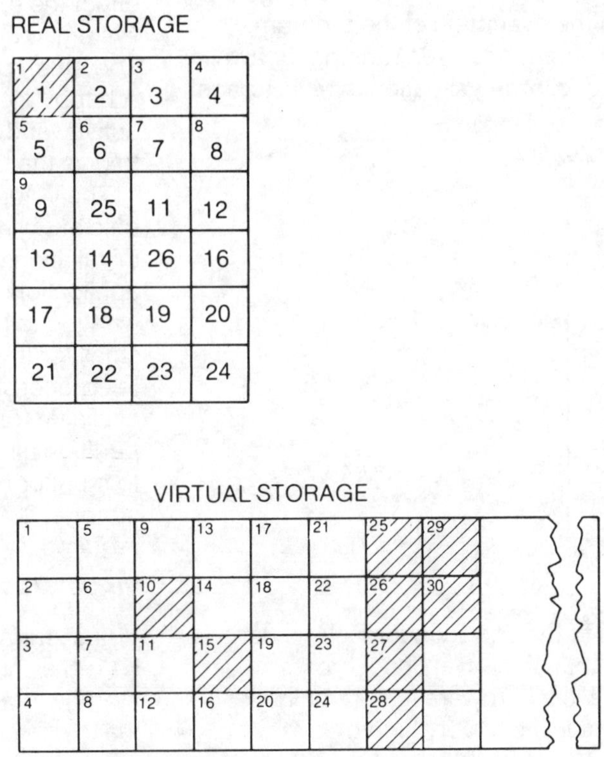

Diagram 15.6 Pages 10 and 15 in Real Storage overlapped by pages 25 and 26 from Virtual Storage

new page is required and it is not already in real storage, the system has to

(1) locate the required page in virtual storage
(2) select a page frame to hold the page
(3) copy the contents of the selected page frame to virtual storage if it is not there
(4) move a copy of the page from virtual storage to real storage
(5) update a table to show that the page is in real storage and the address of its location
(6) perform the virtual address translation.

All this takes place in a fraction of a second and program execution can continue. Pages may need to be copied back into virtual storage or 'paged out' if they have been changed in any way, as well as when they have never been stored there, as with pages 10 and 15 in our example. For example, a counter may have been changed and the page containing this change must be kept correctly in virtual storage for future use during the execution of the program. Thus, after our program has been running for awhile we might have the following situation in real storage:

REAL STORAGE

1 1	2 30	3 3	4 4
29	6 6	7 9	8 8
9 5	10 25	11	12
13	27	28	21
17	18	16	20
10	2	26	24

Diagram 15.7

The translation to the correct addresses is done very much faster than in conventional program translation since it is a hardware feature of the machine and is achieved at very high electronic speeds.

Suppose we extend this idea to a multiprogramming situation. If one of those programs is supporting a teleprocessing network, it might well be occupying a partition for many hours but getting only spasmodic use. Other programs may have to wait for the right size partition to be freed in order that they can be run. None of these space-and time-wasting functions need occur if we employ the virtual storage technique. The teleprocessing network program can be divided into pages as well as other programs, whatever their size, and the execution of several of them can continue concurrently. Naturally there is still a certain section of real storage reserved for the complex control program that is part of the operating system and essential for the running of the computer using virtual storage.

With several programs running at one time as in diagram 15.8 there may be considerable activity in the movement of different pages into and out of real storage. Careful control must be kept so that too much 'paging', as it is called, does not take place, since the additional time taken to change pages may effect the execution time for the program. The entire system could become inefficient if that happened. Too much paging activity is referred to as **thrashing**. A happy medium can be found where the paging activity and the program execution time are balanced to give the best results.

The virtual-storage technique allows much more efficient use of a computer system and provides an installation with a great deal more flexibility in the applications that can be run. Restrictions, such as wanting to run large programs on a machine too small for them, have been removed. Normally, a teleprocessing network that is required to be available for eight to ten hours a day ties up a partition all that time. Now only those pages required to monitor the terminals need be kept in main storage, the other pages being moved in when required.

Virtual Machines

Virtual storage allows more and larger programs to be run using the central processing unit and real storage in a more efficient manner. How can we also make use of all the other units in a more efficient manner and still further increase the usage of the CPU? This can be done by simulating more than one computer using only one real machine. This complete functional simulation of a computer is

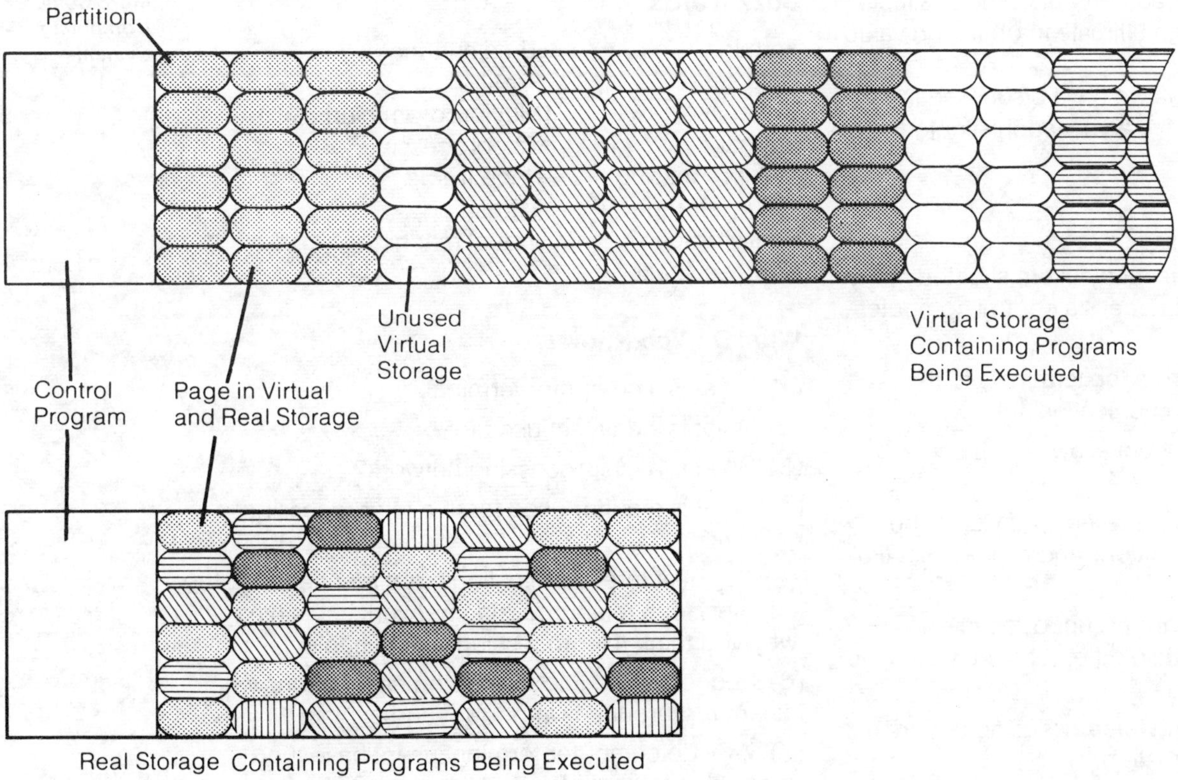

Diagram 15.8

called a virtual machine. Several virtual machines, each with a virtual card reader, virtual printer, and so on, can be running at one time on a real machine using multiprogramming techniques and complex software.

Each user requiring a virtual machine must state what units he requires to be part of the machine. For example, it may consist of a CPU with 256K main storage, disk storage, tape storage, card reader and printer. Of course, each of the units mentioned in any of the virtual machines must be present on the real machine (there are some exceptions to this but we will ignore them). Each virtual machine has its own real console. The user controls his machine using his own console and, as far as he is concerned, he has a real machine dedicated to his use. Each user must also specify the operating system under which his machine is to operate.

All the virtual machines are carefully scheduled by a control program so that they use the real equipment with little or no waiting involved. The real storage now is being used by several machines. The software for a system such as this is probably some of the most sophisticated ever developed. Using such a technique allows much better use to be made of all the equipment—reader, printer, CPU, and so on. It allows an installation to try out new operating systems or to devote a whole machine (virtual) to a teleprocessing network. In a learning environment, this concept can be very valuable. Research personnel, college graduates and undergraduates can have their own virtual machines to perform their own specific applications and try out their new ideas without causing any problems or interference with, for example, a very essential payroll that has to be run. And of course the real computer system is being used nearer to one hundred percent of the available time, which represents the ultimate in obtaining value for money.

Combine all of the ideas we have discussed in this chapter and you really have a very sophisticated computing system.

Points to Review

(1) Teleprocessing allows many users situated many miles from a computer to access a central computer via terminals.

(2) Information passes from the terminals to the central computer via communication lines.

(3) The time-sharing concept allows each user a share of total computing time.

(4) Multiprogramming is achieved by dividing the main storage area into partitions and running several jobs concurrently.

(5) A terminal network can be supported in one partition of a computer while other jobs are run in the other partition or partitions.

(6) Multiprogramming and teleprocessing require a sophisticated operating system.

(7) Multiprocessing is a technique that allows two computers to function as one providing almost twice the computing power, while using only one set of input/output units and auxiliary storage, and running under the control of one operating system.

(8) Virtual storage is a technique using disk storage as an extension of main storage and requiring only active parts of a program to be present in real storage.

(9) Virtual storage allows more efficient use of a computing system and removes size restrictions for programs.

(10) Several computers can be simulated on a real machine by a sophisticated operating system providing every user with his own virtual machine. Each virtual machine consists of all the units the real machine is composed of, as far as the individual user is concerned.

Buzz Words

Terminal
Data set
Buffer
Message
Multiprocessing
Virtual storage
Real storage
Address space
Time sharing
Partition
Multiprogramming
Teleprocessing
Page frame
Thrashing
Virtual machine

What Do You Know?

(1) What is a computer terminal?

(2) What is a data set used for?

(3) What is a teleprocessing network?

(4) What is a buffer used for in a teleprocessing network?

(5) Suggest three applications (not mentioned in the chapter) for a teleprocessing network explaining why you think teleprocessing is applicable.

(6) Suggest three teleprocessing applications where instant turnaround is important and explain why.

(7) Why do computer terminal users have the impression they are the only computer user?

(8) What is a partition?

(9) Why does scheduling jobs to be run become increasingly important in multiprogramming?

(10) Distinguish between multiprocessing and multiprogramming.

(11) Distinguish between real storage and virtual storage.

(12) List all the advantages you can think of for installing a multiprocessing, multiprogramming, virtual storage machine instead of a single partition, single processor, real storage only, computer.

16 Computer Applications

Your phone bill, income tax, hydro bill and bank statements are probably all calculated and produced using a computer. Did you realize that the radio station you listen to may also be following a computer-generated program, and that the hot dogs you eat may have the quantity of ingredients controlled by computer? Rarely are computers rented or purchased by a company for one application, and installations using the computer for specialized jobs typically use it for such general business applications as payroll, inventory control, billing, accounts payable and accounts receivable. Many jobs performed by the computer may only take an hour or two of computer time. In such cases the time can be bought from a company that sells computer time.

Diagram 16.1 Computer terminal in a bank

Some Computer Uses

(1) The National Research Council of Canada uses a huge scale model of the St. Lawrence River to study the effects of environmental changes. Information from dozens of measuring instruments is collected, then processed by computer.

(2) A computer is helping the National Agriculture School in Mexico make impressive progress in increasing the yield of maize and wheat on small farms. The computer is used to study seed quality, soil tests and rainfall patterns.

(3) The Faculty of Dentistry at the University of Toronto collects data from many countries of the world about the size and growth of teeth, enabling statistics to be accumulated about growth patterns, decay, environmental influence, and so on.

(4) In an ancient Venetian square, on-the-scene data is collected for computer study. A team of experts will apply computer simulation in searching for a way to keep the historic and picturesque city from sinking into the sea.

(5) A computer in a sawmill senses the size of cut boards and enables them to be sorted ten to fifteen percent more accurately than was possible before.

(6) Several companies use computer graphic displays to design textile patterns. The designers may experiment economically with many trial designs on the display screen before going into production.

Diagram 16.2 Air traffic control

(7) Computers are being used to study air motion near the earth's surface to determine the effect of pollution. They also analyze water samples from polluted rivers and lakes. The sources of pollution can then be traced and controls initiated.

(8) Signals from electrocardiographs, spirometers and other devices are being analyzed by computer to assist doctors in diagnosing illness. In addition, continuous surveillance of patients in intensive care units is provided by computers that monitor such critical variables as blood pressure, respiration and pulse.

(9) At busy control sectors in air traffic control a radar controller and his assistants follow aircraft by voice contact and radar. A computer provides up-to-date information about the traffic in all areas.

(10) Man would not have landed on the moon without the help of computers. As well as a battery of computers at ground control the astronauts have their own miniature versions on board for the continual calculations required during the missions.

(11) A woman's sportswear manufacturer produces pin tickets for salesmen's samples of their various lines. These pin tickets contain readable and accurate information about the size, colour, fabric, style number and price of the garment.

(12) The shipbuilding industry uses the computer to determine how sheet metal should be cut to obtain the minimum of waste.

(13) University libraries are now controlling their book circulation with the help of a computer. Statistics about the types and number of books borrowed can be produced, and up-to-date lists on overdue books, reserve books, and so on, improve the efficiency of the library.

(14) Jobs in the construction industry can be scheduled in the correct sequence for maximum efficiency, the computer indicating which parts of the job should start at what time, which tasks may overlap and which parts of a job must be finished before others can begin.

(15) A guidance system implemented on a computer is used to provide students with up-to-date information about university and job requirements. Students can brouse through job descriptions until

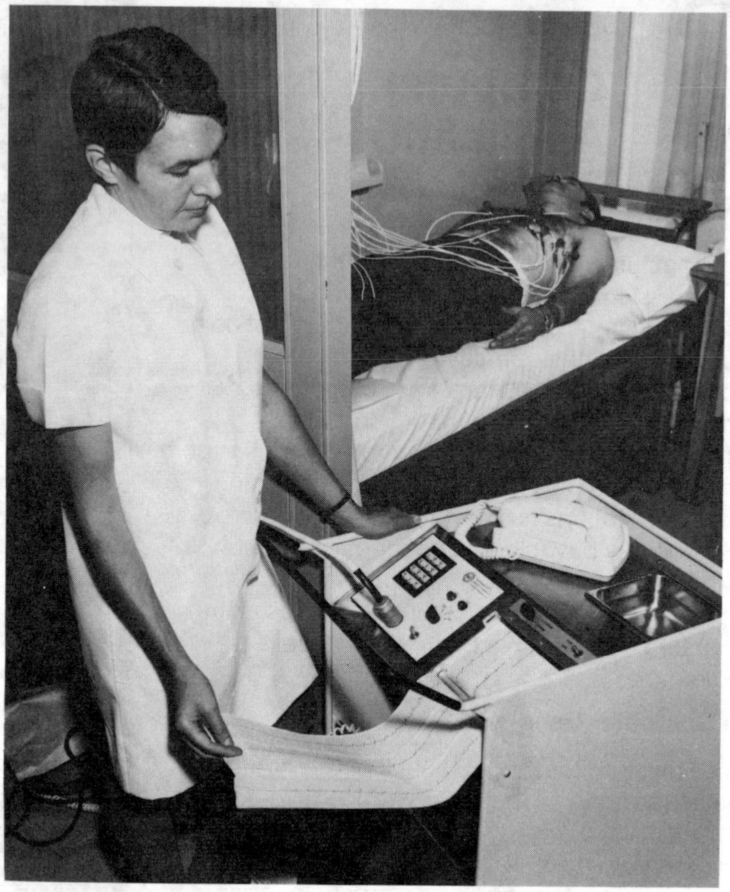

Diagram 16.3 Patient undergoing tests in the hospital

Diagram 16.4 Reporters receiving statistics via computer at the Montreal Olympics

Diagram 16.5 Computer used in controlling Toronto traffic

they find one of particular interest to discuss with the guidance counsellor.

(16) The Royal College of Physicians and Surgeons holds examinations via computer terminals in centres across Canada. Students diagnose illnesses from symptoms given by computer and may request such supplementary information as pulse and blood pressure in order to suggest treatment.

Let us take a more detailed look at some computer applications.

Traffic Control

People listening to the radio early in the morning in the Toronto area occasionally hear the announcer say "It may take you longer this morning—the traffic computer is down." Fortunately this is heard infrequently but it does remind Torontonians that they have their traffic controlled by a computer.

Toronto is a very rapidly growing metropolis and even back in 1957 traffic congestion was a problem. A team of traffic consultants was called in and they came to the conclusion that a computer could help. Starting in 1959 a pilot study was conducted that proved by 1961 that the computer could save both time and money for motorists and the taxpayer. How does it work? Embedded about five cm below the road surface are vehicle detectors. Each consists of a rectangular loop about 1 metre by 2 metres placed approximately 91 metres back from a traffic light. At one of the four corners where the traffic light is situated, there is a control box containing electromechanical equipment. This control box receives signals from the sensors as vehicles pass over them, a '1' indicating the presence of a vehicle, a '0', no vehicle. The signals are received by the control box and transmitted over telephone lines to the central computer. An input scanner receives the combination of ones and zeros and the information from all the sensors is collected by an input/output control unit that checks the scanner several times per second. The data is partially processed and then transmitted to the main computer, a UNIVAC 1107. The computer determines the best traffic light pattern using a complex program and returns information to the control unit. The output distributor is controlled by the input/output control unit and receives unique instructions for each traffic light. These are carried out via the control box at the light. The control boxes are constantly checked to make sure they are sending and receiving information. If at any time this is not so, pre-set timing takes over so that the lights are always working. The mechanism for this timing is housed in the control box. The complete cycle of examining the traffic takes place about once every second.

There are at present 1180 intersections controlled by lights, of which 1100 are under computer control and therefore have the capability of varying the amount of 'green' time to cope with the traffic variations. Intersections are computerized at the rate of 50 per year. As well as providing information for control of the lights the computer obtains statistical information for use by the Traffic Planning Department. Several programs are needed to provide the best possible control because the traffic patterns vary at different times during the day. The morning rush hour for example, differs from the evening rush hour and thus different programs are used. There are various modes of traffic control. For example, lights can be synchronized to permit vehicles to proceed through a series of lights with a minimum of delays. In volume density mode the green light is left on until all cars arriving during the previous red have passed through. The green light will continue as long as the volume of vechicles approaching it is greater than the number stopped at the red light. Some lightly travelled roads have lights that are semi-activated and respond to a single car passing over the sensors or to a push button. The Toronto Traffic Control System is one of the most sophisticated and largest in existence.

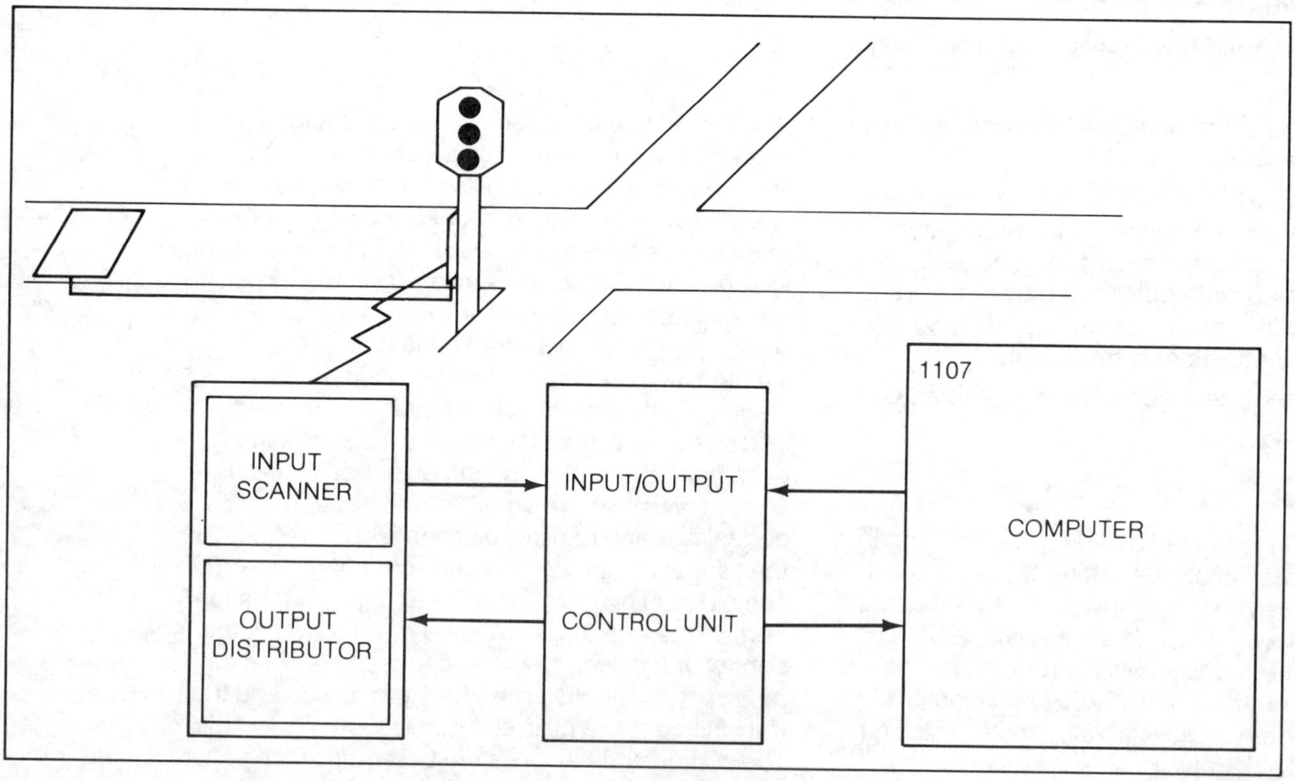

Diagram 16.6 Schematic showing sensing mechanism for traffic control

Can the help the computer gives be measured? There is a measurable saving in the wear and tear on cars, gas consumption and thus pollution. What is harder to measure is the saving of wear and tear on nerves that traffic jams cause. How much time would otherwise be lost 'on the job'? How much would frustration contribute to accidents and thus further tie-ups?

Student Scheduling

Many students in this day and age follow their own individual course of study in high school, which means that they must each have a unique timetable. This makes the scheduling of students even more of a headache than it always has been.

Traditionally the principal or vice-principal and two or three other teachers toiled in August to produce a master timetable, and the secretarial staff typed up home form lists. Everybody in one class had basically the same timetable issued by his or her homeroom teacher on the first day of term. No longer is it that easy. Now every timetable in a particular home form can vary, thus posing a tremendous clerical task and requiring a massive sort to prepare class lists. Let us take a look at the steps in scheduling:

(1) Tally the student requests
(2) Decide which classes can be run concurrently
(3) Build a master timetable
(4) Assign students to classes as efficiently as possible
(5) Prepare timetables and class lists
(6) Issue timetables and file copies in the guidance and student files.

There are several areas where the computer can help. Following the sequence given above we will study how the computer assists:

(1) *Tallying the Student Requests*
Student requests are punched into cards and then tallied by the computer. The program first gives instructions to read in a list of available courses. A table of these courses is set up in main storage or on disk if it is very large. As each card is read it is matched against the table and the appropriate subject counter incremented. A listing is then produced and any error cards listed.

The administration then has the required information to decide upon the number of classes necessary for each subject. For example, ten classes of Grade 9 English may be needed but only one each of Art, Latin and Music in Grade 12.

(2) *Concurrent Classes*
A program is available to check if it is possible to have certain subjects scheduled for the same time slot. The program produces a conflict matrix. For example, suppose 26 students in Grade 12 have selected Music and 24 would like Art. The principal decides that only one class of each is necessary. Can they be run concurrently? The program will check how many students have requested both—perhaps 20. In this case it is not practical to schedule them at the same time. If there were only two students who requested both, then scheduling Music and Art at the same time might be the best solution possible in a complex timetable. Several subjects can be checked against each other in the program, which can be run several times with different sets of subjects if required.

(3) *Building the Master Timetable*
It is possible to have a computer actually generate a master timetable, but few schools make use of it at present. It is a very complex program. Usually the human element enters into the master timetable building process. The principal and his staff may well take into account the fact that Mrs. Jones has always had a certain classroom, Mr. Smith likes his Math class near the gym as he teaches Physical Education as well, and so on. It is very difficult to put these constraints on the computer program and still have it produce a satisfactory timetable on anything but a large machine. Thus the job of building the master timetable is still done by the school administration with the aid of the tally and conflict matrix programs.

(4) *Assigning Students to Classes*
There are several computer programs available to do this, running on relatively small machines and providing a real saving in clerical work. First the timetable is coded and punched into cards. The times when a particular subject is scheduled might look like this:

ENGO9   112135425859

which means
English Grade 9 (ENGO9) meets
Monday Period 1 (11)
Tuesday Period 1 (21)
Wednesday Period 5 (35)
Thursday Period 2 (42)
Friday Period 8 and 9 (5859)

Other information can be coded about the subject on the same card.

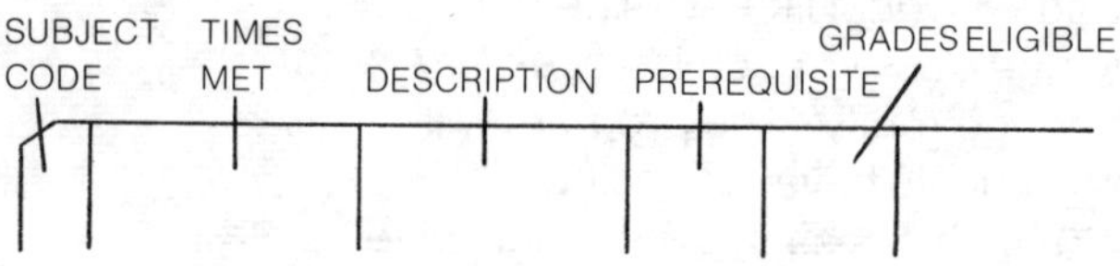

The master schedule is then fed into the computer followed by the requests for each student. When a student is scheduled, single section subjects, that is, subjects where only one class is offered, are scheduled first. There should be no problem scheduling them for the student since those subjects that will conflict should already be known from the conflict matrix and, presumably, the student would not be requesting them. Since there will be more than one class, that is, multiple sections, available in other subjects, many combinations of times can be tried until one that fits is obtained. For example, two sections of Grade 9 French may be scheduled:

Section 1		*Section 2*	
Monday	Period 1	Monday	Period 2
Tuesday	2	Tuesday	1
Wednesday	2	Wednesday	1
Thursday	5	Thursday	4

Two sections of Grade 9 Science may be scheduled:

Section 1		*Section 2*	
Monday	Periods 1, 2	Monday	Periods 5, 6
Tuesday	5, 6	Tuesday	3, 4
Friday	5, 6	Friday	1, 2

Anybody requesting French and Science could be scheduled into either section of French, but must be scheduled into Section 2 of Science. When this student has been successfully scheduled, the number of seats still available in the various classes is updated and the next student processed.

It is probable, as more and more students are scheduled, that certain classes will fill up. The computer can close off the classes and not schedule more students into them. Any errors that occur are printed.

Usually several scheduling runs are made, with adjustments being made in between, to obtain the best possible timetable for as many students as possible. No printed timetables are produced on these runs. The program balances the classes as much as it can; in other words, it makes sure there are 15 students in each of two classes rather than 20 in one and 10 in the other. It will also balance the sexes if required. This is one method of several that are available to load classes.

(5) *Preparing the Timetables and Class Lists*
Eventually when all student requests have been processed, timetables, class lists, teacher timetables and an updated master schedule are printed. The updated master schedule reflects the current numbers in each class. For those students with difficult requests a partial timetable is printed with as many subjects scheduled as possible and the conflict indicated. These students might have to revise their requests or have special timetables made up for them where, for example, they would miss one period a week of one subject.

(6) *Issuing Timetables and Updating Files*
Since the timetables are individualized, issuing them is no problem. Updating student files can be done immediately after the student is scheduled if students' records are kept on disk.

The computer provides a valuable tool in scheduling when freedom of choice is given, but a great deal of care is required in preparing the input. It is still a human function in most cases to produce the master timetable and the better this is done, the larger the percentage of students will be who receive complete timetables. It is quite possible to achieve 100% success in scheduling 1500-2000 students.

AB CENTENNIAL COLLEGE GRADE COURSE REQUEST TALLY

COURSE NO	COURSE DESCRIPTION	SEX	PREFERRED COURSE REQ UNSPFD	SEM 1	SEM 2	ALTERNATE REQUESTS TO OTHER	FR.OTHER
0570	RT3063	B		12			
		G					
		T		12			
0580	RT3093	B		13			
		G					
		T		13			
0590	SS3013	B	60	1		2	
		G					
		T	60	1		2	
0600	SS3063	B		24			
		G					
		T		24			
2010	AC2013	B	77	12			
		G					
		T	77	12			
2020	AC3013	B	1	16			
		G					

C O U R S E S C H E D U L E.

COURSE - GE-101-4 SECTION - 002

...ESDAY	THURSDAY	FRIDAY
		ALBERT 0010
		ALBERT 0010

CENTENNIAL COLLEGE
of Applied Arts and Technology,
651 Warden Avenue, Scarborough, Ontario

S T U D E N T S C H E D U L E.

NAME : HORACE HORSECOLLAR
NO : 66-000-0022

PROGRAM : 211 - BUSINESS ADMINISTRATION. FINANCIAL ADMINISTRATION (90).

TIME	MONDAY	TUESDAY	WEDNESDAY	THURSDAY
8 AM		PY-101-3 SEC - 04 TEAM 13 1166	HR-202-3 SEC - 04 BULLOCK 2050	EN-102-3 SEC - COLOMBO 117
9 AM	AC-201-3 SEC - 02 CHOUINARD 1133		HR-202-3 SEC - 04 BULLOCK 2050	
10 AM		AC-201-3 SEC - 02 CHOUINARD 2091		
11 AM	EN-102-3 SEC - 26 COLOMBO 1177			
12 NOON	HR-202-3 SEC - 04 BULLOCK 2008	PY-101-3 SEC - 04 SPINDEL 1108		
1 PM	DP-201-3 SEC - 04 BURTON 1106	EN-102-3 SEC - 26 COLOMBO 1150		

T E A C H E R S C H E D U L E.

TEACHER - ALBERT

WEDNESDAY	THURSDAY	FRIDAY
AC-201-3 SEC- 001 0010	AC-201-3 SEC- 001 0010	AC-201-3 SEC- 001 0010
		GE-101-4 SEC- 002 0010
BI-101-3 SEC- 001 0030	GE-101-4 SEC- 001 0030	

Diagram 16.7

The Computer at City Hall

At City Hall in Toronto, Ontario, an IBM System/370 is installed with visual display terminals and typewriter terminals as well as disks, tapes, a card reader and a printer. The system was originally installed to process realty taxes, water billing, staff payroll and accounting, purchasing property and planning. One of the immediate improvements made by the computer has been the elimination of duplication in vital record keeping. All the departments at City Hall have access to the information collected at the central location, that is, the data processing centre.

One of the most frustrating tasks of any civic department is answering enquiries from taxpayers who are often not satisfied with "We will answer your enquiry in due course," and a letter a week later. By using the visual display terminals people at City Hall can satisfy the enquiries immediately. In fact many thousands of enquiries per day are being answered at City Hall. Information such as name, address and account number is obtained from the enquirer over the phone or over the counter. This information is keyed in on the visual display terminal and the appropriate record is accessed from the disk. The record is displayed and the enquirer's questions are answered in a matter of seconds. The information given is up-to-date since the records in the file are kept current. Should the enquirer want a permanent record of the information on the display terminal, a typewritten version can be obtained via the typewriter terminal.

Because budget control is a critical function of City Hall, the data processing area keeps a basic accounting file on magnetic tape, which is updated daily. Reports are produced at different levels of detail and these are stored on disk. During the day civic departments have access to this information via the terminals scattered throughout City Hall. The current month's information is available by this means. Previous accounting information is stored on microfilm, which is a method of reducing pages to tiny photographic negatives. 132 characters on each of 66 lines can be reduced to a 13 mm piece of microfilm. The microfilm can be generated directly from magnetic tape. A special viewer is provided for personnel to enlarge the information if required and a photocopy can be obtained on demand. This method of keeping records with the ability to obtain an immediate photocopy of the information has been pioneered by City Hall. All historical information is kept on microfilm. The City Hall computer has also been used to convey election results to the public. Local radio station and newspaper personnel have access to the latest information via the display terminals.

Diagram 16.8 Computer in use at election time

As with any progressive data processing system City Hall is continually expanding its use of the computer. Some new applications include route scheduling of garbage trucks and storage and retrival of council minutes and by laws.

Generalized vehicle scheduling programs exist which can be used to schedule the routes of such vehicles as delivery trucks and school buses. One of these programs is being adapted by City Hall to cope with the specialized problems that exist in refuse collection. For example, unlike a delivery truck, a garbage truck does not carry a known quantity. Since a garbage truck picks up rather than delivers, the quantity can vary considerably. If the garbage truck is full before it reaches the end of this designated route then there is a problem. To enable the computer program to schedule the available trucks such information as street intersections (assigned numbers), street segments (connecting two points), length of street segments, disposal sites and customers (a block of residential units) must be provided. A network is developed and analyzed using this data. A description of the vehicles including total number and estimated capacity, as well as an estimate of expected refuse quantities, is required. Timing information is also provided, such as the length of time needed for pick-up at each block and the time at the disposal site. The computer program then produces feasible routes and assigns them to trucks. Using the computer to schedule the trucks provides better utilization of existing trucks. Situations can hopefully be avoided where some trucks return half full and others have too much refuse to pick-up.

One of the problems that faces governments at any level is the mass of data that exists which has to be searched, referenced repeatedly, and distributed to various departments and individuals. At City Hall there are minutes of Council meetings to be recorded and distributed. The minutes are entered into a database where the data can be edited and manipulated. The edited version is available for printing, and by using a sophisticated computer program any of the stored information can be retrieved by supplying one or more keywords. The by-laws of the city are also stored on disk and can be retrieved by entering key-words or phrases. Such a system allows by-laws to be checked and searches made for any laws pertaining to a certain subject. It is also used for checking on the wording of by-laws which saves time in composing new by-laws to be passed.

The City Hall computer is a good example of how the computer can be used effectively to serve a large number of people in diversified areas. The systems group at City Hall is continually working to solve the problems of the city.

Information Retrieval in the Insurance Industry

Information Retrieval in the Insurance Industry

An insurance company, by virtue of its business, deals with large numbers of records. Insurance policies are issued to a sizeable percentage of the population, sometimes more than one to each person and usually several to a company. The manual system originally used for storing policy information was cumbersome to work with and resulted in long delays in paying claims. The computer has speeded up and improved the accuracy of many operations.

Policy information may be stored on a disk. This information is usually filed by policy number, and the policy file is basic to the insurance industry. However, what happens when people send in claims or enquiries and do not know or cannot remember the policy number? To facilitate the handling of such enquiries, most companies have a back-up system of policy numbers stored in name sequence. But this also presents problems. There may be several persons with the same surname. People are inconsistent in the way they sign or give their names. For example,

Joseph R. Brown
J.R. Brown
Brown, J. Ralph
and so on.

Thus when enquiring into a file several records may have to be checked in order to discover the correct Mr. Brown. This can be achieved easily by programming the computer to display several alternatives. Obviously, name alone is not sufficient to identify a particular individual. Usually, by also checking the date of birth, identification can be established. A married woman may be registered under her maiden name, which means that a cross reference must be supplied.

'Sound alike' names can cause confusion when the enquiry comes from a phone call. For example,

Rogers   Rodgers
Janes   Jeynes
McDonald   MacDonald

Hyphenated names and other peculiarities in spelling must be considered. For example,

Von-Zuben   Vonzuben   Von Zuben

Hence the problem of building an alphabetic or alpha sequence file that will provide accurate information becomes complex. Stringent rules must be followed in loading the file; for example, any name with a hyphen always has the hyphen deleted and Vonzuben is entered no matter how Mr. Von Zuben signs his name. Flexibility must also be provided in accessing the information so that, for example, if the name Tamblin R. is entered, then

Tamblin, R.J.
Tambling, S.R.
Tamblyn, R.
Tamblynn, N.R.

are all listed. The operator can visually check for the correct name identifying the individual by birth date or other information. The policy number can then be noted. This file is merely for rapidly identifying the correct policy, given vague information, and would probably occupy several disks or a data cell. In a large insurance company it is kept on-line, that is, always available for enquiry from terminals. After the policy number is identified, a separate file containing the full policy information is accessed.

This is only one aspect of the use of the computer in the insurance industry. Accounting applications such as premium payments, payment due notices, policy payments, and so on, also make use of the computer and many statistical reports can be produced by it. The basis for all applications is the policy file, so great care must be taken in establishing it in the first place.

Crime Control

The policeman cruising the city notices a man behaving oddly as he gets into his car. Is it his car or is it stolen? The officer radios headquarters giving the licence number and an operator keys in the number, immediately obtaining the information that, indeed, that licence number is on the list of stolen

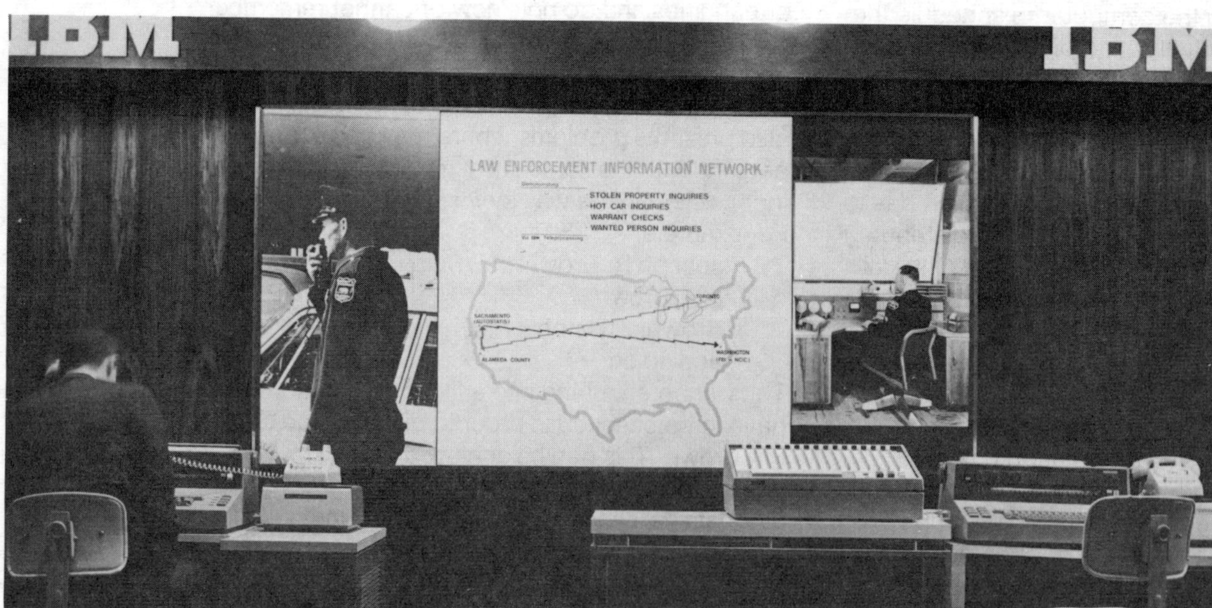

Diagram 16.9 Terminals and computer help the law in controlling crime

vehicles. The policeman takes action. The computer has entered into the field of crime detection.

Files can be kept on wanted persons, lost vehicles and lost property, and can be accessed in a matter of seconds. Not only the list of vehicles stolen in one city can be scanned but also province- or even country-wide lists. Such cities as Vienna, Hamburg, Honolulu, New York and Washington, D.C. already have comprehensive systems. Files kept include

Police Activity
Police Identification
Wanted Persons
Wanted Vehicles

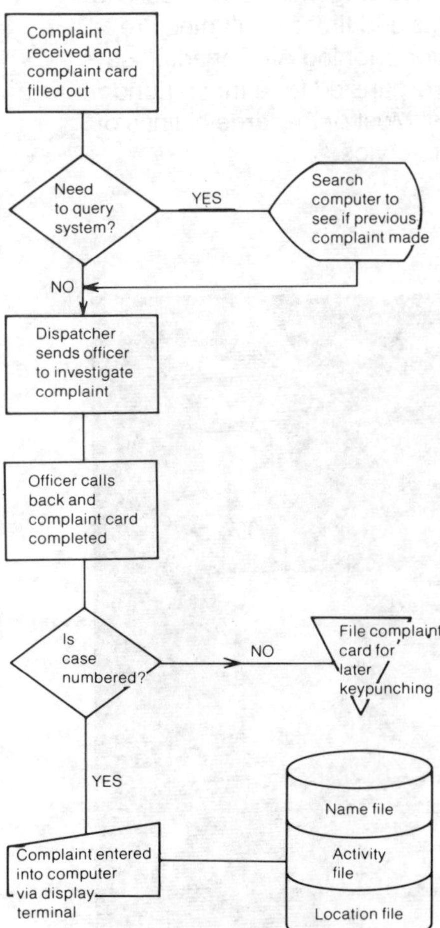

Diagram 16.10 Complaint processing at the Police Department

There are a number of different functions the police perform, one of which is dealing with complaints. Suppose a complaint call is made to a local police station. The operator takes down the necessary details and, if the complaint is serious enough, a visual display terminal is used to enquire into a file kept on disks or data cell to see if a previous complaint has been entered and assigned a number. An officer is then dispatched by radio to the scene, having been given details of the complaint plus any previous complaints. The officer later reports back and the complaint file is updated immediately, or, if it is the first incident, the complaint is given a number and keypunched for entry into the system. As one shift leaves and the next takes over at the station, a report is issued by the computer stating the activity during that shift and reporting on serious activities over the past 24 hours. Activities are filed so that information can be located through enquiry by name, age, offense, date or location of offense.

An identification record file is kept of persons who have been arrested or fingerprinted. Fingerprints are, of course, unique and it is possible to represent the characteristics of each fingerprint by a series of codes and store the information on tape or disk. Records are kept up-to-date on those people on file and are available for court purposes. The file can be used for enquiry and it is also possible to enquire into the files of other cities if the arrested person is from out of town. Reports can be produced from the up-to-date files; for example,

Motor Vehicle Accident Report
Burglary Report
Juvenile Information Report
Missing Persons Report
Stolen Vehicle Report
Robbery Report

With such comprehensive files it is possible to obtain accurate statistics about the incidence of crime, high crime areas, trends in the types of crimes committed, the ages of persons committing crimes, and so on. The police department can then direct their attentions to the trouble spots.

In the United States the Police Department computer frequently issues driver licences and registrations. In Canada this is done by the computer at the Department of Transport.

Airline Reservation System

Booking a trip abroad or just to the next city by air is a very simple matter. Pick up the phone, dial the airline, give the approximate time of departure and within a matter of minutes the seat is booked. The reason a seat can be reserved so quickly is the complex computer system used by the airline. A big central computer with a large amount of disk and tape storage supports many terminals scattered in airports and airline offices throughout the country. The terminals used are cathode ray tube terminals, or typewriter terminals if printed output is required. The reservation system is kept on-line at all times; in other words, the computer is always running a program to service the terminals.

Suppose you wish to travel from Windsor, Ontario to London, England. You phone Air Canada in Windsor where you are informed that you will have to change planes in Toronto. The agent keys in a request for flights from Toronto to London using codes for the cities. A list of available flights is given, together with pertinent information.

```
BA  600  707  FY  20:00  07:45  D,B  820./486.
AC  856  D8   FY  21:00  08:45  D,B  820./486.
```

Since these are evening flights the agent requests afternoon flights from Windsor to Toronto and a suitable combination is chosen. Return flights are discussed and decided upon in the same manner. The agent asks you for your name, home phone number and business phone, and this information is entered via the terminal forming a record for you consisting of your name, phone contact and confirmed flights. "Where would you like to collect your tickets?" You make arrangements for receiving the tickets and the flights and times confirmed are repeated. "Thank you for phoning Air Canada," says the agent, and you are organized for a trip to London in less than ten minutes. Most of the large airlines of the world offer a similar service.

Diagram 16.11 An airline reservation terminal in use at Toronto International Airport

There are many files required to operate an airline system efficiently:

(1) *Passenger File*
Every passenger requesting a flight has a record on file containing such information as

name
home phone
business phone
payment made or date for payment
city code of agent
agent code
date of transaction
flights and times

As a flight is made, the information connected with it is moved to a section of the record for historical data.

(2) *Flight Inventory File*
This is the information about each flight offered by the airline. One part of each record contains information about the entire flight such as

flight number
flight date
equipment code (type of aircraft)
terminating airport
percentage of overbooking allowed

For each leg of the flight detailed information is kept:

boarding airport
departure time
arrival time
indicators for controlling sales, waitlist

If applicable, information by class is held:

seats available
class of service code
seats authorized for sale
indicators for overbooking, limit of sales

Records are kept for up to a year ahead. If you take a look at the flights offered by any of the world's major airlines, you will begin to have some idea of the enormous files involved.

(3) *Flight Schedule File*
Information to answer passenger enquiries is readily available. Since most people know where they want to go and the approximate time, the agent can query the system and obtain such information as the applicable flights, fare information, departure and arrival times, and stops and meals served. If the particular airline does not have a flight to the destination required, then data for other airlines is available. When departure time arrives the departure processing agent requests from the system the number of passengers booked so that meals and/or beverages can be ordered and put on board. He also requests information to control the boarding of passengers and receives full details about the flights:

departure time
flight number
date
departure city
flight information
numbers of passengers, waitlisted passengers
names and destinations, connecting flights of passengers
meal information
connecting flights
other miscellaneous information

Passengers are checked off as they arrive at the departure gate and waitlisted passengers are accepted at the appropriate time. After departure the agent updates the appropriate files with the actual flight and passenger information: no shows, missed connections, number boarded, departure time, and so on.

Because of the complexity of such a system, control programs keep tight control on the operation of the system. For example, indicators must be set to stop agents booking a flight that is already full, information must be transferred to historical rather than current status when a flight takes off, passengers failing to collect and pay for tickets must be deleted or alerted and waitlisted passengers must be informed as seats become available.

Since total information is kept about flights and passengers, statistics about the running of the airline are a valuable by product of a reservation system.

Banking

The job of the bank teller has certainly changed over the past few years. All the charter banks in Canada and many other banking institutions in Canada and the rest of the world now have installed sophisticated computer equipment to take care of most banking transactions. Now, when you ask such questions as: "What is the balance in my chequing account?", the teller types in your account number on a typewriter-like keyboard and within seconds he/she checks that you are the owner of that account and tells you your balance.

The computer systems used vary from bank to bank but all have a central computer installed or access to part of a central computer with the usual supply of disks and tapes, a printer and a card reader. Also, there are a varying number of terminals with the capability of accessing the system. There are terminals with keyboard entry through which the teller can make enquiries and process transactions. These terminals can usually update pass books which are slotted in at the top. They may also have a video display screen. One terminal is usually shared by two tellers. Other terminals may be available in the bank to provide printed output of reports pertaining to that bank from the central computer. The 'latest' in bank terminals is the 'do it yourself' banking terminal found installed on the outside walls of many banks. It is sometimes called a bankette. Let us take a look at what happens in the bank when you conduct your business with the teller, and outside when you 'do it yourself'.

Suppose you go to your local bank to withdraw some money from your account. First you hand the cheque or withdrawal slip to the teller. The teller identifies the transaction on the keyboard either by a special key or a particular code. Your pass book is now placed in the slot. Your account number, date of the last transaction, the balance and the new transaction are entered followed by the indication for end of transaction (a special key or code). The information is transmitted to the computer. The program in the computer will find the customer record that matches the account number. The customer records are stored on a disk so that they can be rapidly located. Any transactions after the last balance are transmitted back to the terminal to update the pass book, followed by the new transaction and the new calculated balance. The customer record is also updated to reflect the last transaction and updated balance. The transaction data is recorded on an electronic journal or current transaction file, probably another disk file. The customer is now handed the amount of money requested, his/her pass book, and, with a smile from the teller, is ready to leave two or three minutes later.

Should the computer system fail for some reason, there is often an intermediary unit called a controller or control unit present which is capable of storing the data received from several terminals on a mini disk or diskette. When the computing system is again functioning, then the information temporarily stored on the mini disk is transmitted to the system. During the temporary failure your pass book cannot be updated or reflect the latest transaction, but the customer file is updated as soon as the system is again fully operational.

Suppose you have left it too late to go to the bank one evening and need some cash before the next day. There is a terminal installed on the outside wall of a bank near you, a branch of the bank at which you have an account. It does not have to be at the branch that you normally deal with. If you are authorized to use these terminals you will have received a personal ID (identification) card from the bank. The card has a magnetic stripe on it that contains your account information. This stripe is readable by the terminal, not by people.

First you insert your ID card in the slot provided, having first ascertained that the terminal is OPEN; that is, it is not disabled. A panel will slide up exposing a keyboard with a number of keys and a small display panel. The display panel shows a message asking you to

ENTER YOUR PERSONAL ID

This you do using the numbered keys provided. You must know your ID since you cannot read it off the ID card!

The terminal displays

SELECT TRANSACTION

You choose and press the appropriate key, namely one saying

WITHDRAW CASH

Your interaction with the terminal continues as follows:

Terminal Display	*Your Response*
SELECT ACCOUNT	press FROM CHEQUING key.
ENTER AMOUNT	key in $50.00 (or required amount)
$50.00	press PROCEED key (or CORRECTION key if you have keyed in the wrong amount)

The terminal now transmits all this information to the central computer. Your record is checked—the ID on your card must match the ID you keyed in, and of course you must have money in the account to be withdrawn. The money is counted out and checked. You remove your ID card and the money, which projects out in a cash dispensing slot. If you loose your card and somebody else tries to use it, the computer can stop all processing against your card if you report the loss. The terminal does some police work on the side!

Computerization of banking has many advantages and of course some disadvantages. It can be very annoying to go into the bank and discover that the computer is not working—a power cut can really foul up computers! There is no way the teller can give you your current balance since manual records are seldom kept and the latest print-out of all accounts may not be up-to-date and is time consuming to search through.

The advantages fortunately out number the disadvantages. It is very useful to be able to withdraw money any time of the day or night. Transactions in the bank are speeded up and human error greatly reduced since the computer can perform all arithmetic. Your account is kept up-to-date and as terminal networks increase you will be able to deposit and withdraw money at any branch of your bank without a phone call to see if you are solvent. This could be very useful to those of us who run out of cash on holidays. The auditing and balancing functions that are time consuming and tedious can be automated, speeded up and performed with increased accuracy.

Are we moving towards a cashless society? Will we soon pay all our bills at the bank? Our accounts could be debited and the hydro, phone and oil company accounts credited. The cashless society makes an interesting subject for discussion.

Diagram 16.12 **Updating an account by computer.**

Diagram 16.13 **"Bankette" terminal**

Typesetting

Publishing companies are making use of the versatility of the computer, particularly its ability to accept a variety of input. This book was typeset with the aid of a computer.

One of the most tedious jobs associated with publishing is preparing the edited manuscript for printing. Using a traditional method, the typesetter selects each individual metal character from a typecase, and assembles the characters "backwards" in a case, surrounded by pieces of metal to take up the spaces. From these galleys, galley proofs—sheets of text—are printed. The galley proofs are used to proofread the text and to do a paste-up of the final book.

There is now available a variety of new methods for preparing the text; some of which utilize the computer. One such method is to type the manuscript and various typesetting commands on what appears to be a regular typewriter. The typewriter is connected to either a paper tape or

Diagram 16.14 **The manuscript for this book and various typesetting commands typed onto O.C.R. (Optical Character Reader) sheets**

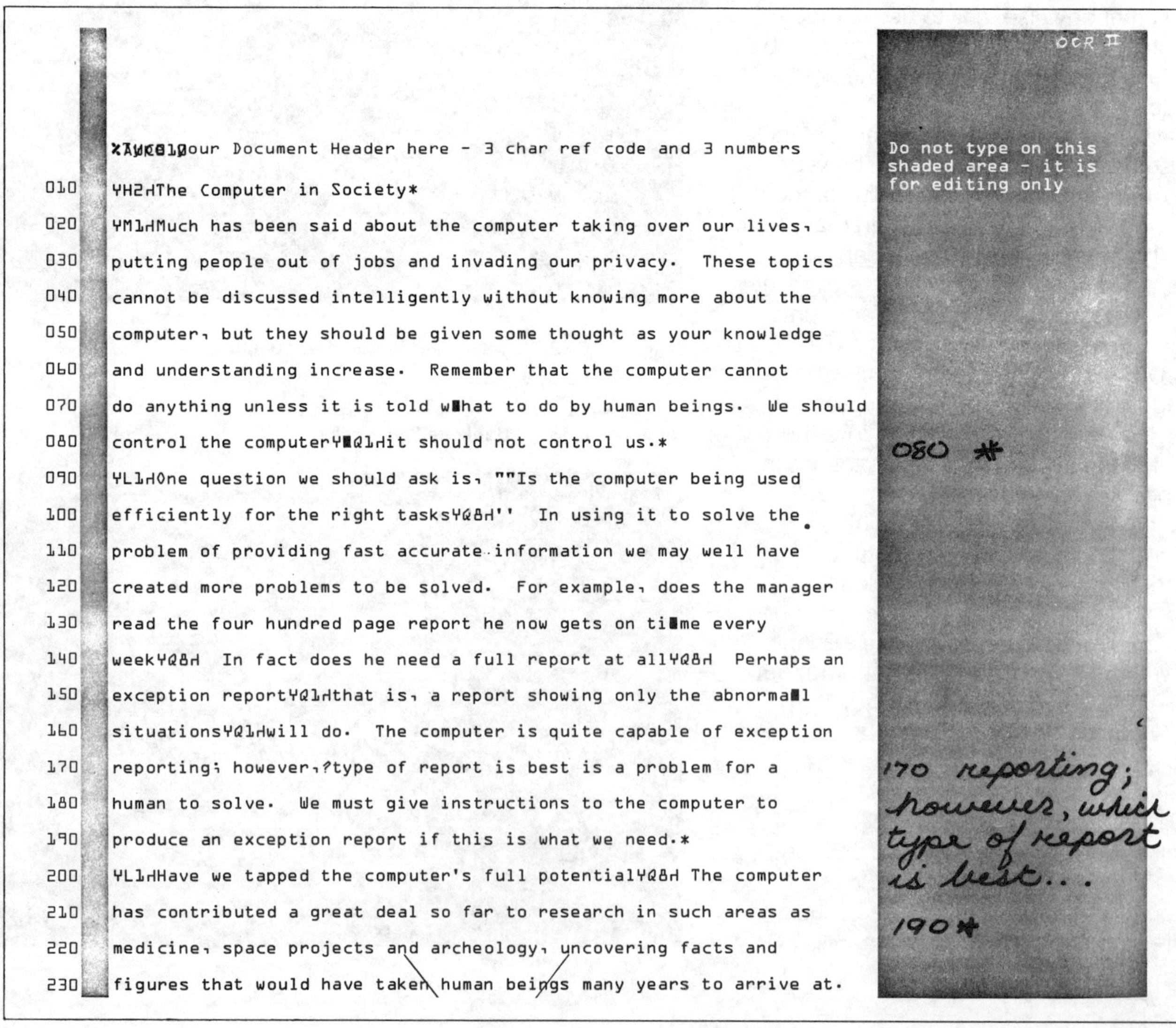

```
    %AYC010our Document Header here - 3 char ref code and 3 numbers
010 YH2HThe Computer in Society*
020 YM1HMuch has been said about the computer taking over our lives,
030 putting people out of jobs and invading our privacy.  These topics
040 cannot be discussed intelligently without knowing more about the
050 computer, but they should be given some thought as your knowledge
060 and understanding increase.  Remember that the computer cannot
070 do anything unless it is told w■hat to do by human beings.  We should
080 control the computerY■Q1Hit should not control us.*
090 YL1HOne question we should ask is, ""Is the computer being used
100 efficiently for the right tasksYQ8H''  In using it to solve the
110 problem of providing fast accurate information we may well have
120 created more problems to be solved.  For example, does the manager
130 read the four hundred page report he now gets on ti■me every
140 weekYQ8H  In fact does he need a full report at allYQ8H  Perhaps an
150 exception reportYQ1Hthat is, a report showing only the abnorma■l
160 situationsYQ1Hwill do.  The computer is quite capable of exception
170 reporting; however,?type of report is best is a problem for a
180 human to solve.  We must give instructions to the computer to
190 produce an exception report if this is what we need.*
200 YL1HHave we tapped the computer's full potentialYQ8H The computer
210 has contributed a great deal so far to research in such areas as
220 medicine, space projects and archeology, uncovering facts and
230 figures that would have taken human beings many years to arrive at.
```

magnetic tape device. The tape then forms input to the computer. Alternately, the manuscript can be typed on special sheets, and transformed to tape by a scanning device (Optical Character Reader), which is an input unit to the computer.

Once the text is in computer readable form it can be stored on a disk as a series of files. The stored information is direct input to a photocomposition system. Special disks called typemasters provide a tremendous variety of letterforms. Under computer control these typemasters spin at approximately 2400 r.p.m., and the required characters are exposed to photosensitive film or paper to produce galley proofs.

The text will be left-justified, that is, lined up with every line on the left starting at the same place. Sometimes it will be right-justified as well, as in newspapers, in which case the computer will calculate how many letter spaces can be fitted in one line, and insert the correct number of characters for that line. Often, however, the right hand side is left ''ragged'' as, for example, in this text. The words can be correctly hyphenated, using a special routine which follows logical rules. There is a file of some 300 000 words which are exceptions to the logical rules, and this is referred to first. The computer can even handle hyphenation of English and French words!

The galleys will be carefully scanned by the editor and author before the book is printed. The disk files are indexed and can be accessed for correction by using a video display terminal. The correction process is assisted by the use of special keys on the typewriter for particular functions such as insert, replace and delete. The delete function deliberately requires two keys to be depressed to provide a safety factor.

Once the galley proofs are finally corrected, a clean galley proof of the text may be produced. This is combined in a paste-up with the photographs and diagrams, and the book is printed from plates made from film of the paste-up.

Other printed materials such as catalogues and directories are published with the help of the computer. The information is stored on disk, and after being corrected and updated, a new edition can be produced. The computer provides a flexible tool for the publishing industry.

Diagram 16.15 Paper tape used in controlling photocomposition systems.

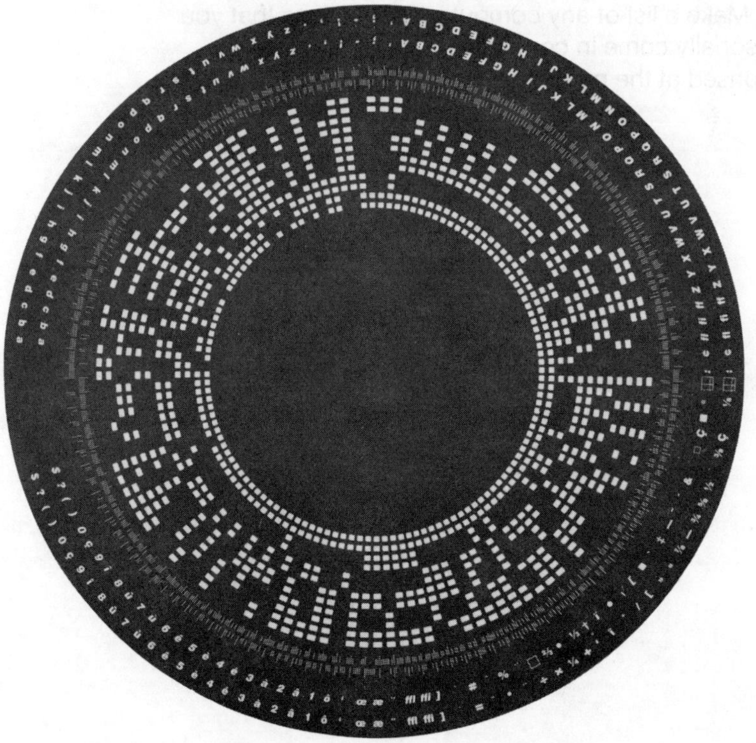

Diagram 16.16 Typemaster

Projects

(1) Research a computer application that is not dealt with in the text (in any chapter) and give a 15-minute presentation to the rest of the class. Use your resource centre, local library, newspapers and magazine articles to find information.

(2) Without the computer we could not have put a man on the moon—so what. Discuss.

(3) Make up an imaginary conversation between Mr. Smith, who cannot see how a computer can help him solve his 'paper pollution' problem (customer record keeping, billing, accounts receivable, and so on), and Mr. Jones, who enthusiastically believes it can.

(4) What effect would a three-hour power cut have on the sixteen computer applications mentioned at the beginning of the chapter? Which, if any, would require auxiliary power to provide back-up during such an emergency?

(5) Which computer application that you have read about do you consider has contributed the most towards improving the world we live in. Give reasons.

(6) Make a list of any computer applications that you personally come in contact with. (You may be surprised at the number!)

17 Techniques For Solving Complex Problems

Simulation

Before a commercial airline pilot flies an actual aircraft with live passengers, he spends many hours at a simulator. This is a very intricate machine using a computer, among other things, to check out the pilot's reaction to 'what if' situations. What if engine number one fails? What happens to the aircraft? What must the pilot do? In what sequence must he respond? The simulator can indicate exactly what will happen when the engine fails. As the pilot sits at the controls he views his surroundings just as they might be 25 000 feet up. He feels the craft tip as the engine fails, he hears warning buzzers and the different sound now being emitted by the engines, he sees the warning lights flash. He learns to react immediately, in correct sequence, to the emergency. If he does *not* react correctly, once again the simulator responds and the student pilot is vividly reminded of the consequences. All this is being achieved with no risk to man or aircraft.

Simulation of a project or situation and the ability to answer the 'what if' question without actually experiencing the event is a very valuable tool. Suppose city planners decide to develop a new subdivision. What form should it take? Naturally there will be houses, shops, apartments, and schools. Electricity, gas, water and other facilities will be needed. Will there be enough people to require a hospital? What transportation will be required? What effect will building highrise apartments, as opposed to 3- or 4-story units, have on transportation, school requirements, sewage, and so on? The effects can be simulated. There will be a larger number of people in a smaller area if high-rise apartments are built, and consequently more schools, hospital facilities, water, power, transportation, and so on, will be needed. Will the roads support the increase in traffic? This tool for planning, if properly used, means that new developments should be practical and suitable places to live. However, although the computer can simulate the traffic problems, the facility requirements, the population density, and so on, it is incapable of checking to see if the subdivision will be pleasing to the eye. Neither does it make the decision as to what will *actually* be built. It merely produces statistics enabling us to make practical decisions to improve our living conditions. We still have the capability of ignoring the sterile practical statistics in favor of a beautiful but impractical solution. Obviously we need a combination solution giving us the best of both worlds.

Simulation

An example of simulation now widely used in schools and colleges is in timetabling. The process for doing this is explained in Chapter 16. Trial runs are, in fact, simulations. 'What if', for example, in a college timetable English 101 is moved to 4 o'clock each day? We may find that, although no conflicts occur, there are many students with two hours to spare most afternoons waiting for their English class. This is not very acceptable to the student population. Of the ten sections for History, there are four that quickly fill up while others remain almost empty. This is a situation that needs checking out on the master timetable. All these situations can be corrected after the simulations are run until an optimum solution is obtained.

The space voyages involve countless simulations. Minute adjustments in the trajectory of a spaceship may be needed. Their effect must be calculated before they are made. As the actual voyages are made we are able to watch a simulation. The simulated model is produced by a computer with a cathode ray tube displaying the results, which are then relayed via television.

The technique of simulation is being increasingly used in medical schools in the training of doctors. Patients are simulated by a computer program. Supposing a real patient enters the emergency department of a hospital. A doctor examines the patient and notes certain obvious symptoms—pulse, bleeding, state of breathing, swellings, bruises, breaks, colour of skin and so on. Then he takes action—stops the bleeding, orders an x-ray, takes samples for tests and so on. Further action may be taken when x-ray results are seen, blood pressure checked or the results of tests are available.

All of these things can be simulated by the computer with time lapses built in if they are significant. A student can learn all about the patient via a display terminal. Sophisticated programs control audio visual equipment allowing students to view x-rays and hear heart beats. If a student does not react correctly to the symptoms new symptoms may appear on the screen. If he is really slow in an emergency situation or makes the wrong diagnosis his simulated patient may die! The computer can simulate many more situations than can be seen by the average student during his stint in an emergency ward. These patient simulations are of course, only part of a doctor's training. There is also a great deal of practical work with live patients!

Special languages have been produced for using the computer for simulation. In many cases the language applies to a specialized class of simulations. It is more difficult to produce a generalized language since the applications are so diversified. However, when you think about it there are many similarities between what appear to be very different applications. Take, for example, airline reservations and a supermarket. Both are selling something (a seat on a plane or an item stocked). Both must predict future requirements, adjust prices and expenditures to try and maintain a profit margin, and so on. There is a parallel between boarding a plane and entering a supermarket—frequency, number of entrances, and so on. The languages developed allow the simulation to be done by people who are neither computer experts nor programmers. They can define what they need in either English terms or the jargon of their industry.

Some of the simulations made are a little frightening—world population and air pollution, to name two. Hopefully we shall use the simulation capabilities of the computer to make the world a better place in which to live. The computer can tell us 'what if' and we can decide what to do.

Computer Assisted Instruction

One of the frustrations experienced by a teacher, particularly in a junior school, is the lack of time to help students who have been absent or who need extra help on a specific topic. No two students learn at the same rate, and trying to keep all 30 or 35 students moving along at the same pace in Mathematics for example, is impossible. Here the computer can help. Suppose a student has trouble in simple addition. Once he understands how to do simple addition, he requires plenty of practice until he has mastered the rules and can come up with the answer in a reasonable time. It is possible to write a computer program to provide this practice. The student can sit down at a terminal—a typewriter or a visual display terminal—and work through practice problems at his own pace.

The following could be a segment from such a program:

Please type your name
□ John

If you wish to stop, type STOP
9 + 20
□ 29

Good!
14 + 27
□ 44
No that isn't right—try again
□ 41

Good!
13 + 54
□ 77
No that isn't right—try again
□ 66

Still not right—the answer should be 67
41 + 35
□ STOP

So far John you have got 24 out of 30 questions correct.
Keep trying

This is a very simple drill and practice example of Computer Assisted Instruction or CAI. Notice the English used is minimal and simple. When CAI programs are constructed it is necessary to take into account the age of the students and how much they can already understand. The numbers presented in this segment can be restricted to below 100. All John's responses can be kept for the teacher to analyze later. John is given a summary of his efforts to date—he could be shown the result of today's practice or an accumulation over a period of time. Computer assisted instruction lends itself particularly to subjects where drill and practice are needed—Mathematics, English Grammer, Physics.

Special computer languages have been developed to help in preparing course material. The languages are such that the preparation of courses can be done by non-programmers. Computer experts and manufacturers can provide hardware and language capabilities to help the educators. The course material should be written, or at least designed, by educators, *not* by computer personnel. Teachers are the people who know what they want students to learn, to what depth it should be taken, the degree of difficulty required for the problems, and so on.

CAI course material needs a great deal of testing before it can be considered of value to a teacher. Ambiguities must be ironed out. If a teacher is in the classroom, an ambiguous question can be rephrased immediately. An ambiguity in CAI, however, may cause a student at a terminal to puzzle over the meaning for a long time with nobody to ask.

All situations of students providing wrong or unexpected answers must be covered. For example, suppose you were asked for the capital of Japan and replied TOKIO—you have a spelling mistake but had you spoken the answer, it would have been correct. A reply such as

'Yes that is correct but it is spelled TOKYO'

would save the situation. Thus many answers must be anticipated. Subjects such as Mathematics tend to be easier to program since there is only one answer to such questions as 12 + 13!

Diagram 17.1 Young student learning arithmetic with the help of the computer

A good teacher usually can anticipate the types of errors students will make and can have the computer respond just as he might. For example, suppose the question was

What is the capital of Canada?
Correct Answer: OTTAWA
Anticipated wrong answers: OTAWA
OTTOWA
TORONTO

By branching to specific replies for each answer the teacher can accept 'near misses' and explain some incorrect answers:

To the student's reply OTTAWA the program would reply

GOOD

To the student's reply OTAWA and OTTOWA, the program would reply

Yes—but it is spelled OTTAWA

To the student's reply TORONTO, the program would reply

No—this is the capital of the province of Ontario—try again

With this type of dialogue to be composed for each question, and the necessity of keeping track of many students using the system, CAI becomes a complex program. It can take anything up to 200 hours of teacher's time to compose one hour of work for the students. Many teachers do not have that sort of time to spare. People are continually working to improve this time ratio. Why bother? One advantage, of course, is that when it is completed and tested, the course or course segments can be used by countless numbers of students. Also, it is a method of helping people who have little chance of getting the help any other way. As well, the computer is an unemotional 'teacher'. It does not shout at you, laugh or react to your temper. It does not rush you or slow you down, but allows you to proceed at your own rate.

Many subjects do not lend themselves to CAI, particularly those subjects involving a great deal of dialogue or opinion. To have a terminal produce masses of information on a topic is a waste of time—a book on the subject would be much more practical. A combination can be achieved by requiring the student to study certain books before proceeding to the next section of the computer program.

Remember we are talking of computer *assisted* instruction. There are definite limits to what the computer can be used for and nothing will replace a good teacher in the classroom and the human relationship between students and teacher.

Sensor-Based Systems

In all the applications we have studied, the computer concerned has been dealing with data consisting of numbers or characters and manipulating them—in fact we have seen that all the characters can be represented as digits. We have been dealing with digital computers. The computer can also be used to measure and control continuous physical quantities. The computer would then be dealing with analog data gathered from what is termed the real world.

Analog data can be defined as data represented in a continuous form. An analog computer can measure heat, light, sound and other physical quantities and respond accordingly. The measurement is achieved by duplicating the action by mechanical or electrical means. For example, heat can be measured using a thermometer, the rise and fall of mercury measuring heat by indicating a temperature. The height of mercury is analogous to the amount of heat.

In many cases analog computers are built for specific applications as, for example, in the production control of chemicals or the measurement of earthquakes. It is often desirable to have a combination of analog and digital capability in the same system. Such a system is called a sensor-based system, or sometimes event driven system. The input to the system is measurements taken from the real world, translated to the ones and zeros the digital computer can use in calculations. The digital computer is said to have a sensor-based front end. Sensor-based systems are used in traffic control, control of automatic welders, process control in the pulp and paper industry, lab automation, atomic energy control, pollution control, and many other areas.

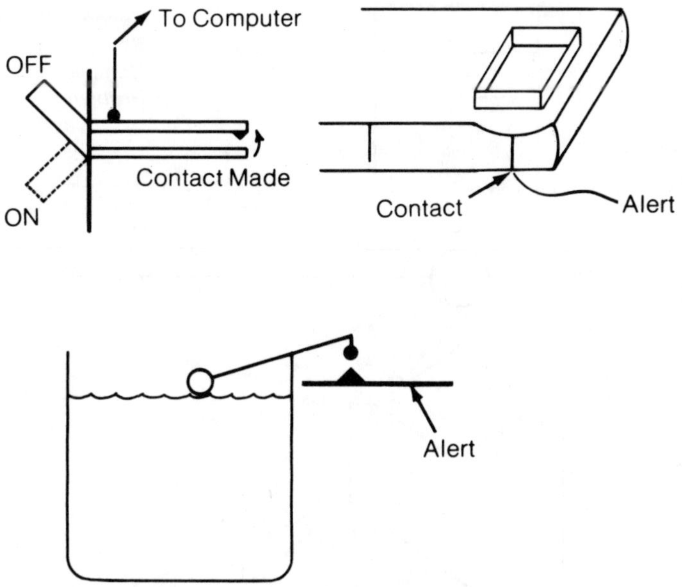

Diagram 17.2

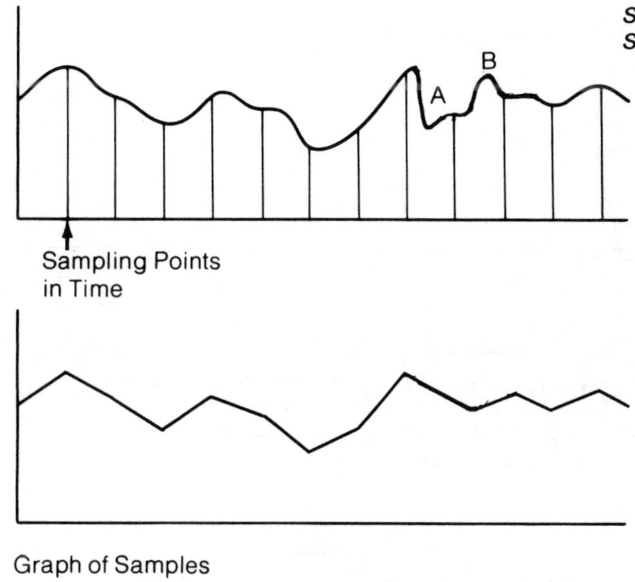

Diagram 17.3

The front end may immediately convert certain conditions to digital information: For example, is a switch on or off, has an item reached the end of a conveyor belt, is a vessel full or not (see diagram 17.2)? In these cases the information is available to the computer as a one or a zero and action can be taken according to the program.

Other front ends may sample voltages that are proportional to some physical circumstances, for example, temperature or pressure. The interval between samplings can be altered according to the degree of accuracy required. The voltages are converted to digital form and can be analyzed, graphed or used in calculations as required. In diagram 17.3 the sampling may not be adequate since the dip at A and the peak at B are not reflected in the graph formed.

As well as accepting input, the front end of the system can produce output. Switches can be turned on or off, current can be allowed to flow or be restricted, pressure can be increased or decreased, the mix of certain chemicals can be regulated, and so on.

Sensor-based systems usually run continually since they have one job as opposed to the stream of jobs performed by a digital computer. Frequently back-up systems are required because of the critical jobs performed. They are required to be extremely reliable under the most rugged circumstances since they are often exposed to extremes of heat and cold, and to damp and dirt.

Timing is very important. If a digital computer is an hour behind producing the payroll, it is a nuisance but not a disaster. If a sensor-based computer fails to react immediately to alerts, there could be explosions or other serious consequences.

Sensor-based systems are widely used in many industries but their potential is largely untapped and it is expected that their use will grow tremendously in the next decade.

Structured Programming

A technique called structured programming which has been in existence for a number of years is becoming increasingly popular in computer installations. Its increasing popularity probably relates to the increasing cost of writing and maintaining programs. Although the cost of computer hardware has been steadily decreasing the cost of programming and producing software has

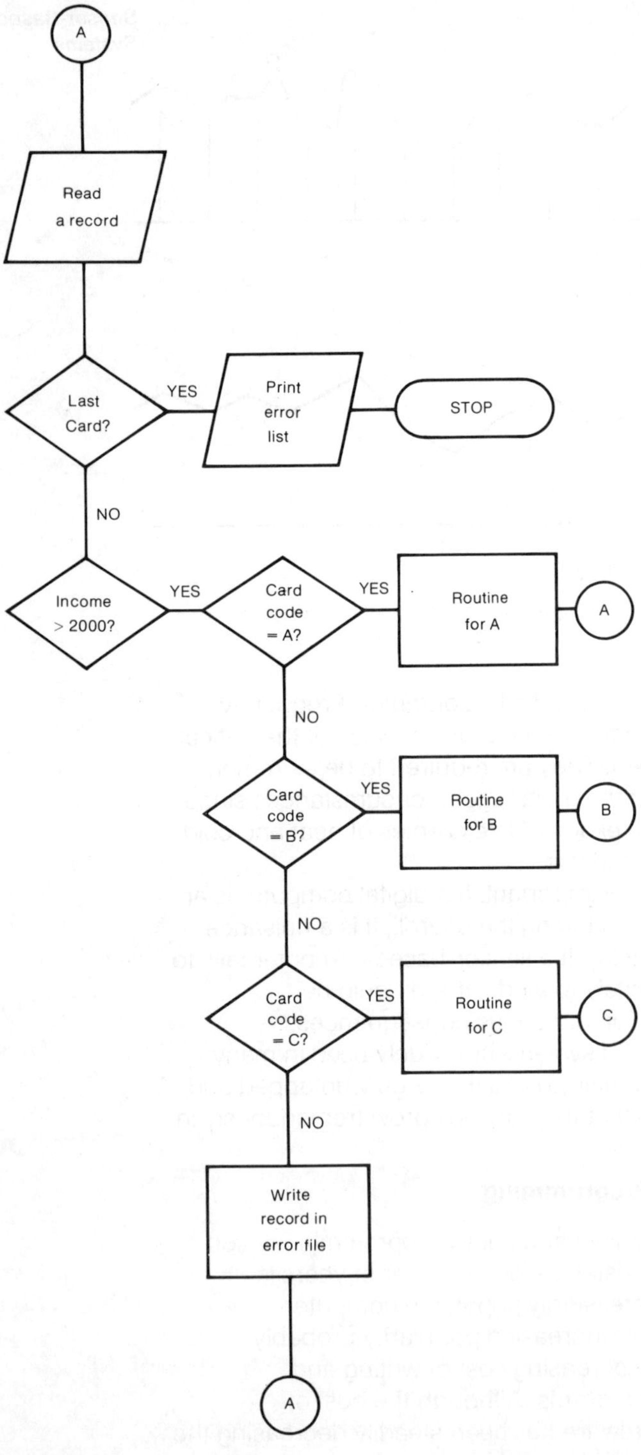

Diagram 17.4 Traditional flowchart: tax calculation according to province

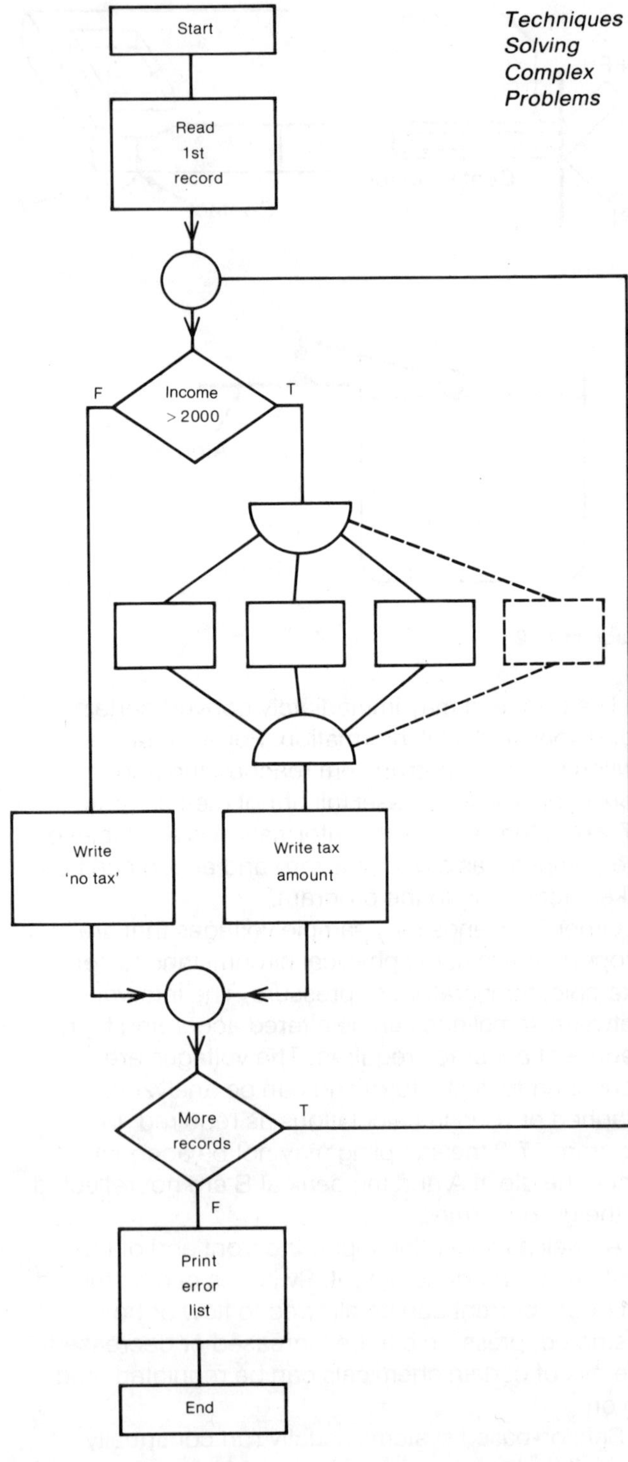

Diagram 17.5 Structured flowchart: tax calculation according to province

been steadily increasing, mainly because of the increase in the salaries paid to programmers and analysts. The complexity of the programs has increased and therefore the cost of maintaining them is steadily rising since it directly relates to people costs. Small sophisticated programs are no longer required since the cost of main storage and rapidly accessed direct access storage is declining. The emphasis has switched to the production of error free, easily maintained programs since maintenance and correction of errors are where the high costs occur.

Some of the problems that could exist in a typical installation are:

– flowcharts and programs which don't really match. This could be due to changes in the programs that were not correspondingly made in the flowchart.

– programs that work but are badly organized, for example overlapping branching, insufficient comments, meaningless labels.

– the changing of one label in a program without all references to it being found and changed.

– sophisticated, but not easily understood programs, which were written by a programmer who has now left the company.

All of these problems make the task of program maintenance time consuming and very costly. Programming has grown up as an art when it really should be a science!

Structured programming is an attempt at a scientific approach to programming in that it requires the programmer to stick to a number of simple rules making his/her programs easier to write without bugs, easier to follow and self-documenting to a large extent and therefore easier and less costly to maintain. The following is a list of the main rules to be followed in writing a structured program:

(1) use a limited number of statement types
(2) eliminate GO TO statements (to discourage poor branching techniques)
(3) code only one segment per page
(4) use one entry at the top of the page and one exit at the bottom
(5) use indentation and paragraphing to improve readability
(6) use meaningful names for variables and labels.

Obviously the so-called rules might have to be bent a little to adapt the technique to a specific, already existing programming language. Some languages have had language words added (plus the appropriate code added to the translator) to allow the structured programming techniques to be used. Diagrams 17.4 and 17.5 show the same problem flowcharted using standard flowcharting and structured programming flowcharting.

Structured programming uses three basic building blocks which relate directly to sections of the flowchart.

(1) IFTHENELSE Statement

Pronounced IF THEN ELSE, this statement is pseudocode; that is, it does not appear in any language although its equivalent will be found in most high level languages. For example:

IF CARD CODE IS 'A' **THEN**
    ADD 1 TO THE A-CARD TOTAL
ELSE ADD 1 TO THE X-CARD TOTAL
ENDIF

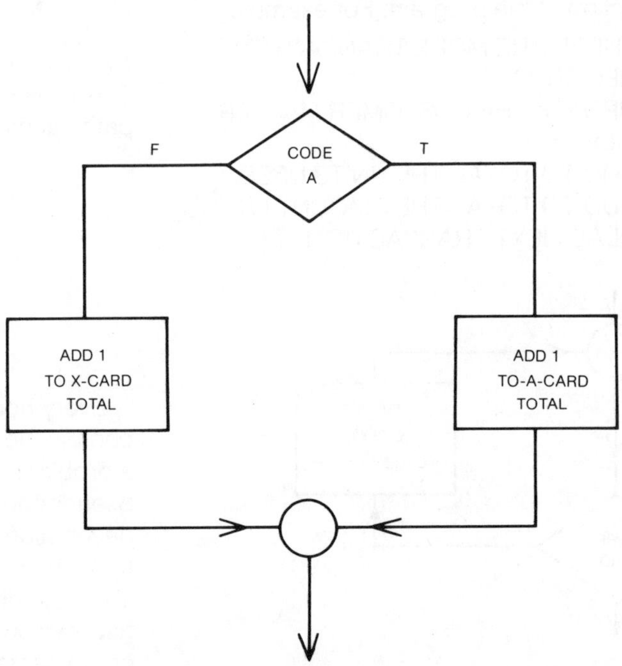

Diagram 17.6 **Flowchart: IFTHENELSE**

(2) *SEQUENCE*
This statement indicates a number of functions to be performed one after the other. For example:

CALL ROUTINE TO UPDATE TRANSACTION FILE
CALL ROUTINE TO UPDATE CUSTOMER FILE

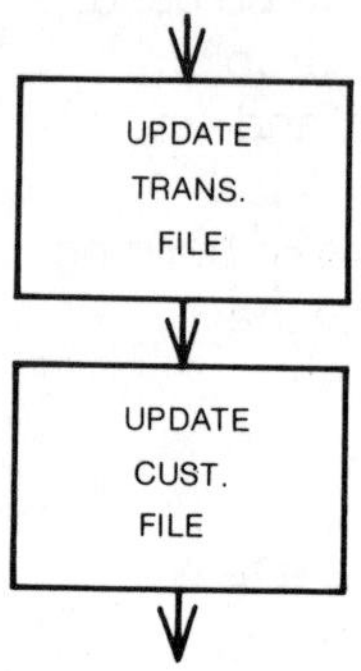

Diagram 17.7 Flowchart: SEQUENCE

(3) *DOWHILE*
Pronounced DO WHILE, this statement says DO *the following functions WHILE a certain condition is true—otherwise continue with the next function or statement.* This provides a facility for looping and repeating a section of the program. For example:

DOWHILE THERE ARE MORE TRANSACTION RECORDS
UPDATE THE CUSTOMER MASTER FILE
ADD TO TOTAL THE UNITS USED
ADD TO TOTAL THE AMOUNT OWING
READ NEXT TRANSACTION
ENDDO

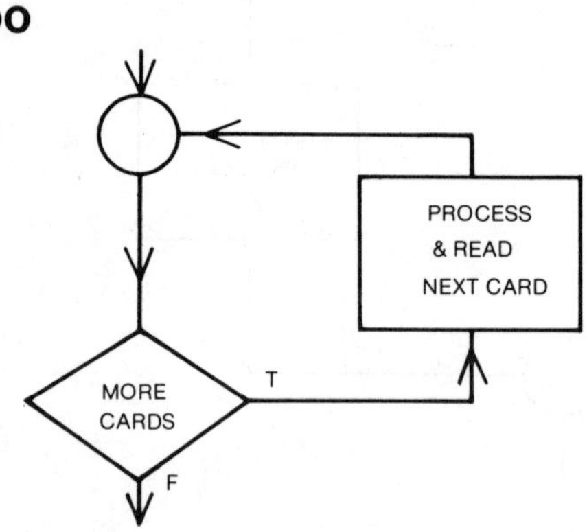

Diagram 17.8 Flowchart: DOWHILE

You will notice that the number of flowchart symbols has been reduced to three so far, and they are often referred to as **nodes**.

Nodes

Function or Process Node
This indicates that a function, subroutine or some processing is to be performed; that is, some data processing to take place.

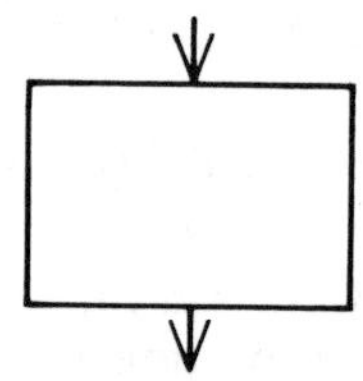

Predicate or Decision Node
Data is to be tested resulting in a true or false condition. The result of the test influences the logical path to be followed.

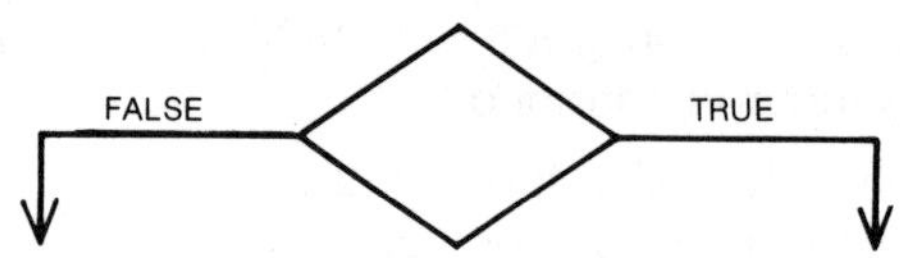

Connector Node
This is merely a junction which always has two entry paths and one exit.

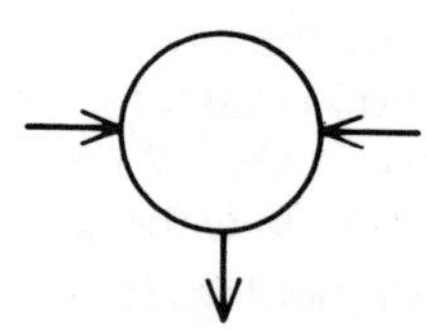

Every node has a path through it, and a combination of these nodes will completely describe a problem, preparing it to be translated into pseudocode. The pseudocode provides an English description of the problem employing some standard terms such as DOWHILE and IFTHENELSE, but it is still readable to a non programmer. Then the pseudocode can be translated into the code of the computer langauge to be used. Following is pseudocode for Diagrams 17.3 and 17.4.

Pseudocode - Traditional:

```
START: Read a record
       IF end of file GO TO FIN
       IF income is greater than 2000 GO TO TAX
       Otherwise write 'no tax' on file
       GO TO START
TAX:   IF card code is A GO TO CALCA
       IF card code is B GO TO CALCB
       IF card code is C GO TO CALCC
       —
       —
       —
       Otherwise write record in error file

       GO TO START
CALCA: Tax calculation for province A
       GO TO START
CALCB: Tax calculation for province B
       GO TO START
CALCC: Tax calculation for province C
       GO TO START
FIN:   Print error list
       End of program.
```

Pseudocode - Structured

```
Read the first record
DOWHILE there are more records
    IF income is greater than 2000 THEN
    CASENTRY   card code
        CASE A
            Routine for province A
        CASE B
            Routine for province B
        CASE C
            Routine for province C
            —
            —
            —
        CASE OTHER
            Write record in error file
    END CASE
    Write tax amount on file
    ELSE write on file no tax to be paid
ENDDO when all records have been read
    Print error list
    End the program
```

Do we really need to flowchart? Well, that is a debateable point. The concensus of opinion seems to be that it still provides a pictorial view of the problem, organizes thoughts and ideas and is useful as part of the documentation, particularly for a complex program. However, flowcharts for very large programs tend to get out of hand. Traditional programming is still very much alive and well, since it is easier to learn for a beginner who can then graduate to the more formal structured flowcharting for structured programming.

Let us examine a more complex program where we have nested IFTHENELSE functions. The problem is to check for card codes A, B and C, adding 1 to appropriate counters, and counting the remaining cards.

Pseudocode:

IF CARD CODE IS 'A' **THEN** ADD 1 TO COUNTER A
ELSE IF CARD CODE IS 'B' **THEN** ADD 1 TO COUNTER B
    ELSE IF CARD CODE IS 'C' **THEN** ADD 1 TO COUNTER C
        ELSE ADD 1 TO COUNTER X
        ENDIF
    ENDIF
ENDIF

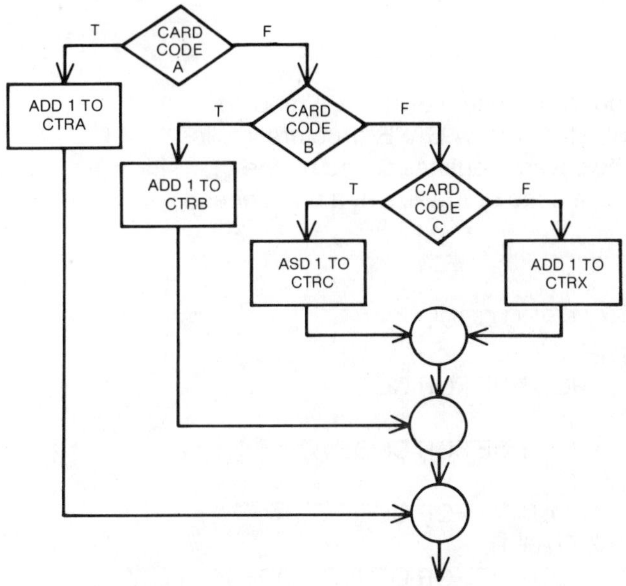

Diagram 17.9

Obviously this could get very tedious if there were many codes to be tested. To avoid this we use the **CASE** structure.

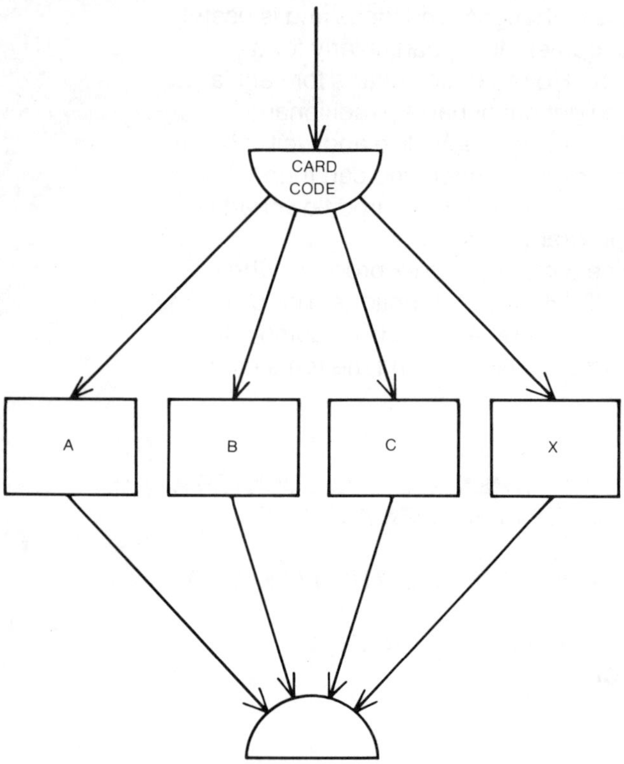

Diagram 17.10

We have introduced another flowchart symbol to indicate a CASE structure. A CASE structure implies that there will be several routines based on the results of testing a code or the size of a number and so on.

Psuedocode:

```
CASENTRY CARD CODE
    CASE A
        ROUTINE FOR CODE A
    CASE B
        ROUTINE FOR CODE B
    CASE C
        ROUTINE FOR CODE C
    CASE OTHER
        ROUTINE FOR OTHER CODES
ENDCASE
```

In the translation of the pseudocode for the CASE structure to a high level programming language it is sometimes necessary to use a GOTO statement because the languages do not have a true CASE structure implemented. It is however, a very restricted use of the GOTO.

In summary, structured programming is an attempt to finalize and improve the science of programming. It cannot consist of a rigid set of rules because there must be integration with existing software, but it should provide guidelines for more efficient programming so that programmers can achieve a higher level of productivity.

Projects

(1) Write a short paper on an application which uses a sensor-based system.

(2) What advantages does CAI have over traditional classroom teaching? What are its disadvantages?

(3) "CAI is a dangerous weapon, since mass education can be controlled centrally." Discuss.

(4) Write a short paper on an application that uses a simulation technique.

18 Living With Computers

There are many controversial subjects associated with computers and we will take a brief look at some of them.

Can Computers Think?

Take a look at the dictionary definition of the word think. Many definitions are given depending upon the context: (1) consider, be of opinion, (2) exercise the mind otherwise than by passive reception of another's ideas.

Has the computer an opinion of its own? Other chapters in the book have described in a fair amount of detail how the computer works and mentioned its limitations and capabilities. It should be obvious that any 'opinion' the computer expresses is merely a logical deduction based on information it has received. It makes the deduction because it has been given instructions that lead it to do so. Who is really doing the thinking?

Can the computer answer any questions posed to it (that is, exercise its 'mind')? A definite no is the answer to that one. The only way a computer can answer questions is to be programmed to recognize the question and produce the answers accordingly. Such programming is required when course material is prepared for computer assisted instruction (see Chapter 17). Can the computer 'exercise its mind' in any way? This is debatable. Logic ability is often confused with thinking ability. It is probably true to say that logic ability is a part of thinking ability. Yes, the computer is extremely logical and it is our ability to be illogical when necessary that makes us very different from a computer. The computer will always make the same decision given the same set of circumstances. Computer dating is a good example. You may be paired with somebody who has the same interests, is the right age, intelligence, shape and size, but when you meet face to face that is the end of everything. She thinks he looks terrible and he thinks she has an awful squeaky voice! All circumstances were great for the match but the human element had a couple of illogical thoughts.

Unfortunately many people feel that computers can think. This is a potentially dangerous situation implying that 1984 will become reality. Computers play a very important part in many areas but they do not have the ability to weigh one circumstance against another, to consider human emotions when making a decision, to decide to stop work for an hour and go for a walk because it is a beautiful day.

It is possible, however, to have computers learn by their mistakes. A computer can be programmed to play chess. It is a very complex program because of the tremendous number of moves possible—estimated at 10^{120}. It is not possible to program for each move *all* the possible results of that move. As the game is played between computer and a human being the computer stores each move made, rating it according to whether it is a good move or one leading eventually to defeat. As more and more games are played, the library of moves grows and by checking each move in the current game against this library the computer can improve its game. It takes many years to make the computer a really good chess player. Would you now consider the computer is thinking?

The human brain is a very sophisticated thinking machine. The computer is logical, fast and accurate—and can always be stopped by pulling out the plug.

The Privacy Question

Privacy is very much a debatable subject. Individuals have a right to privacy, but the organizations representing them, to the extent that they must preserve law and order, control crime and disease, and so on, have a right to information.

With the introduction of storage units capable of storing massive amounts of information, it is possible to store comprehensive information about every citizen (even in a country as large as the U.S.A.), accessible instantly by one computer. That is a frightening thought. Who will have access to this information, what type of information will it be, and how accurate will it be? The majority of people give the matter little thought until something happens and they realize their privacy has been violated. Let us look at a couple of examples.

There are many instances of incorrect credit ratings due to human errors. We all know the frustration of trying to find a human being who will check out the problem and feed the appropriate correction into the computer. The person concerned

probably didn't realize such information was kept without his specific knowledge and of course inaccurately.

Many banks have computerized the majority of their operations. It is therefore possible to trace financial transactions for an individual or company over a period of time, showing trends and discrepancies. This could be very valuable information to the police in the case of fraud. Where did Mr. X get $10 000 in March? His pay is only $1000 a month and there are several more deposits of large amounts. Does the fraud squad have a right to such information?

The privacy question has caused comprehensive studies involving computer users, governments and computer manufacturers to be done in several countries to try to find an answer. Sweden is one country that has had privacy legislation since 1973. Personal files may not be kept without permission of the Data Inspection Board. Many other countries are actively working on legislation to protect the privacy of the individual. The legislation being drafted will probably include such items as:

(1) No secret data banks (or databases) can be maintained – their existence must be known.

(2) Those maintaining the databanks must be responsible for the integrity of the data and providing adequate security for preventing misuse.

(3) The individual to whom the data pertains, must:
(a) be able to update it and check its accuracy.
(b) know what information is being kept and who is using it.
(c) be able to prevent use of the information by other unauthorized people.

Stored data, in most cases, can be divided into the following broad categories:

Critical data
– such as airline reservations, credit card data, accumulated statistics. This data, if lost, could cause a great deal of aggravation, loss or disruption of business but is not necessarily confidential in nature.

Personal data
– confidential information such as medical histories and financial data.

Proprietary data
– confidential information such as research information and customer listings.

When personal information is to be kept then a critical study should be made about each item of data:

(a) Is it necessary?
(b) Who needs it?
(c) Why do they want it?
(d) Does the individual know it is being kept?

There is no technical reason why the individual's privacy cannot be preserved. Remember, *people* control the operation of computers. What is required is the implementation of high standards of security. The standards for control of information will vary with its value and the degree of privacy required. This brings us to the next topic—security.

The Security Problem

Good security procedures can ensure privacy. Security of data is attainable. Security of data implies that the data can be trusted to the computer department and that it will be correctly processed, not destroyed, and kept confidential. Recent studies in the U.S.A. have shown that problems with data security can be divided into the following broad categories, in order of importance:

Errors and ommissions
Dishonest employees
Fire
Disgruntled employees
Damage by water
Theft and damage caused by outsiders.

You will notice that most of these are human caused problems as opposed to problems with computer hardware or software. Let us take a look at some of the people-caused problems that contribute to lack of data security.

Input

- control cards incorrect (could cause tape to be erased)
- lost cards due to handling
- cards entered upside down (still giving valid data)
- incorrectly repaired cards after a card jam in the card reader.
- poorly documented instructions for the operator.
- jobs run in the wrong sequence.
- incorrectly labelled tape.

Processing

- insufficiently tested programs (causing production data to be processed incorrectly)
- multiprogramming systems that are not reliable
- back up procedures that are not sufficient (no sure means of recovery if there is a power or system failure)

Output

- printer output that can be read by anybody
- output which is sent to the wrong terminal
- output which is wrongly routed manually.

Users

- easy access to passwords and terminals
- no check made for appropriate clearance to access data

Physical

- easy access to the computer room, terminals and tape libraries

All of these problems can be solved, and a good installation will have few lapses in data security. Those companies that act as data servicers have probably got the biggest security problem. A data servicer sells computer time and related services to users. If they have a large computer they have hundreds of customers. If the company runs a terminal network with customers accessing their own data via their own terminal, data integrity and software integrity is of prime importance. The data servicer will soon lose customers if output is wrongly routed or one customer is able to gain access to another's confidential data.

In order to provide a secure environment installations must provide:

(1) good training for operators, programmers and other computer personnel with access to the data.
(2) division of responsibility (to prevent information theft by collusion).
(3) good documentation
(4) audit procedures on a regular basis
(5) a security manager (to control the issuing of passwords and control the access to data).
(6) a log of events so that checking can be done
(7) physical protection

(8) implementation of software to prevent access to data files without proper authorization.

There is a cost attached to a secure system. All of the suggested requirements listed above will cost the installation money–directly, for example, training and facilities; or indirectly, for example, computer time to run the password checking program. The debatable point then is, can the installation or company afford security?

In many cases people are complacent about data security. "Nothing has ever gone wrong, do I really need to improve security?" That is much the same argument as can be made for insurance, preventative medicine, flood protection and so on. Another issue that arises is responsibility for the security of the data. Is the installation responsible? Do I sue the manufacturer whose software was unreliable? Is it my own fault for giving control of confidential data to somebody else?

In summary, the security problem is really a communication problem—man to man, man to machine and machine to machine. The computer becomes the scapegoat when data is lost or incorrect but as we have seen, most of the problems are with people and can be solved.

Have We Accepted the Computer?

People's attitudes towards the computer have been changing over the last decade. The fear that existed for many years is being replaced by tolerance, with the inevitable frustration with errors supposedly caused by the computer but probably caused by people. We are becoming increasingly dependent on computers. For example, airline reservations are instantaneous when computerized. Would we be prepared to return to a manual method? Banking by manual methods is gradually disappearing. Will the

cashless society be a reality? It is possible even now to exist without cash, and at least one credit card company uses this approach in their advertising. Certain car rental companies will only rent you a car using a credit card—no cash transactions. However, it is not completely convenient to exist without cash since you can't pick up a newspaper or a quart of milk at the corner store.

Although there would be disadvantages to a cashless society there would also be advantages. There would be no purpose in robbing a store or bank if there was no money to steal. Robbing somebody of their pay would be impossible. Many companies already deposit employees' pay directly in the bank. However, there is still some resistance to such a method as many people have a distrust of banks and cheques and like their pay in an envelope. Although theft of one sort would be eliminated there could be a growth of theft connected with the computer. Are we prepared to hand over all our money transactions to a bank? Will the corner store be swallowed up? There are many sides to this discussion and of course the privacy question also arises again. It would appear that a compromise is feasible. There is much to be gained from automatic transactions in certain areas but *not* in all areas.

The computer is part of a new era in living where automation and advanced technology in many areas have shortened working weeks and increased leisure time to the extent that it is not just a break from work and a time to recoup for the next day. This is creating a whole new social problem. The computer takes care of the time-consuming repetitive jobs. Can we take care of the leisure time we now have? Can we make use of the computer to improve the world we live in? There have been a number of social revolutions in history. Is this another—the computer revolution? The computer was invented by human beings, surely we can exploit it for our own benifit.

Projects

(1) The individual has a right to privacy. Society has a right to be informed. Discuss.

(2) The computer is a high speed idiot not a giant electronic brain. Expand on this statement explaining any computer jargon used.

(3) List other possible breaches of security connected with a computer installation—there are many more than have been mentioned in the chapter. Suggest possible solutions.

(4) Draft privacy regulations for school records, covering what information they should contain and who should have access to this information.

(5) Patients' records should not be shown to the patients. Discuss.

(6) List all the advantages and disadvantages that you can think of, of a cashless society.

(7) Computers will eventually control our lives. Discuss.

19 Past Present and Future

How many of the predictions made for the seventies have come to fruition? Certainly landing a man on the moon and reaching Mars are two that did, both greatly assisted by the computer.

Looking Back

The computer has been in existence commercially for twenty-five years and in those years it has become **smaller, faster and cheaper**. Below is a table of comparable costs (compiled by IBM) and processing time for a variety of jobs over two decades.

	1955	1960	1965	1976
Cost	$14.54	$2.48	$.59	$.28
Processing Time	375 secs.	47 secs.	37 secs.	5 secs.

This reduction is mainly due to the development of smaller circuits which speed up processing and reduce cost. Back in 1946 vacuum tubes were thousands of times faster than the original electrical relay. Vacuum tube computers multiplied two numbers in one tenth of a second. It was predicted at that time that the U.S.A. would need about forty computers in the foreseeable future! The transistor was incorporated into the computer at one two-hundredth of the size of the vacuum tube. Two ten digit numbers could now be multiplied in one one-hundred-thousandths of a second. Next came solid logic technology (SLT) where tiny circuits were placed on a 13 millimetre square ceramic base. This increased the speed by a factor of at least 2. The reliability also improved to the extent that these SLT modules ran for many millions of hours without failing. Finally, present day computers have monolithic storage chips, once again fractionally smaller than SLT modules. The latest technology for producing these incorporates metal oxide semi-conductor field effect transistors (MOSFET) technology.

Size, speed and cost of other units have also dramatically changed. Printer speeds have increased by a factor of at least 100. The latest printers use laser technology and electrophotography.

Diagram 19.1 Vacuum tube

Diagram 19.2 Metal Oxide Semi-conductor Field Effect Transistor (MOSFET) has about 40 times greater circuit density in less space than Monolithic Systems Technology (MST).

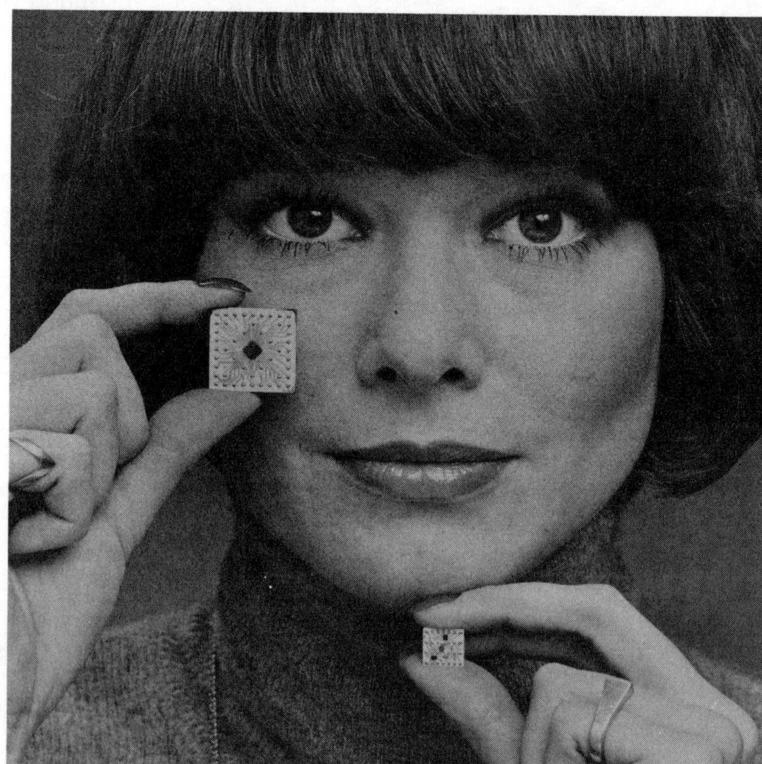

Diagram 19.3 Devices for performing logic have become increasingly smaller: from vacuum tubes to components connected on cards to Solid Logic Technology to Monolithic Systems Technology. One MST module, lower right, is equal to five SLT modules.

Main storage capacity is now in the millions of characters; auxiliary storage in the billions (mass storage units). The density of packing data on disks has increased from over one hundred bits of data per square centimetre to over two-hundred thousand. We have gone from a computer in the fifties having a mass of 90t to a 22.5 Kg mini which is considerably faster and more powerful.

Programming has progressed from a series of numbers (machine language) coded laboriously by the programmer, to near English resulting in readable sentences which the computer can reduce to its own language. Initially programs were run one at a time. Now it is possible to run many programs written in different languages concurrently, fully controlled by a sophisticated operating system.

The first generation of computers were very much function oriented. There were scientific computers and commercial data processing computers but no general purpose computers. These first specialized computers were not compatible with each other. If you had a set of programs for one computer and had

Diagram 19.4 Cutting out patterns for making monolithic circuits

to get a more powerful model the chances were that you would have to rewrite all your programs! This represented a large investment in time and money. The first really general purpose compatible computers appeared in 1965 although a few previous to that might have qualified. Now the user could run both scientific and commercial jobs and if he needed a larger computer then more power and capability was available without having to re-program.

Smaller, Faster and Cheaper

Monolithic Storage

Monolithic technology is one of the advances that has contributed to the smaller, faster and cheaper computers. How is it possible to make the tiny components used in monolithic storage? The first step in this process is seen in diagram 19.4. The circuit design is cut on a sheet of polyester consisting of an opaque layer and a clear layer. It is 200 times the size of the finished component. The design is then reduced photographically and placed on a piece of glass less than two millimetres square to form a silicon wafer. The wafer is thoroughly cleaned in a chemical bath and coated with photosensitive material. Acid is then used to etch away all but the original circuit design. The wafer has such chemicals as gold, arsenic and boron deposited on it to form devices such as transistors. Aluminum is deposited to form the connections. Between each process it is baked in a furnace. The wafers are then sliced in two and are ready for mounting and testing. More than one hundred steps are gone through in producing the monolithics. When it is completed, the tiny chip can easily pass through the centre of a pen nib — in fact on one chip there could be enough devices to build forty transistor radios!

One of the main problems to be overcome in the manufacturing process is keeping the monolithics absolutely clean. Even a speck of dust could blot out a connection and cause a short circuit. A rejection of 1% for each step produces a very poor yield when you consider there are over one hundred steps—in fact less than 30% of the original would be left. This

Diagram 19.5 **Josephson Tunnel Junctions**

is, of course, uneconomical and very strict rules are followed to keep dust and dirt out of the manufacturing area. All workers wear surgical gowns and the air is filtered continually. When transistors were mounted separately as in earlier methods, those that were substandard could be disregarded. With monolithics both circuitry and the devices such as transistors are produced already integrated and there have to be very precise controls. An error of one millionth of a centimetre is not acceptable. In spite of these problems storage and logic monolithics are cheaper than preceding methods.

It must be remembered that decrease in size allows increase in speed. It takes time for electrical signals to travel along the connectors. The most powerful computers can now process one instruction in less that 60 billionths of a second—light travels about 18 metres in the same time. Monolithics are used both in the central processing unit and in main storage, giving us computers that can operate as much as four or five times faster than their predecessors.

There are technical limitations using monolithic technology. Research is now being directed towards devices called Josephson Tunnel Junctions, developed by two scientists who subsequently won a Nobel Prize for their work. These junctions are a few square microns (a micron is one fifty-thousandth of a centimetre) and operate at low temperatures. Switching (on/off) can be achieved in an estimated ten trillionths of a second.

Mini Computers

If you ask five people for their definition of a mini computer you will probably get five different answers!

- under $60 000 (purchase price)
- small CPU with limited input, output capability
- small in size and light in weight
- capable of running only one program
- all of the above.

A typical mini might have 4-128K of main storage, fit on a table, be easily moveable, have relatively slow input and output (paper tape, video display terminal, card reader and printer), will not require air conditioning and have some tape or disk storage. The languages implemented on a mini are usually limited to one or two. BASIC, FORTRAN or RPG are frequently used and nearly all have an assembler type language. There is a relatively unsophisticated operating system, often called a monitor.

What are minis used for? Every field of computing has made use of minis. There are scientific-oriented, engineering-oriented, process control, numerical control, industrial control and commercial minis ... and many more. A mini can control the processing in a manufacturing plant, control the heating in a building or run a typesetting program. Many minis are used in universities by individual departments for research. Minis with terminals are used, for example, in CAI, engineering applications, problem solving and data collection.

Minis are frequently used to process local data, for example, at a branch office, with summary data being transmitted later to a central computer. This reduces the cost of data transmission since it need only be done once or twice a day instead of continually. Only centrally required data need be transmitted. Many companies will dedicate a mini to one application since it is easier to control and maintain. The tendency seems to be towards small, portable machines. You can take them home and finish your work.

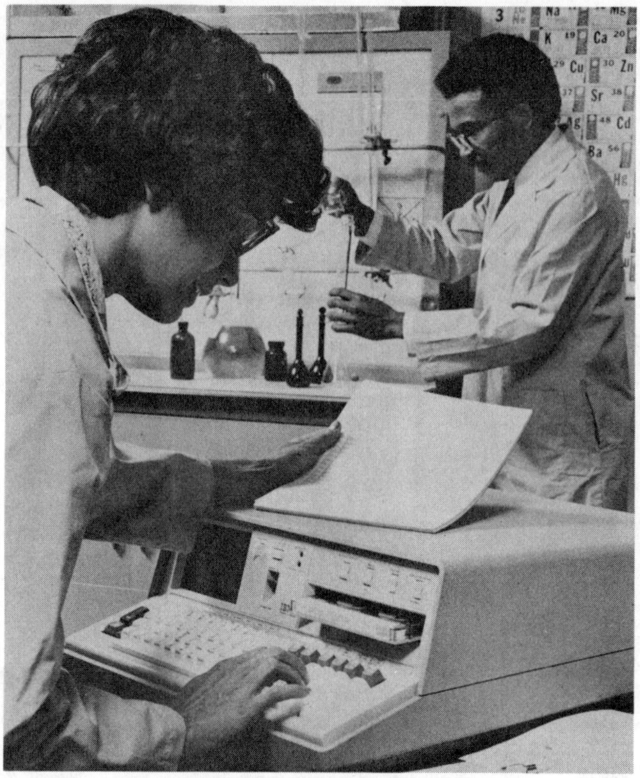

Diagram 19.6 A portable computer

Computer Networks

Advances in telecommunication methods and the use of satellites together with the reduction in size and cost of terminals and storage media has contributed to the growth in size and number of computer networks. There has been a tremendous increase in the variety of terminals available with a parallel decrease in cost. We have already mentioned in earlier chapters terminal uses in such areas as banking, airlines, CAI and hospitals. Every industry makes use in some way of terminal networks both large and small. Networks of terminals are common with up to 600 or 700 terminals scattered across continents, controlled by a central computer (or computers). Networks exist whereby a series of medium-sized computers will each control a number of terminals, communicating with the central machine only part of the time. Minis are often used as terminals in networks. When equipment such as minis and medium sized computers are used as terminals they are referred to as intelligent terminals since they are capable of processing data on their own as well as being used to transmit data to the central computer.

With the development of such networks there is an increased need to produce stable software to run them since many are used in critical applications such as moon landings and medical monitoring. If, for some reason, a user at a terminal cannot get an answer, where in the network is the problem? The software is complex and must be reliable. There must be adequate backup, and recovery procedures are essential (both software and hardware).

The sort of problems being solved today in the computer industry are different from those 25 years ago. There is more emphasis on reliability, stability, security, telecommunications problems and user-oriented languages. A network can offer terminal users a tremendous variety of help in their everyday tasks — supplying languages for problem solving, enquiry into files, record storage, file updating and so on — all on the same computer at the same time.

User Oriented Program

Computer	*User*
Enter Cust No	
	1374
Enter Field/Contents	
	Name/John Doe
Enter Field/Contents	
	End
Enter Cust No	
	13824
Error—Entry Too Long	
	1384

Looking Forward

It is difficult to predict the computers' future since there are so many variables involved, both social and technical.

Certain trends will obviously continue, such as miniturization and cost reduction. Hardware will become increasingly modular so that one set of circuits can be changed in a few seconds and whole units can quickly be replaced if faulty.

Magnetic bubble storage is one area of research, where it is hoped to replace the traditional disk and tape storage with a more reliable storage with no moveable parts, only moveable magnetic domains. This would provide storage at a density of fifteen million bits per square centimetre. Security of data in the transmission of data between terminal and CPU will be improved with the use of cryptographic techniques.

Great attention is being paid to software. If the cost of hardware is such that anybody who would like to use a computer can afford it, then it must be made useable to those people without the additional cost and time involved in training. The trend is towards computer languages resembling natural language so that very little training is required. There is a large increase in package programs which are user-oriented, and which are generalized so that many different users can adapt them to their own problems. The computer is being used as a productivity tool to try and keep costs down and production up.

A technique called microprogramming is increasingly being implemented. Microprogramming makes use of micro instructions which are pseudocode built into the computer and stored in a special area of the computer. They are directly translated to machine commands. Frequently used routines, sometimes even language translators, are micro programmed, considerably speeding up their execution.

The use to which the computer is put is ever increasing, and the cost decreasing in spite of inflation. The overall trend seems to be to bring the computer to the end user; that is, the person who really wants a problem solved. After all—it is an everyday machine.

Projects

(1) Discuss the advantages and disadvantages of one big computer versus several small ones (minis).

(2) Prepare a fifteen-minute presentation entitled 'What is a Computer?' to be given to a group knowing nothing about a computer.

(3) The year is 2001. Using your visual telephone you confer with your business associates in Montreal and Vancouver. Then you enquire via your computer terminal about the latest stock market figures and....

Prepare a presentation (written or oral) about two or three aspects of the year 2001 in connection with the computer, communication or information processing.

Standard BCD Interchange Code

CHARACTER		CARD CODE	BCD CODE						
		PUNCHES	C	B	A	8	4	2	1
.		12–3–8		B	A	8		2	1
⌑		12–4–8		B	A	8	4		
[		12–5–8		B	A	8	4		1
<		12–6–8		B	A	8	4	2	
≢		12–7–8		B	A	8	4	2	1
&		12		B	A				
$		11–3–8		B		8		2	1
*		11–4–8		B		8	4		
]		11–5–8		B		8	4		1
;		11–6–8		B		8	4	2	
Δ		11–7–8		B		8	4	2	1
—		11		B					
/		0–1			A				1
,		0–3–8			A	8		2	1
%		0–4–8			A	8	4		
\		0–6–8			A	8	4	2	
⧻		0–7–8			A	8	4	2	1
#		3–8				8		2	1
@		4–8				8	4		
:		5–8				8	4		1
>		6–8				8	4	2	
?		12–0		B	A	8		2	
A	LOW	12–1		B	A				1
B	↑	12–2		B	A			2	
C		12–3		B	A			2	1
D		12–4		B	A		4		
E		12–5		B	A		4		1
F		12–6		B	A		4	2	
G		12–7		B	A		4	2	1
H		12–8		B	A	8			
I		12–9		B	A	8			1
J		11–1		B					1
K		11–2		B				2	
L		11–3		B				2	1
M		11–4		B			4		
N		11–5		B			4		1
O		11–6		B			4	2	
P		11–7		B			4	2	1
Q		11–8		B		8			
R		11–9		B		8			1
S		0–2			A			2	
T		0–3			A			2	1
U	Collating Sequence	0–4			A		4		
V		0–5			A		4		1
W		0–6			A		4	2	
X		0–7			A		4	2	1
Y		0–8			A	8			
Z		0–9			A	8			1
0		0				8		2	
1		1							1
2		2						2	
3		3						2	1
4		4					4		
5		5					4		1
6		6					4	2	
7		7					4	2	1
8	↓	8				8			
9	HIGH	9				8			1

Glossary

Address. A label, name, or number which identifies a location in storage.

Address space. The complete range of addresses that is available to a programmer.

Algorithm. A series of organized, logically defined steps representing the solution to a problem.

ANSI. American National Standards Institute.

APL. A programming language. A problem solving language designed for use at remote terminals; it offers special capabilities for handling arrays and for performing mathematical functions.

Arithmetic/logic unit. That part of the central processing unit designed to carry out arithmetic and logical operations.

Assembler language. A source language that includes symbolic machine language statements in which there is a one-to-one correspondence with the instruction formats and data formats of the computer.

Auxiliary storage. Data storage other than main storage; for example, storage on magnetic tape or direct access devices. Synonymous with external storage, secondary storage.

BASIC. Beginners All-purpose Symbolic Instruction Code. An algebra-like language used for problem solving by engineers, scientists and others who may not be professional programmers.

BCD. Binary Coded Decimal notation. A method of representing decimal numbers using sets of binary digits.

Bit. From the words **bi**nary digi**t**, used to describe the smallest definable unit connected with computer storage.

Branching. A programming technique used to transfer control from one sequence of a program to another.

Buffer. An area of storage that is temporarily reserved for use in performing an input/output operation, into which data is read or from which data is written.

Bug. A term used to reference an error in a computer program.

Byte. A grouping of adjacent bits (usually 8) which are operated on as a unit. In certain computers, the smallest unit that can be addressed, processed or store information.

Cathode Ray Tube. An electronic vacuum tube, such as a television picture tube, that can be used to display graphic images. Often used in a visual display unit.

Card hopper. That part of a card processing machine which holds cards ready for them to be fed singly into the machine.

Card punch. A device to record information in cards by punching holes in the cards to represent letters, digits, and special characters.

Card reader. A device that senses and translates into machine code the holes in punched cards.

Card reader/punch. One unit combining the functions of a card reader and a card punch. Reading and punching are under program control.

Central Processing Unit. CPU. The computer unit containing circuitry for interpreting, controlling and executing instructions.

Chained records. A system of storing records in which each record belongs to a list or group of records and has a linking field for tracing the chain.

Character. Any symbol which a

data processing machine can read, store, or write.

Chip. In microcircuitry, a single electronic device that has been cut from a larger wafer of silicon.

COBOL. **C**ommon **B**usiness **O**riented **L**anguage. A programming language allowing the use of English words to describe the problem. Used for programming business applications.

Collating. The arranging of information in a predetermined sequence.

Communications common carrier. A government-regulated private company that furnishes the general public with telecommunications service facilities; for example, a telephone or telegraph company.

Compiler. A program that translates high level (near English) computer languages to the machine language of a particular computer. Several machine language instructions will be generated for each high level statement.

Computing system. A central processing unit, with main storage, input/output channels, control units, direct access storage devices, and input/output devices connected to it.

Control card. A punched card containing input data or parameters for initializing or modifying a program.

Control program. A program that is designed to schedule and supervise the performance of dataprocessiing work by a computing system.

Control unit. A device that controls input/output operations at one or more devices OR the portion of the central processing unit controlling the operation of the entire computing system.

Core storage. A form of high-speed storage using magnetic cores.

Cryptographic. Pertaining to equipment that transforms data to conceal its actual meaning, usually by secret conversion.

Cursor. A movable spot of light on the cathode ray tube of a console or display unit that indicates where the next character will be entered.

DASD. Direct Access Storage Device. A device in which the access time is effectively independent of the location of the data.

Data. Units of information which can be processed or produced by the computer.

Data base. A collection of data fundamental to an enterprise.

Data file. A collection of related data records organized in a specific manner. For example, a payroll file (one record for each employee, showing his rate of pay, deductions, etc.).

Data processing. The execution of a systematic sequence of operations performed upon data.

Data processing system. A network of machine components capable of accepting information, processing it according to a plan, and producing the desired results.

Data set. A device that performs the modulation/demodulation and control functions necessary to provide compatibility between business machines and communications facilities.

Debugging—debug. To locate and correct all errors in a computer program and any malfunctions in the computing system itself.

Directory. An index that is used by a control program to locate one or more blocks of data that are stored in separate areas of a data set in direct access storage.

Disk pack. A removable direct access storage medium containing magnetic disks on which data is stored. Disk packs are mounted on a disk storage drive.

Drum storage. A direct access storage device that records data magnetically on a rotating cylinder. A type of addressable auxiliary storage associated with some computers.

Electromechanical. A system that combines both electrical and mechanical principles.

Field. A column or group of columns in a punch card allocated for punching specific information.

Flowchart. A graphic representation of the flow of information through a data-processing system.

FORTRAN. **For**mula **Tran**slation. A problem-oriented programming language designed for programming scientific-type problems.

Gangpunching. Punching information read from a master card into following detail cards.

Hash total. A summation for checking purposes of one or more corresponding fields of a file that would ordinarily not be summed.

Hexadecimal. Pertaining to a number system with a base of 16; valid digits range from O through F, where F represents the highest units position (15).

Input Unit. A device used to introduce information into the central processing unit.

Installation. A particular computing system, in terms of the work it does and the people who manage it, operate it, apply it to problems, service it, and use the results it produces.

Interpreting. Causing the information recorded in code in punched cards or tape to be printed on the cards or tape.

Keypunch. A device for punching holes in cards in a specific code to record data.

Machine language. A language that requires no further interpretation by the computer.

Main storage. All program-addressable storage from which instructions may be executed and from which data can be loaded directly into registers.

Mass storage. The storage of a large amount of data which is also readily accessible to the central processing unit of a computer.

Matching. Checking two files to determine if there is a corresponding card or group of cards in each file.

Merging. Combining two files in like sequence into a single file.

Message. In telecommunications, a combination of characters and symbols transmitted from one point to another on a network.

Microprogramming. A method of operation of the CPU in which each complete instruction starts the execution of a sequence of instructions, called microinstructions, which are generally at a more elementary level.

Mnemonics. The symbolic representation of instructions which are designed to aid the memory.

Monolithic storage. Composed of monolithic integrated circuits which are a type of circuit fabricated from an active material such as silicon.

Multiprocessing. Simultaneous execution of two or more sequences of instructions using a computing system employing two or more interconnected processing units.

Multiprogramming. Concurrent execution of two or more sequences of instructions using a computing system wherein main storage is divided into partitions.

Network. In teleprocessing, a number of communication lines connecting a computer with remote terminals.

Operand. That part of an instruction qualifying the specific operation to be performed, usually an address.

Operating system. Software controlling the complete operation of a computing system; scheduling jobs, controlling input/output units, providing security checks, assigning storage and so on.

Operation code. The part of an instruction which designates the operation to be performed by a computer.

Output. Information transferred from a computer's internal storage unit to an external storage medium.

Page frame. In virtual storage systems, a block of real storage that can contain a page. Synonymous with frame.

Parity Bit. A check bit added to binary digits that form bytes or words to make their number either uniformly odd or even.

PL/1. A high-level programming language, designated for use in a wide range of commercial and scientific computer applications.

Pointer. An address or other indication of location.

Printer. A device that writes output data from a system on paper or other media.

Program. A series of instructions given to a computer in a logical sequence to perform a certain task.

Random access—or direct access. Retrieval or storage of data by a reference to its location on a recording medium, rather than relative to the previously retrieved or stored data.

Real storage. The storage in a computing system from which the central processing unit can directly obtain instructions and data, and to which it can directly return results.

Register. A temporary storage device used by the computer during the instruction and execute phases.

Reproducing. To prepare a duplicate of stored information, especially for punched cards, punched paper tape, or magnetic tape.

RPG. Report Program Generator. A processing program that can be used to generate object programs that produce reports from existing sets of data.

Segment. A continuous area of virtual storage that is allocated to a job or system task.

Sensor based system. An organization of components, including a computer whose primary source of input is data from sensors and whose output can be used to control the related physical process.

Sequential access. Accessing data in the same logical order that it was originally stored, eg. in alphabetic sequence or numeric sequence.

Software. Programming aids supplied by the manufacturer for optimum utilization of computing systems.

Solid logic technology. Miniaturized modules used in computers, which result in faster circuitry because of reduced distance for current to travel.

Sorting. Arranging data in a specific sequence using one or more fields eg. branch sequence within district sequence.

Source program. A computer program written in nonmachine language form.

Supervisor. The part of a control

program that coordinates the use of resources and maintains the flow of CPU operations.

Teleprocessing. The processing of data that is received from or sent to remote locations by way of telecommunication lines.

Terminal. A device, usually equipped with a keyboard and some kind of display, capable of sending and receiving information over a communication channel.

Thrashing. In virtual storage systems, a condition in which the system can do little useful work because of excessive paging.

Throughput. The total volume of work performed by a computing system over a given period of time.

Time sharing. A method of using a computing system that allows a number of users to execute programs concurrently and to interact with the programs during execution.

Translator. A device that converts information from one system of representation into equivalent information in another system of representation.

Utility program. A problem program designed to perform an everyday task, such as transcribing data from one storage device to another.

Variable name. The name given to an entity; storage area that can assume any of a given set of values of the same type.

Virtual machine. A functional simulation of a computer and its associated devices.

Virtual storage. Addressable space that appears to the user as real storage, from which instructions and data are mapped into real storage locations. The size of virtual storage is limited by the addressing scheme of the computing system (or virtual machine) and by the amount of auxiliary storage available, rather than by the actual number of real storage locations.

Word. A collection of binary digits treated as a unit that can be addressed, processed or store information. Sometimes the smallest addressable unit. Sometimes a number of bytes.

Index